Marcello Mastroianni

MARCELLO MASTROIANNI

His Life and Art

Donald Dewey

A Birch Lane Press Book
Published by Carol Publishing Group

For Julian Bees

A Birch Lane Press Book
Published by Carol Publishing Group
Birch Lane Press is a registered trademark of Carol Communications, Inc.
Editorial Offices: 600 Madison Avenue, New York, N.Y. 10022
Sales and Distribution Offices: 120 Enterprise Avenue, Secaucus, N.J. 07094
In Canada: Canadian Manda Group, P.O. Box 920, Station U, Toronto, Ontario M8Z 5P9
Queries regarding rights and permissions should be addressed to Carol Publishing Group, 600 Madison Avenue, New York, N.Y. 10022

Carol Publishing Group books are available at special discounts for bulk purchases, for sales promotion, fund-raising, or educational purposes. Special editions can be created to specifications. For details, contact: Special Sales Department, Carol Publishing Group, 120 Enterprise Avenue, Secaucus, N.J. 07094

Manufactured in the United States of America

10 9 8 7 6 5 4 3 2 1

Library of Congress Cataloging-in-Publication Data

Dewey, Donald.
    Marcello Mastroianni : his life and art / by Donald Dewey.
        p.   cm.
    "A Birch Lane Press book."
    ISBN 1-55972-158-8 (cloth)
    1. Mastroianni, Marcello, 1924–   2. Motion picture actors and actresses—Italy—Biography.   I. Title.
PN2688.M33D48   1993
791.43′028′092—dc20   92-37468
[B]   92-37568   CIP

Contents

Preface

M arcello Mastroianni is an Italian word meaning work. Since he
first appeared as a fourteen-year-old extra in a movie musical
in 1938, Mastroianni has been involved in an estimated 140 motion
pictures; more astonishing, in about 90 percent of them he has had
the starring role. Between film assignments, he has performed on the
stage in Italy and France and shown up on European television as
both a dramatic actor and a song-and-dance man. Along with these
appearances have gone thousands of television, radio, magazine, and
newspaper interviews. If there is another actor-star in either Europe
or America who has worked and talked about his work as much as
Mastroianni has, he or she can only have reached critical mass and
disappeared from memory.

Mastroianni: *His Life and Art* is an attempt to put into focus
what is arguably the most remarkable career of any film actor in the
second half of the twentieth century. In line with Mastroianni's own
insistence over the years that "work is what my whole life is about,"
the book's main narrative line follows his film and theater experiences, with minimal editorial comment. Observations on particular
aspects of the Mastroianni persona, his impact on the motion picture
industry, and the frequently contradictory images that he has generated in different parts of the world, have been concentrated in
"Close-up" chapters separating the most distinguishable phases of
his professional career.

The material for *Marcello Mastroianni: His Life and Art* comes
from two general sources. The first has been the author's conversations with Mastroianni and professional colleagues, within the
framework of both the present book and of earlier writings for magazines and newspapers. Among those of assistance in one or the other
categories have been Theo Angelopoulos, Bernardo Bertolucci, Laura
Betti, Victor Cavallo, Alexander Cohen, Federico Fellini, Geraldine
Fitzgerald, Jay Hoffman, Lauren Hutton, Beeban Kidron, Jack Lem-

mon, Richard Levine, Pia Lindstrom, Francesco Rosi, Gene Saks, Billie Whitelaw, and Shelley Winters. Also, the late Trevor Howard, Elio Petri, and Ugo Tognazzi.

The second source has been the almost literally myriad of interviews that Mastroianni has granted to the media over the years. In working through this Everest of material, the author has had invaluable assistance from numerous people in various countries. Among those who deserve thanks are Amelia Antonucci, Gyula Barsony, Daniela Bönsch, Ida Cicalà, Lila Dlaboha, Mauro Gobbini, Gino Gullace, Matilde Hochkofler, George Kalogeroboulos, Wendy Keys, Dominic Lord, Franco Pantarelli, Giampaolo Pioli, Giancarlo Riccio, Roberto Silvestri, Gabriella Steiger, and Carlos Varela. Very special thanks go to Silvana Silvestri for her forays into morgues that collect defunct newspapers as much as old clippings and to my wife Marta for translating Hungarian and German materials.

It goes without saying that the book would have been impossible without the cooperation of Marcello Mastroianni. In addition to our personal conversations, he found the time to fax answers to niggling questions from several locations in Europe and South America. My gratitude, as well, to Giovanna Cau for facilitating these communications.

Next to the subject himself, if there is one person who has made *Mastroianni: His Life and Art* possible, it is Julian Bees, whose efforts in tracking down material and coordinating research in Italy were indispensable.

Naturally, all the errors, arrogances, and unwarranted leaps in logic belong solely to the author.

January 1993

Marcello Mastroianni

Introduction:
Stars and Spectacles

The emergence and longevity of Marcello Mastroianni as a leading man, for all his international standing, has remained an anomaly for Italy. Prior to Mastroianni, for various cultural and economic reasons the Italian film industry had not only not produced a comparable male star familiar to world audiences; it had even failed to sustain someone of his caliber for domestic audiences for more than a few years at a time—particularly curious for a nation that was second only to Denmark (and ahead of the United States) in promoting a movie-star tradition at the dawning of the century.

Before there were Italian films, there was an Italian film industry. This owed to the almost monopolistic hold that France had over Italian film activities from 1895 to 1905. With rare exceptions, screen initiatives in the medium's infant decade were financed and distributed by the French; more often than not, Italian actors and directors were employed directly by Lumière or by some other Paris-based company. It was also because of the French connection that Italy's first conspicuous production center was not Rome but the far more northerly Turin. Most of the work produced in the period consisted of street-scene fragments, music-hall numbers, and optical-effects games; there were also forays into recording passion plays and religious ceremonies—as much for winning over the Vatican to the new medium as for entertaining the general public.

Italy's equivalent of Thomas Edison was Filoteo Alberini. Between the summer of 1894 and the following spring, Alberini perfected what he called the *cinetografo*, a machine that recorded, developed, and projected animated films. Some years later, the Turin native also devised the *autostereoscopio*, a 70-mm projection process that represented one of the world's first wide-screen technical endeavors. But as important as he was as an inventor, Alberini had equal impact as an entrepreneur and producer. In 1905, he initiated the gradual shift of serious Italian movie production away from Turin by financing the construction of Cines, the Rome studio that remained synonymous with the country's motion-picture industry until well into the 1930s. The first Cines production that same year— and the first truly Italian film—was *La Presa di Roma* (The Taking of Rome), a 700-foot narrative that dramatized the consolidation of the Italian state by depicting the arrival of infantry troops in the capital in 1870. The success of *La Presa di Roma* encouraged scores of production companies to spring up in Rome, Naples, Milan, and Turin, almost all of them with local financing. When foreign buyers caught a whiff of the new creativity, distribution deals were hammered out throughout Europe and the United States, often for films that had not been seen by their importers.

In glorifying the Garibaldian forces that seized Rome, Alberini's film also set the pattern for the rhetorical costume stories that would dominate Italian production for decades. Almost uniformly grandiose, the pictures made up in posturing what was missing in historical accuracy or in faithfulness to literary sources. Although many producers of the era claimed sophisticated tastes, it was mainly costume and heroic spectacle that marked such productions as *The Last Days of Pompeii* (four versions between 1908 and 1926), *Garibaldi, Othello, Romeo and Juliet, El Cid, Giordano Bruno, The Fall of Troy, Hamlet, Frederick Barbarossa, Anna Garibaldi, Macbeth, Lucrezia Borgia, Joan of Arc, Dante and Beatrice, Parsifal, Siegfried,* and *Spartacus.* The most noteworthy of the epics—direct influences on the work of D. W. Griffith and Cecil B. De Mille—were *Quo Vadis?* (1912) and *Cabiria* (1914). The first of numerous screen adaptations of Henryk Sienkiewicz's novel, Enrico Guazzoni's *Quo Vadis?* was an eight-reel spectacular that cost more than $700,000 and literally employed a cast of thousands. But although marketed as a feature that would never be eclipsed in production values, it was, and quickly—by *Cabiria.*

Two years in the making and budgeted at $1 million, *Cabiria* was the crown jewel of Turin film production, setting international box-office records that stood in many countries until well after World War I. Directed by Giovanni Pastrone (working under the pseudonym of Piero Fosco) and shot on location in the Alps, Sicily, and Tunisia, the epic, set against the background of the Second Punic War, was arguably responsible for more technical innovations than any single film in the twentieth century. Pastrone himself, for example, earned patent rights to the elaborate tracking shots that he introduced to world filmmakers in *Cabiria.* The director also went to his grave insisting that his use of parallel cutting had preceded Griffith's credited initial employment of this editing technique. In addition, *Cabiria* was significant for its persuasive shooting of scale models, its unprecedented aesthetic lighting, and its elimination of the archaistic painted backdrops that, until then, had been de rigueur. The integration of all these elements, according to one continental critic, made Pastrone "the Giotto of the cinema."

But its innovations notwithstanding, *Cabiria* was also typical of the period for both its pompous storytelling and its celebration of the star system. The script, written primarily by the megalomaniacal, proto-Fascist, poet-novelist Gabriele D'Annunzio, included such card captions as "The Latin ships set out once again onto the sea where their first naval triumph had shouted the name of Rome to all the waters of the earth." The film's protagonist, a valiant soldier of Arnold Schwarzenegger proportions, was played by Bartolomeo Pagano, a Genoa longshoreman with no previous acting experience. When Pagano's *Cabiria* character of Maciste identified him to the public more readily than his own name, he adopted the screen name altogether. To put it mildly, leading roles in such epics had little in common with choral performance, so that the historical character's dominance over his contemporaries (at least as depicted) was paralleled by the star's dominance over the rest of the cast. In this way, the costume dramas proved basic to the evolution of *divismo* (the star system) on the Italian screen.

Both Pagano personally and his herculean character of Maciste (later played by others) had sturdy careers, if in increasingly negligible productions and in stories that abandoned the original premise of Hannibal's campaigns against Rome. Aside from Maciste, the most notable male personalities over the first couple of decades of Italian filmmaking were Mario Bonnard and Alberto Capozzi, the prototypical Latin Lovers, and Emilio Ghione, the star, writer, and director of a series of fantasy thrillers. For all their popularity, however, none of these actors had the drawing power of such leading ladies as Lyda Borelli, Francesca Bertini, Hesperia (Olga Mambelli), or Maria Jacobini; even the success of Bonnard and Capozzi stemmed in good part from being paired with Borelli or Bertini. Long before there was a Jean Harlow, Audrey Hepburn, or Madonna "look," the hairstyles and fashions of Italy's most prominent actresses were setting the pace in Rome, Paris, and Berlin. If a Hesperia or Jacobini asked for a script or contract revision even in the middle of shooting, there was little hesitation about acceding to the request—the alternative being a complete shutdown of production. Almost always it was the actresses, not the actors, who received primary billing.

The decidedly female emphasis given to *divismo* grew out of a number of cultural and industrial factors. One was Italy's opera tradition, with its stress on tragic heroines. Another was the reluctance of noted male theater performers to test the new medium, particularly if they had companies with strong regional associations. A third was the profoundly ironic attitude of the Italian public toward the swaggering of Maciste and other characters accredited with moving history. But if, instead of the Roman Empire or Troy, the object of vicarious conquest was a beautiful woman, such as a Borelli or Bertini character? That prospect did not make for so much irony in the mainly male audiences that flocked to Italy's early silents. More than merely a complement to the superman of the battlefield, the superlover of the bedroom, the divan, and the campfire blanket represented a far more tenable screen surrogate for the spectator: first, because the *dive* being romanced were more appealing to the eye than spears and horses; second, because the superlover did not pretend that the spectator identify with some dubiously historical self-aggrandizement; third and most important, because the superlover as surrogate was in the final analysis far more *dispensable* to the fantasies suggested by the film screen. If the superlover was in fact as much of a self-delusion as the superman and if sexual self-aggrandizement was as deceptive as the historical kind, there remained for the spectator an emotionally more plausible association with the beautiful neighbor across the hall, the beautiful co-worker, or the beautiful pedestrian waiting on the corner for the light to change. Latin Lovers of Capozzi's stripe were useful only to the extent of gaining access to a Bertini; after a while, they became only an embarrassing mockery of unfulfilled desire and were best ignored until they were replaced.

The relatively subordinate role played by male stars continued through the 1920s, the consolidation of the Fascist regime, and the advent of sound. For a while, the premier male box-office attraction was theater-trained Tullio Carminati, who starred in numerous "passion films" with titles that translated as *The Lie, The Abandoned Woman, Love Betrayed,* and *Madness.* Tired of playing the Latin Lover in such soap operas, Carminati returned to the stage, where he worked frequently with Eleonora Duse. Later on, he went to Hollywood, where he was typed even more relentlessly as a Don Juan, prompting him to pull up stakes still again—this time to Broadway, where he was a matinee idol until the mid-1930s. Carminati kept working well into the 1960s, appearing in character parts in many American productions shot in Europe.

The entrenchment of Mussolini's regime gave impetus to still more screen glorifications of the deeds of historical and fictionally historical characters, but at least until Italy's invasion of Ethiopia in 1935, more as voluntary exercises by sympathetic or toadying directors than as mandated policy. Initially, the sound era was dominated by melodramas and glossy comedies known as White Telephone films for their customary upper-middle-class settings. The chief male star of the period was Vittorio De Sica, whose dashing looks and boulevard charm had already made him popular with silent-film audiences and whose theater training had eased his transition into talkies. De Sica's persona of the light-footed wag proved especially attractive to a growing female audience, making him one of the few bankable male performers of the decade. After his popularity began to wane under the progressively intrusive demands of life under Fascism, he went on to a rich career as a character actor and, even more markedly, as the director of such postwar classics as *Sciuscià* (Shoeshine), *Ladri di Biciclette* (The Bicycle Thief), *Miracolo a Milano* (Miracle in Milan), and *Umberto D.* As both an actor and a director, he was also what Sophia Loren once called "the third leg of the triangle" in her successful comedies with Mastroianni in the 1950s and 1960s.

In coincidence with his aggression against Ethiopia and Spain in the latter half of the 1930s, Mussolini lost patience with the banal and timid escapism of the White Telephone films, insisting on more explicit political and military propaganda. Declaring that "cinema is our most important weapon," the dictator clamped down on the industry and authorized an expenditure of millions of dollars for the building of Cinecittà, an enormous studio complex on the outskirts of the capital that effectively swallowed up the Cines operations begun by Alberini. In another decision that would have ramifications for decades, he permitted foreign movies into the country only on condition that they be redubbed into Italian before being exhibited. Although originally aimed at preventing anti-Fascist sentiments from slipping into theaters, the reliance on the dubbing studio, continued to this day for both inscribing all the dialogue of domestic films and translating that of foreign imports, has made it harder over the years for any number of Italian performers to persuade producers abroad that they are capable of working with the live sound customary in most other countries. Conversely, some Italian performers who might have pursued careers as profitably abroad as at home have turned down offers precisely because of apprehensions about working without the net of a dubbing studio.

Mussolini's more oppressive interest in the film industry resulted in slews of features about Italian war heroes in Africa and Spain, soap operas about home-front war widows, and yet more costume epics trumpeting the glories of individual warriors during the days of the Roman Empire or some other moment of national military pride. In various guises, such regime favorites as Fosco Giachetti and Osvaldo Valenti played lost souls who found meaning to their lives by joining the Fascist party or sacrificing their lives for the greater good. Valenti and his actress-wife, Luisa Ferida, equally ardent off-screen apologists for the regime, ended up making just such a sacrifice when they were executed by partisans in the closing days of the war. The busiest actor of the period was Amedeo Nazzari, who played the stalwart patriot in such films as *Luciano Serra—Pilota* (Pilot Luciano Serra) and *Il Cavaliere Senza Nome* (The Warrior Without a Name). Nazzari remained active until his death in 1979, but the same hard handsomeness and somewhat rigid bearing that had made him ideal as a military man in the 1930s and as the star of a number of postwar moralistic melodramas left him out in the cold with neorealistic directors in the late 1940s. By the time commercial melodrama and comedy returned to dominate the Italian industry in the 1950s, he was regarded as fairly weathered; it didn't help, either, that many 1950s features were coproductions in which Italy accounted for the female lead and France or West Germany the male star. Nazzari wound down his career as a featured player in costume and gangster pictures (notably, *The Sicilian Clan* in 1969 and *The Valachi Papers* in 1972) and as the star of turgid Italian television mysteries.

The 1940s were a patchwork of hard-bitten, naturalistic dramas (*Ossessione*, or Obsession) and costume spectaculars (*La Corona di Ferro*, or The Iron Crown) produced during the most chaotic years of the war, postwar neorealism, and toward the end of the decade, another return to big-screen pseudohistory in costume. As a prominent player in *Ossessione* and in the epics *La Corona di Ferro*, *I Dieci Commandamenti* (The Ten Commandments, 1945), and *Fabiola* (1948), polo and swimming champion Massimo Girotti enjoyed a brief box-office vogue but then spent years as the hero or villain in a series of increasingly tatty mythical sagas. It was only in the latter part of the 1960s that Girotti once again obtained contemporary roles of some substance, as a featured player in the works of Pier Paolo Pasolini, Luchino Visconti, and Bernardo Bertolucci. Another actor in demand in the 1940s was Rossano Brazzi, who appeared in both costume pictures (*I Dieci Commandamenti*) and contemporary melodramas (*Il Passatore*, or A Bullet for Stefano) before going to Hollywood. Working for American studios, Brazzi had appreciable roles in such films of the 1950s as *The Barefoot Contessa*, *Three Coins in the Fountain*, *Summertime*, and *South Pacific*, but more often than not found himself flirting with caricature as a Latin Lover. Between the 1960s and 1990s, he appeared as a feature player in numerous big-screen quickies and TV movies, sometimes as a decadent aristocrat, almost as frequently as a priest.

With their emphasis on ensemble playing and nonprofessional

performers, the neorealist films of Roberto Rossellini, De Sica, and others were hardly fertile terrain for memorable leading men; only actress Anna Magnani, in fact, emerged from the genre with the visibility of a traditional screen star. On the other hand, it was from the relatively slight form of music-hall comedy that the Neapolitan Totò arose to become the country's most popular male performer by the end of the decade. A master of machine-gun patter, dialect lampoons, and physical humor, the squash-faced veteran of variety theaters was Italy's equivalent of France's Fernandel. Unlike Fernandel, however, Totò's stress on verbal humor more than on mugging made him less translatable than the Frenchman to foreign audiences. Ultimately, he achieved his greatest international recognition from his featured role as the bumbling safecracker in *I Soliti Ignoti* (Big Deal on Madonna Street), a 1958 caper comedy.

Also emerging in the late 1940s was Raf Vallone, who had the leads in two tempestuous melodramas—*Riso Amaro* (Bitter Rice) and *Anna*—that brought world attention to Silvana Mangano. With a burly build and vulnerable looks, Vallone negotiated more than one tale as an impassioned lover who was doomed to be hurt but who would also exact vengeance before going down. Although he, too, appeared in a number of costume epics in the early 1950s, he went on to divide the majority of his time between an acclaimed stage career in France and prominent supporting roles in Hollywood productions (*The Cardinal, Nevada Smith, Cannon for Cordoba, The Godfather, Part III*, etc.), frequently as an extremely worldly cleric. Vallone's most prestigious moment probably came in 1962, when Arthur Miller chose him to play the lead in the playwright's film version of *A View from the Bridge*. (The actor had played the part on the French stage.)

In both *Riso Amaro* and *Anna*, Vallone's main antagonist was portrayed by Vittorio Gassman, prior to Mastroianni the Italian actor who came closest to having his cake at home and eating it abroad. Principally because of his success in the Mangano films, Gassman was pursued avidly by Hollywood, where he ended up in several glossy tearjerkers (most conspicuously opposite Elizabeth Taylor in the 1954 production of *Rhapsody*) that did him a great more harm than good. In the moralistic and xenophobic atmosphere of McCarthyite America, his stay in the United States was also undermined by a rowdy affair, marriage, and divorce from actress Shelley Winters. Back in Europe in the middle of the decade, he appeared in American-financed spectaculars, such as *War and Peace* and *The Tempest*, as a second or even third lead; well into the 1990s, he continued working for U.S. companies, most notably in Robert Altman's *A Wedding* (1978) and in the same director's *Quintet* (1979).

But there was more to Gassman's checkered fortunes in the United States than his saccharine scripts and public scenes with Winters. Even as the stereotypical Latin Lover sought by American producers, he was something of a failure because of a screen persona that was not so much self-assured (à la Brazzi) as it was impenetrably arrogant, providing little plausibility for Hollywood's preconceived notions about Lotharios being ultimately tamable or deeply repentant. Reinforcing this persona was the theatrically trained Gassman's penchant for going over the top—a tendency that the actor did not harness until his return to Italy. Once he did rein it in, he launched what was in effect a second career, first by going back to the stage as one of the country's most celebrated showmen (his specialty being one-man performances of classic European dramas and literature) and then as the star of such box-office-bonanza comedies as *I Soliti Ignoti* and *Il Mattatore* (Love and Larceny, 1960). *Il Mattatore*, in particular, was a signature film not only for showcasing the first of big-sized Gassman performances in scores of bittersweet comedies over the next couple of decades but also for spawning the term *matador* to describe several Italian male stars of the 1960s and 1970s who were viewed as so dominating their surroundings that they killed off everyone around them. The connotation was not (necessarily) that of a ham performance but of the kind of star vehicle that had until then been associated in Italy primarily with actresses, going back through Magnani to Isa Miranda and Alida Valli, all the way to the silent era of Borelli and Bertini. Aside from Gassman, the main matadors were Alberto Sordi, Nino Manfredi, and Ugo Tognazzi—all of them commercial insurance policies individually and even more so when, as occurred regularly, they were teamed in various combinations. Except for Sordi's appearances in internationally cast comedies (*Those Magnificent Men in Their Flying Machines*, 1965) and Tognazzi's success in France (*La Cage aux Folles*, 1978), the matadors were largely a national phenomenon, with their popularity ensconced in frequently hard *commedia all'italiana* satirical perspectives on urban, provincial, and regional customs and hypocrisies.

With the matadors not yet in the arena in the 1950s, Italy's screens were even more of a woman's world than usual; among those exerting the greatest star power were Magnani, Mangano, Gina Lollobrigida, Loren, Lucia Bosè, Silvana Pampanini, and Eleanora Rossi Drago. Unlike the men, the women found it relatively easy to move in and out of American and British projects, though only occasionally (Magnani in *The Rose Tattoo* in 1955 and *The Fugitive Kind* in 1959; Loren in *Desire Under the Elms* and *The Key* in 1958) in parts that stressed dramatic abilities rather than physical endowments. Actors of the 1950s also suffered from Hollywood's financial and production invasion of Italy: Not only did U.S. companies shake the local film industry's economy to the core by setting higher cost and salary standards and by ransacking Rome's distribution systems, but as a condition of coproduction deals, they imposed American leading men on otherwise Italian casts. Even modest-budgeted sandal-and-sword epics starred the likes of the faded Alan Ladd and B-movie leads Rory Calhoun and Guy Madison instead of genre veterans Girotti and Vallone. While usually insisting that they themselves had sought out the performers in question for purely artistic reasons, directors as noted as Federico Fellini and Michelangelo Antonioni also eschewed Italians for Americans; for example, Anthony Quinn and Richard Basehart in Fellini's *La Strada* (1954), Broderick Crawford and Basehart in the same filmmaker's *Il Bidone* (The Swindle, 1955), and Steve Cochran in Antonioni's *Il Grido* (The Outcry, 1957). Still another American, former Mister America and Mister Universe Steve Reeves, played Hercules in a series of costume spectaculars that were as big in box-office profits around the world as they were long on gimcrack sets, clumsy use of scale models and back projection, and inept acting. Indeed, aside from Totò, the Italian actor of the period with the biggest domestic or foreign following was the chunky, fifty-year-old Gino Cervi, who portrayed the Communist mayor Peppone in the treacly Don Camillo comedy series with Fernandel.

The launching of Mastroianni in the early 1960s as the longest-reigning international male star from Italy was no overnight happening. The actor had, in fact, been working steadily before the cameras since the late 1940s, following an initial speaking role in an Italian version of Victor Hugo's *Les Misérables*. Prior to gaining notice for performances in the somber *Le Notti Bianche* (White Nights) in 1957 and the zany *I Soliti Ignoti* with Gassman and Totò the next year, he had been regarded in some quarters as something of an Italian Louis Jourdan for his spare-cheeked, glistening-eye look; some photos of the late 1940s and early 1950s also evoke a pretty boy in the Alain Delon mold, although his actual screen appearances failed to support this impression. Pretty boy or not, for many years directors tended to view him as fit only for roles as well-meaning innocents who get involved in situations bigger than they are. Despite triumphs such as *Le Notti Bianche*, this typecasting did not really disappear until his appearance as the dissolute journalist in Fellini's *La Dolce Vita* (1959), seconded immediately by *Il Bell'Antonio* the next year and by *La Notte* (The Night) and *Divorzio all'Italiana* (Divorce Italian Style) in 1961. Taken together, the four pictures provided an instant demonstration of Mastroianni's range, extending from the morose writer of Antonioni's *La Notte* to the wildly scheming husband in Pietro

Germi's *Divorzio all'Italiana*. Equally important, the four films were at the forefront of an Italian-industry renascence that was welcomed throughout Europe and the United States by critics who had tired of Britain's "Room at the Top" morality sermons and who had sometimes been less comfortable than they had cared to admit with the technical jarrings of France's New Wave. The Italian features *told stories*, usually in a traditional, linear fashion, without apologies for the sensuality that suffused even the less orthodox, intellectual works of Antonioni. It also helped that films like *La Dolce Vita* and Visconti's *Rocco e i Suoi Fratelli* (Rocco and His Brothers) radiated the kind of production size normally associated with Hollywood and that these two pictures, along with Antonioni's *L'Avventura*, opened in New York, London, and other major cities within days of each other, reinforcing the sensation of a new artistic phenomenon.

As it turned out, Mastroianni lasted much longer than the industry's renascence. By the mid-1960s, overextended production companies (Titanus and Galatea were the biggest) were collapsing faster than the sets on a Hercules movie. While even the Fellinis and Antonionis had to go scratching for capital for their projects, American actors were once again brought in as box-office saviors—this time not to take over the lead roles in toga tales but in the so-called spaghetti westerns pioneered by producer-director Sergio Leone. Basically operatic variations on Hollywood westerns in which a sinuous musical soundtrack (especially if composed by Ennio Morricone) was as important as the plot, the Leone productions gave new impetus to the careers of Clint Eastwood, Charles Bronson, and Lee Van Cleef and provided novel roles for everyone from Henry Fonda and Jason Robards to Rod Steiger and Eli Wallach. But although hundreds of the action features were turned out between the mid-1960s and early 1970s (many of them produced only as tax shelters and never distributed), few were the Italian actors who emerged from them with hardier careers. One was Giuliano Gemma, who became a standby in medium-budgeted action stories of all kinds. Another was Gian Maria Volonté, who parlayed prominent roles as Eastwood's nemesis in Leone's *Per un Pugno di Dollari* (A Fistful of Dollars, 1964) and *Per Qualche Dollaro in Più* (For a Few Dollars More, 1965) into leads in such bristlingly political features as the Oscar-winning *Indagine su un Cittadino al di sopra di Ogni Sospetto* (Investigation of a Citizen Above Suspicion, 1970), *Sacco e Vanzetti* (1971), and *Todo Modo* (One Way or Another, 1976). Most symptomatic of all was the case of Mario Girotti, who, after years as a featured player in costume sagas, dyed his hair blond, took the name of Terence Hill, then went on to star in a number of western spoofs. The most successful of the slapstick ventures, which costarred Carlo Pedersoli, rebaptized as Bud Spencer, were *Dio Perdona, Io No* (God Forgives, I Don't, 1967) and *Lo Chiamavano Trinità* (They Call Me Trinity, 1971). Following the critically applauded *Il Mio Nome È Nessuno* (My Name is Nobody) with Fonda in 1973, Hill signed a Hollywood contract but got little beyond a tepid comedy with Jackie Gleason before returning to Europe.

The loss of leading male roles to Americans wasn't felt solely in the westerns; in fact, by the mid-1970s, there were few Italian films with pretensions to major international distribution that did not import their star players. Where the meaty roles were, even for characters drawn from classic Italian literature, one could find Burt Lancaster, Marlon Brando, Jack Nicholson, Sterling Hayden, Donald Sutherland, and Robert De Niro to play them. The reliance on familiar American faces even extended to B-budget police mysteries and erotic thrillers in the 1970s, with veteran supporting actors along the lines of Lee J. Cobb, Karl Malden, James Whitmore, Martin Balsam, and Edmond O'Brien getting the key parts. The dependence on the Hollywood character players, none of whom had the world box-office clout that had justified the signing of Lancaster for *Il Gattopardo* (The Leopard, 1963) and Brando for *Quemada!* (Burn!, 1969), reflected still another pressure on Italy's own actors—the shooting of all features in English. For Italian producers with an eye on the international market, it was infinitely more economical to sign an American actor, dub his role into Italian for domestic audiences, and then present the rest of the world with a subtitled feature in which the salient performers were already using their native tongue.

Inevitably, the greater use of English made some Italian actors far more in demand than others for their ability to speak the language. Among leading men, one beneficiary was Franco Nero, who overcame an early, dewy-eyed Hollywood role as Sir Lancelot in *Camelot* (1967) to work regularly in pictures shot in Italy with international casts. On the other hand, Volonté and Manfredi, aside from other reservations they had about scripts having only the most approximate of cultural contexts, found the language problem obtrusive to their careers. Tognazzi didn't fare too well, either, although he sought to overcome his problems with English by merely mouthing a series of numbers during actual shooting. At that, his solution was not all that bizarre, since even many of the Italians who were at ease speaking English were later redubbed by Americans or Canadians to erase what were considered offensive accents.

Among Italian character players, probably no one gained from the English-language requirement more than Gabriele Ferzetti, the lead in Antonioni's *L'Avventura* who ended up doing scores of gangster and *patron* roles (where a light accent was acceptable) on both sides of the Atlantic, including several made-for-TV movies in the United States. Like Ferzetti, Adolfo Celi also worked frequently for American and British productions, most prominently as the villain in the James Bond action film *Thunderball* (1965). Among those losing out because of the language problem was Enrico Maria Salerno, a character player of equal weight in Italy who had to surrender the role of the crippled heavy in Leone's *C'Era una Volta il West* (Once Upon a Time in the West, 1968) to Ferzetti.

The situation did not get any better in the 1980s. With even the matadors aging or dying (e.g., Tognazzi), cable television competing for evening attention, and continental coproduction deals all the more de rigueur with the European Community's moves toward integration, few were the Italian actors who maintained a regular starring presence in theatrical features. The handful of exceptions included Giancarlo Giannini, who continued to play leads at home, especially in the works of director Lina Wertmuller, while appearing more often as a supporting player in American pictures; Paolo Villaggio, a television-born comedian who did a number of programmers with little export resonance; and Roberto Benigni, another television-born performer of a droller, more unorthodox appeal who became associated with such Jim Jarmusch American satires as *Down By Law* (1986), then undertook to succeed Peter Sellers in the role of Inspector Clouseau. For once, even Italian actresses found themselves being squeezed on local marquees: After the post-Magnani waves of Monica Vitti, Claudia Cardinale, and Virna Lisi and then Mariangela Melato, Stefania Sandrelli, Laura Antonelli, and Ornella Muti, Rome-produced features were as likely to star an Isabelle Adjani, an Isabelle Huppert, or the latest British or American fashion model as a native performer. Some actresses, such as Isabella Rossellini and Valeria Golino, became more identified with their work in the United States than with that at home.

Through it all, Mastroianni kept working, defining himself as much by what he declined to do as by what he did. To begin with, he waved off countless opportunities to join the ranks of the matadors, largely sticking to films in which his costar (almost always a woman) was as much of a presence as he was. The primary exceptions were in such Fellini pictures as *8½* (1963) and *La Città delle Donne* (The City of Women, 1980), in which production values and directorial glitz served as at least a rival source of attention. Second, the actor generally refused costumers and period epics—a choice confirmed for him conversely when he made an ill-advised foray into a bad remake of *Scipione Detto Anche L'Africano* (Scipio the African) in 1971. Third, apart from *Scipione Detto Anche L'Africano* (in which he had to shave his head) and a couple of other features, he turned down practically all offers that involved altering his physical appearance in any dramatic way; as he once told a reporter, "When you begin to change your looks, it's usually a sign that you are tired of yourself. How long after that will it be before the public senses what you are feeling and also gets bored with you?"

Until the early 1990s, Mastroianni also rejected all attempts to get him to work in Hollywood, confining himself to occasional U.S.-financed projects shot in Italy by non-Americans. Among these films were *The Poppy Is Also a Flower* (sponsored by the United Nations and directed by Britain's Terence Young in 1966), *Rappresaglia* (Massacre in Rome; costarring Richard Burton and directed by the Greek George Pan Cosmatos in 1973), and *Maccheroni* (Macaroni; costarring Jack Lemmon and directed by Italy's Ettore Scola in 1985). While acknowledging that the Hollywood heroics of the Gables and Coopers had transformed his childhood into a brilliant garden of fantasies, he produced reason after reason for not working in Southern California, including his bemused credo that "all of us ought to have at least one thing in old age that we regret not having done, and mine will be that I never accepted an offer to go there."

But if Mastroianni went out of his way to avoid Hollywood, he didn't avoid too many other places, even boasting of his ability to get both Italian and foreign producers to finance his travelings around Europe and other continents. In 1970, he was drawn to De Sica's *I Girasoli* (The Sunflowers) in part because it was the first Soviet coproduction with a Western country since the onset of East-West tensions. In 1987, he was back in Russia for his award-winning role in Nikita Mikhalkov's *Oci Ciornie* (Dark Eyes). His apprehensions about language (one of the reasons given for not going to Hollywood) did not prevent him from speaking English in the British films *Diamonds for Breakfast* in 1969 and *Leo the Last* the following year. In addition to taking on numerous leading roles in French features over the years, he had triumphant Paris stage runs in 1984 in François Billetdoux's *Tchin-Tchin* (under the direction of Peter Brook) and in 1987 in an amalgamation of Anton Chekhov's writings (under Mikhalkov). In 1983, he went to Brazil for Bruno Barreto's Brazilian production of *Gabriela*. In 1986, he undertook the first of two Greek films for Theo Angelopoulos and the following year camped down in Budapest to work with Hungary's Pal Sandor. If he long disdained the idea of going to work for Americans in Hollywood, he was more than agreeable to acting for Italians in New York and Chicago. Other roles over the years have taken him to Algeria, Morocco, the Congo, Canada, Argentina, and Uruguay. Audiences have heard soundtracks of his voice in English, French, Portuguese, Greek, and Russian, as well as in an array of Italian dialects.

Although he has shrugged off some of his more exotic ventures as merely being in keeping with an actor's obligation to go where the roles are to be found, Mastroianni was also careful until the 1980s to entrust himself only to the most prominent directors, whatever the promise of a script. "It is very unusual for me to get excited about what is on the page," he has said repeatedly. "I don't even bother reading the script sometimes. Everything depends on my relationship with the director." Among non-Italians, this has meant a readiness to work primarily for the likes of such internationally recognized talents as Angelopoulos, Mikhalkov, John Boorman, Roman Polanski, and Louis Malle. With regard to the Italians, in a career that had totaled more than 125 films by the onset of the 1990s, it meant a scrupulous preference for a handful of directors who came into their own with him in the 1950s and 1960s and who have constituted as much of an artistic elite as the country's industry has ever had. With a regularity reminiscent of some Hollywood collaborations between star and director back in the years of the big studios, Mastroianni has worked with Scola ten times, with Mario Monicelli and Marco Ferreri seven times, with Fellini six times, and with Dino Risi on four occasions. Among the older guard, he performed before the camera for Luciano Emmer five times and for DeSica and Alessandro Blasetti four times each. In fact, aside from Roberto Rossellini and Bernardo Bertolucci, there had been hardly an Italian director worth the name that the actor had not worked for by the early 1990s. The now deceased Rossellini spent a considerable part of his career making semidocumentary historical films that Mastroianni once declared beyond his range. Bertolucci had reached agreement with the actor to play the Fascist leader in his *Novecento* (1900) [1976], but the plan had to be scrapped when Mastroianni went into a debilitating depression after his breakup with Catherine Deneuve.

But there has been much more to Mastroianni's endurance as Europe's most recognized male screen performer than his willingness to travel for good parts or his carefulness about working with Italy's directorial elite. Hollywood ideas about Latin Lovers aside, he initially drew attention for a graceful handsomeness that had none of Gassman's threat or Brazzi's archness. More to the point, he aged with equal gracefulness, permitting directors to use his looks as a counterpoint to an artistic versatility unmatched on the European screen. It has been this latter quality, more than his friendship with director-contemporaries or their heirs, that has kept him in demand. For every cigarette-wielding sophisticate that he has played, he has portrayed innumerably more priests, con men, rabble-rousers, drunks, assassins, addicts, and policemen. He was the screen's first pregnant man, the suicide who did nothing but play with balloons, and the narcissist who never retired for the evening without putting his hair in curlers. The fabled lover of beautiful women has been an impotent cuckold, a homosexual, and a rapist. He has raged as much as murmured, sung and danced as deftly as crooned sweet nothings, and in the process carried off dozens of acting awards from an equal number of countries, even becoming the first continental to get a Best Actor Oscar nomination for work in a foreign film, then doing it twice more. Some film festivals, notably those in Cannes and Venice, have become regular sources of tribute. In 1988, a continental panel in Brussels named him as Europe's best actor over the last thirty years, then selected Fellini's *8½*, in which he starred, as the best film over that stretch of time.

To hear Mastroianni, none of this requires special comment. He declines to think of himself as a star, or, more important, to act like one, even though nobody in Europe or North America in the last three decades has been so emulative of the professional choices once made by the Gables and Coopers (the difference being that Mastroianni has made them for himself rather than having them made for him by a studio or an agent). When he has not ridiculed the importance of the actor, he has relished recounting tales such as Fellini's approach to him in the casting of *La Dolce Vita*, when the director reportedly declared that "I need a face with no personality—like yours." He has also attributed his longevity to "merely being who I am, letting myself be passive for whatever the director has in mind to do with me." If this smacks of the falsely ingenuous, it is Mastroianni himself who has pointed it out, reflecting in other conversations that he would have never gotten anywhere without his theatrical training in the late 1940s and 1950s under Visconti.

In 1991, Mastroianni agreed to undertake the first project that could be said to be a Hollywood picture. At the age of sixty-seven, the accord for making *Used People* added his name, finally, to the long list of Italian actors who have sought to trump a European success in America. Unlike his predecessors, going back to Tullio Carminati, however, in Mastroianni's case, it was a question of the mountain coming to Mohammed.

Part One

Marcello

1

Extra Places

If Marcello Mastroianni's career has displayed a penchant for sponsored vagabondage, the pattern was set in his earliest years.

The first of two sons of Ottorino Mastrojanni and Ida Irolle, Marcello Vincenzo Domenico Mastrojanni was born on September 28, 1924, in the town of Fontana Liri, a modest production center for laced footwear some fifty miles southeast of Rome. At the time, Fontana Liri belonged to the province of Caserta in the region of Campania (Naples); three years later, administrative reshuffling assigned the community to the province of Frosinone in the region of Latium (Rome). Although the gerrymandering abetted the later identification of the star of *La Dolce Vita* with the Italian capital, he himself has often claimed warmer feelings for Naples, even bristling at the notion of being considered a Roman.

> In Italy, if you're from the Ciociaria, as I am, you're regarded as something of a peasant from the outskirts of the capital. There is an insult in that attitude, but I have never let it bother me. On the contrary, where I was born, everyone regards himself as superior, more Roman than the Romans. Yes, we're a race of peasants and merchants, but we've never had to put up with the great invasions that Rome has, and we've never gone through the bastardization of races and cultures that has afflicted the big cities. I've always been proud of the fact that I come from Fontana Liri, that I have a little piece of country soul that nobody can ever take away from me.

The father's side of the family had a strong artistic résumé. One of Mastroianni's uncles was a successful sculptor; another, an accomplished painter. Before World War I, a granduncle named Domenico had been very much in vogue as a sculptor. A paternal grandmother came from a clan that produced, among others, American screen actor Richard Conte. For all that, however, the Mastrojannis (film distributors changed the *j* to an *i* in the early 1950s) were like most of their neighbors—poor. The father worked at a series of jobs, mostly of a fetch-and-carry kind. As the actor once recalled:

> We accepted poverty as a natural condition of our lives. My mother liked saying my father was a cabinetmaker, but he only repaired broken furniture. He also repaired the holes in my shoes with pieces of aluminum, so that I sounded like a horse when I walked. A lot of my clothes came from an uncle in Turin, and my arms hung out of them so much that the kids in the neighborhood called me Skinny Paws.

In 1928, Ottorino Mastrojanni lost a job as a chemist's assistant for purportedly offending a number of locals with his anti-Mussolini sentiments (a reason given by his mother that the actor confesses to never having been able to confirm). With little alternative, the family accepted an offer to move to Turin to live with the uncle who had been supplying Marcello with his clothes. It was in Turin that Mastroianni's brother, Ruggero, was born on November 7, 1929.

Aside from beginning school there, the actor's strongest memories of Turin centered around the hand-me-down clothes that he remained largely dependent on until his father began picking up some work as a carpenter. One particularly mixed blessing was what was given to him by his uncle the sculptor.

> He had incredibly gaudy taste. I would go around dressed like a jockey—all bright reds and greens and blues and usually in the same shirt and pants. I'm embarrassed to think of what I must have looked like. I suppose some people might say that it was then and there that I had to make some kind of peace with being a public spectacle. But back then we were mostly grateful to get whatever we could.

They remained grateful until 1933, when Ottorino Mastrojanni again moved the family, this time to the Tuscolano section of Rome, to the house of a brother-in-law who worked for the state railway. In the capital, the father turned his carpentry talents to a small furniture-making business, where Marcello helped out after school.

> It was nothing special as a job, mainly sawing and staining. My father was hardly in a position to hire somebody as a full-time assistant. The smells of the wood and varnish made it worthwhile. I don't think I've ever walked past a carpentry shop without thinking of my father's place.

When he wasn't sitting in a classroom or using a saw, however, the preteen Mastroianni was doing what he did best:

> I was a street kid. Left to ourselves, my friends and I were very happy. We would go strutting around thinking that we were the

bravest and healthiest boys in the world—certainly braver and healthier than the rich kids who always seemed confined to some big house with a wall around it. We'd sneak into gardens or any- where else there was to sneak into. We'd swipe stuff off the stands in front of stores or in the markets. My own specialty was knives; I had a passion for them. We never considered any of it stealing in a real sense. The whole point was just to grab something and be able to boast that you had pulled it off. Of course, when your parents asked you where you got that brand-new knife, you always told them something like "Oh, I borrowed that from Sergio." I'm sure my mother's heart went into her mouth every time I went out the door, but there was really very little that she could do about it.

It wasn't exactly that way, according to Ida Mastrojanni. Inter- viewed in the late 1970s by Italian television, she declared:

> He never really knew how to lie. He would tell me so many stories, but with so little conviction that I'd tell him not to bother to go on. He had such a simple face, like an open book. I always thought that he was more of a little girl than a little boy in that way.

Rainy days made a special impression on the street raga- muffin.

> It was a feeling, a smell. When it rained, everything seemed coated with an odor of adventure. The sticky horses, the wet clothes—we had the feeling on those days of setting out to conquer the Hima- layan Mountains.

Not that his imagination obscured from view those who seemed to be better off than he was.

> There was a *rosticceria* on Via Appia Nuova. It was called the Ros- ticceria Catena. I never felt so envious as when I would look through the window there and see them serving *supplì* [fried balls of rice, cheese, and tomato sauce]. I'd stick my nose against the glass and think to myself, "When I'm rich, I'm going to buy myself a *supplì*." I could feel it melting on my tongue. I would picture eat- ing it very slowly, with the cheese dripping down over my chin. It was so hot, so perfect. Those *supplì* drove me crazy.

Another status symbol was a chambermaid.

> There was this colonel who lived across the street from us. His win- dow faced on ours. I would see this chambermaid in there, and that to me meant rich. I don't mean like today, when you're always reading about rich people sailing off in yachts or having holidays in Sardinia or the French Riviera; no, just the fact that this colonel had this woman come in to clean up for him—that's what made him

rich as far as I was concerned. My mother said the colonel could afford the woman because he had a pension, and that made him a Signore. I believed it, I really did. I had a friend named Valentino, a kid my age. He used to go off with his family for vacations to exotic places (at least to me) like Ostia, and he had an accordion and a radio and who knows what else. But mainly because he, too, had a maid to come in and clean up his room, I thought that Valentino was a Signore, too.

As he would say later of his film career, the actor discerned a touch of luck in his early years.

It was lucky of me not to get into any trouble, or even to be tempted by it. I was also lucky in gambling games. Every Sunday, my father gave me a few lire, and I usually got by on it because I knew a little something about playing cards and billiards.

In school, he had a little more than luck; he also had the memory that would one day make him a quick study on dialogue.

I was one of those who studied without studying. I was hardly a genius, but I usually remembered what I had to do. Arithmetic, dates, that kind of thing came to me fairly easily.

More generally, Mastroianni has depicted his earliest schooling as a stressless time, filled with companionship—a reminiscence reflected in his frequent references over the years to "classmates" as an example of a model human relationship. (In particular, he has used this term often to describe the nature of his ties to director Federico Fellini.)

Of course, there was one area that produced *some* stress.

When I think of my first great love, I think of Silvana. Silvana was beautiful, and I was only twelve years old. What struck me most about her was the way her long blond hair would jump up and down whenever she played hopscotch. It took me a long time to declare my love, to tell her that she was part of my every waking thought. That wasn't something just blurted out, not with all the other kids around.

He finally found his way to Silvana's heart with the help of his uncle's garden.

He had everything—dahlias, geraniums, even some roses. I felt like such a criminal taking my knife to them one afternoon. But Silvana was very happy when I presented her with my bouquet. When she sniffed the flowers, she turned completely red in the face. The next day, she gave me a small medallion of the Madonna. It was tucked into a red piece of silk shaped like a heart. I ran home to show it to my mother, who was very impressed. She decided that Silvana was a nice girl.

But still just one girl.

I guess I had a taste for complications even back then. At four o'clock I would be with Floriana, at six o'clock with Carla. Not that I didn't pay for it sometimes. One day, a brother of one of my "conquests" showed up and belted me so hard that I decided right then and there never to go near another woman who had a brother bigger than I was.

Although raised as a Catholic and prone to church imagery for conceptualizing his attitudes toward himself and others in his later years, Mastroianni's only vivid memory of practicing his religion as a boy was of trying to be more papal than the pope.

I got it into my head that if people were supposed to be closer to God by taking communion, then I would get closer than any of them by receiving it twice on Sunday. So that's what I did—up to the altar rail, back and swallow, then back up to the rail again for another Host. I was so proud that I made the mistake of telling the priest. Instead of congratulating me, he exploded! Maybe it was from that point on that I usually spent most of my time in church looking at the girls.

Following grade school, Mastroianni enrolled in the Duca d'Aosta vocational institute in his district. Because of his facility with numbers, he was soon on a track for a career as a technical engineer, obtaining a diploma in building survey and construction from the Carlo Grella Industrial Institute in 1943. He seriously contemplated going on with studies in architecture, and even long after he had established himself as a screen star, he insisted that would have been his profession of choice. "I'll continue to make movies just for the money," he told Rex Reed in the *New York Times* in 1970, "but architecture will always be my first love." In the same vein, he told a French periodical around the same time:

Whenever I'm bored, I imagine that I'm an architect. How I would like to build something solid, with solid materials! Bricks, cement, wood—their odors—just to touch them makes me feel wonderful. To mix cement with a trowel, to build something that would really last—that's what I would really like to do.

(In other interviews, and in the contradictory style that has habitually marked his declarations to the media, Mastroianni has claimed to retain only a passing interest in architecture, extending no further than an opportunity to visit the studio of some architect acquaintance to glance at blueprints. But most evidence would argue otherwise; although he has not been known to do much cement mixing, his enthusiasm for architecture led him to help design several homes in the 1960s and 1970s.)

A second option following his graduation from the technical institute was to go into accounting.

> Becoming an accountant was a common goal for someone with the petit bourgeois background that I had. I still have moments when I think that one of these days somebody is going to stand up in a cinema, point to me up on the screen, and yell out: "That's no actor, that's just a public accountant trying to pull the wool over our eyes!"

But Mastroianni the teenager also had a third choice.

> Being an actor always attracted me. I wasn't the class clown or anything like that, but I didn't go out of my way to avoid attention, either. For a while, I liked very much being in the church choir. The church was the place for us to hang out, and it didn't cost anything to sing. Then, on Thursdays, there was a parish priest, his name was Virgilio Caselli, who figured that the best way to keep young scoundrels off the road to hell was to make them part of these little theatricals he wrote about the saints and martyrs. They were really only homilies in dialogue form, and we would perform them for all the children in the neighborhood. I was practically in every one of them, but I never got a lead role. I was usually just a supporting martyr. I loved the exhibitionism of it all, especially when I noticed that it seemed to make an impression on the girls in the neighborhood.

In 1938, the fourteen-year-old Mastroianni gave his first performance outside the parish theatricals when he got a part as an extra in Carmine Gallone's film musical *Marionette* (Marionettes). The opportunity came his way through the mother of one of his friends, who worked as a cashier in one of the restaurants in the nearby Cinecittà complex. *Marionette* starred opera tenor Beniamino Gigli.

> It was a grape-harvest-festival scene. They had a lot of young people sitting around as Gigli came through the vineyard booming out his song. For one night of work, I got paid ten lire, and that was a fabulous sum as far as I was concerned. My mother and a lot of my friends were in it as extras, too. After we finished shooting, we were allowed to eat as many grapes as we wanted.

But the experience of *Marionette* amounted to significantly more than ten lire and a stomachful of grapes.

I was fascinated by this exotic world I had stumbled into. Making movies seemed like a game played by adults. I was very proud of myself for being part of it. I also remember feeling that everything I saw that night had somehow been arranged specifically for me, that everything had a meaning with a capital M, and that all I had to do was to pay attention and I would pick up some valuable pointers for life. Maybe I did, because it was from that work as an extra that it always seemed important to me to stay in the middle of people, never to withdraw like a snob.

The money was no small factor, however, not with the war conditions in Italy practically reducing to zero the demand for Ottorino Mastrojanni's furniture-making services. In fact, from the age of thirteen, Marcello had been called on to help the family's finances with summer jobs; among the places he worked at between school terms were the Italian army's artillery division headquarters and the Rome sanitation department. But once through the door of Cinecittà with *Marionette*, he had little doubt how he preferred making money.

Sometimes when I mention to people how young I was when I began working, they look like they want to take pity on me for not having been there at the time to give me some money. They're absolutely crazy. I never had so much fun in my life. For just one day, I'd be anything at all—an Indian, a pirate, whatever. I *liked* working.

Among the films he appeared in as an extra were Alessandro Blasetti's costume epic *La Corona di Ferro* (The Crown of Iron, 1940) and Mario Camerini's *Una Storia d'Amore* (A Love Story, 1942), the latter experience a particularly memorable one.

What I had to do for Camerini was nothing more than to stand in an elevator in a Rome department store with five or six other extras. It was the simplest thing in the world: Camerini calls for the action to start, the door opens, and out we go. But suddenly there's the door opening, and I walk right into Assia Noris, who was the star of the film and one of the great beauties of the period. I started trembling. Then I remembered she was married to Camerini and felt like a double fool. Fortunately, Noris was more professional than I was, so nobody said anything.

On another occasion, however, he had little patience with what he deemed the lack of professionalism by another actor.

We were doing something called *I Pirati della Malesia* (The Pirates of Malaysia), and I was standing around in this tavern scene. Massimo Girotti, who was a great athlete but who didn't know how to act for anything back in those days, was supposed to say a line, then jump up on a table and run out. He was great at the jumping, but he couldn't say this simple line. Finally, the director calls a halt and tells his assistant to go get a bottle of orange soda for Girotti. "Maybe that will relax him and loosen his tongue," he says. Well, I'm standing there thinking, What the hell kind of a shithead is this? He can't say a single line? To hell with the bottle of soda. Give him a kick in the ass. That'll loosen his tongue, too.

The fledgling actor's first important contact in the industry was Vittorio De Sica, whose sister Maria had remained close to Mastroianni's mother since their early years of working together at the Banca d'Italia.

I never stopped bothering Maria with business cards and the like to pass on to her brother. My mother got annoyed at the way that I was breaking balls, but not Maria. She introduced me to Vittorio and never once complained about being used as a middleman. Finally, Vittorio hired me as an extra for *I Bambini Ci Guardano* (The Children Are Watching) in 1942. I think he thought that was the only way of getting rid of me.

On the contrary, his work on the De Sica film only persuaded Mastroianni that he would be able to find even steadier work as an extra if he applied himself to it, so he deluged production companies with pictures and résumés. He didn't let the actor-director forget about it, either.

I always knew where Vittorio was shooting, so I'd wait until the crew was taking a break, then I'd go marching in on him in the middle of a snack or a nap. He was incredibly tolerant. In his place, most people would have thrown me out on my ear. But all he'd say to me in that stentorian voice of his was, "Study, study, study. Get your degree and then we'll see." When I think back on it, I can't believe how pathetically relentless I was.

Even though Mastroianni ended up starring in several films for De Sica in later years, the basis of their relationship was established during the actor's days as a job-seeking extra, and it had little in common with his familiarity with "classmate" Fellini.

De Sica always remained something of an uncle to me. Afterward, when we were shooting things like *I Girasoli*, I saw nothing wrong in still thinking of him in that way. I could never use the intimate form of address with him when we talked. I always gave him the respectful, third-person *Lei*. At the same time, I found it perfectly natural that he would use the familiar *Tu* form with me, the way an adult addresses a child or somebody with less experience of the world. I didn't dare do anything to change that, even when I was well into my forties.

For all his determination to make it as an actor, the shaky financial situation of his family deterred Mastroianni from totally abandoning his formal training, particularly when his hunt for film work turned up little beyond a couple of vague promises. His compromise solution was to enroll in the University of Rome's Economics and Trade Department in 1943.

It seemed like the only way of getting near the university's theater company, where I could do some real acting on the stage. It was free, and I certainly didn't have the money for an acting school. Maybe I was also calculating that if things didn't work out for me as an actor, I was still within a study area where I could make a living. I didn't dwell too much on the possibility of failing, but it was in the back of my head.

The theory turned out to be better than the practice. With the Italian army suffering rout after rout and Mussolini's regime collapsing, the university theater became a luxury. After a brief period of financing his studies with a job as a draftsman for the municipality of Rome, Mastroianni was recommended for a post with the Istituto Geografico Militare in Florence; his main task was to assist in drawing maps for Italy's retreating armed forces. When the Italians surrendered to the Allies in September 1943 and the Nazis occupied the peninsula of their erstwhile Axis partners, the institute position exempted him from being drafted into the German military. Instead, together with other males employed at the Florence center, he ended up being shipped north to Dobbiaco in the Alpine region of the Alto Adige and forced to dig trenches. This lasted until early 1944, when he got word that he was about to be transferred to another labor camp in Germany. Using the graphic skills that he had honed as a mapmaker, he forged documents for himself and painter Remo Brindisi, and the two of them escaped to Venice, where they began a year's hand-to-mouth existence while eluding the Germans and diehard Fascist thugs.
Mastroianni:

It was a bohemian time in some respects, and I'll sometimes let myself get nostalgic about it. But it was also an extremely bitter time. I was cut off from my family; we never knew when a tap on the shoulder meant that we were under arrest. An old tailor by the name of Calzavano gave us a small room in the attic of his house. I never did decide whether he was an anti-Fascist or just someone who understood our situation and wanted to help us as a fellow

human being. We made ends meet by tracing postcard scenes of the
bridges onto handkerchiefs and selling them to tourists as genuine
Venetian handicrafts. Brindisi, who was a great painter, did most of
the art, and I did the selling, but sometimes I'd try my hand at the
designing, too. I wasn't the worst artist in the world. Our private
joke was that we mostly did the Ponte dei Sospiri (The Bridge of
Sighs), since it was named after the despair of people who were
about to be executed back in the old days.

But at least in retrospect the worst part of the Venice hiding was
not knowing what was happening with his family.

I had never been cut off from them for so long before. Many nights
in that attic I would think about not just my parents and my brother
but about so many gatherings where the grandparents and aunts
and uncles and cousins would be around the same table. Especially
when I was young, I thought of those occasions as real feasts. It was
a nuclear family in the classic sense, somewhat patriarchal, with
my grandfather having the last word on everything.

Then, too, there had been his more recent memories, immediately before leaving Rome for Florence.

Things had really been bad in Rome when I had left. Food, everything, had gotten scarce. One time, a bomb hit a coal yard near
where we were living, so I got a wheelbarrow and ran out into the
street to fill it up with all the coal that had been blown out of the
coal yard. There was a black marketeer in the neighborhood who
always had pasta, so I pushed and pulled the wheelbarrow up four
flights of stairs to his apartment to see if he would trade me some of
it for the coal. We did some bargaining, he gets the coal, and I get
the spaghetti. I go running back home so proud of the deal I've
pulled off. It's only when I open the boxes in the kitchen that I see
that there are more worms than pieces of spaghetti inside.

With such images in mind, he took the liberation of Rome on
June 4, 1944, as a signal to gather up as many beans and potatoes as
he could find and hurry to the capital with his emergency supplies.
But when he arrived, he found his family eating much better than he
had been.

The Americans had brought food, so the starvation crisis was over.
On top of that, my brother had gotten a job as a waiter at the Hotel
Excelsior, and through all the Americans and other people he met
there he had been able to pick up a few extras. With my beans and
potatoes I felt like a total idiot.

Although deflated in his self-importance by finding his family in a better state than he had expected, Mastroianni had the consolation of a cousin's connections to land a position as a bookkeeper in the Rome office of J. Arthur Rank's Eagle-Lion Films. Once reestablished at home with his Eagle-Lion salary (the equivalent of forty dollars monthly), he picked up the old thread of seeking movie work and also dusted off his plan of getting into the university's theater company.

> It wasn't the greatest time in my life, and I really hated going to that office. Fortunately, there were five women there, and they did most of my work for me. For the most part, I sat there looking at all these pictures on the wall of James Mason, Margaret Lockwood, and Phyllis Calvert and recited poetry aloud. I must have read fairly well because one day a woman in the office next to ours mentioned me to her brother-in-law, who was then connected to the university theater. Otherwise, though, there were not too many laughs. Most of my salary went for medicine for my father, who was suffering a good deal from diabetes. I never had enough even to go to the cinema. My idea of a big night was to play billiards and *boccette*.

For two years, sitting in the same room with the portaits of James Mason and Margaret Lockwood was as close as Mastroianni got to the film world; not even De Sica was good for more than a lament that he wasn't old enough to take one of the prominent supporting roles in *Ladri di Biciclette*. Finally, in 1947, he got the small part of a revolutionary in *Tempesta su Parigi* (Storm Over Paris), the second half of director Riccardo Freda's two-part adaptation of Victor Hugo's *Les Misérables*.

> I'd been walking up and down the streets of Rome with pictures and résumés for more than two years. I suppose I should have been excited to get the job, but I couldn't help thinking how desperate those people must have been to hire me.

By the time the picture was released, he had become much less iconoclastic.

> It was due to open at the Supercinema, and I was pacing up and down outside the theater for an hour before the place opened. When I got inside, there I was—the second-to-last name on the cast list, but still there with Gino Cervi and Valentina Cortese and everyone else.

It was also around this time that Mastroianni encountered the first two of the numerous noted actresses with whom he would be associated, onscreen or offscreen, for the rest of his life. One was Silvana Mangano, then a seventeen-year-old with ambitions for a film career; according to the actor, their relationship was "more of a flirt than a fling." The other was Giulietta Masina, a member of the university theater troupe. It was Masina who helped him be noticed for his acting potential rather than merely for his persistence in seeking a job.

2

Close-up: Home

In February 1965, *Esquire* magazine transformed an interview with Mastroianni into a bylined "article" in which he recommended an ideal itinerary for Barbra Streisand in Italy. The celebrity-slick initiative had the actor declaring in part:

> I'd say skip the north, Milan, and even Florence. It is undoubtedly a good quality to be so intellectual and cultural the way they are up there, but it can also get on your nerves. I love the south—Naples, especially. I would take her down to Naples.

The statements published by *Esquire* reflect a common reverse snobbery of central- and southern-peninsula Italians toward northern regions of the country, where condescension toward the south has always been mandatory. But, over the years, Mastroianni has shown uneasiness over more than the "intellectual and cultural" north; just as often, he has been cavalier toward Rome, his home for more than sixty years, and in a comparable tone of the perpetual outsider. In the same *Esquire* piece, for example, his recommendations to Streisand concerning the capital all but stop and start with the cafés and restaurants in the historic center that he has patronized for decades. In this connection, an associate once chided him and members of his immediate circle, particularly director Federico Fellini, for behaving as though Rome extended only from the Piazza del Popolo to the Campo de' Fiori, the tourist node of the city. Mastroianni himself has acknowledged that he no longer has any taste for the various Rome neighborhoods that he called home until the 1960s, that he is happiest in his villa near the Tuscan city of Lucca; his pet peeve about the metropolis is "the twenty-four-hour traffic and noise."

The irony in all this, of course, is that, aside from Rimini native Fellini, nobody has become more identified abroad with the Italian capital than Mastroianni. Even omitting all the momentous personal events in his life that have been tied to the city (his family's move from Turin, his schooling, his wartime experiences, his initial jobs and theater work), the geographic focus of the Italian motion-picture industry and specific scripts have contrived to see an appreciable number of his films produced in Rome. Moreover, he has often complained about assignments that have required him to work in the Cinecittà studios rather than in the streets and piazzas of what he has termed "the real Rome."

> I don't like working in a studio. They remind me of government offices. Going to a studio in the morning is like reporting to a desk. That's not the same thing as being out with real people.

But neither has he ever regarded working in the city as the same thing as belonging to it. Repeatedly, he has branded Rome a necessary evil, gone on to enumerate all the administrative, political, and temperamental insufficiencies of the city that amount to a civic primer for Italians (including Romans), then expressed gratitude that he had no natal attachment to the place. More often than not, it has been within such diatribes that he has also confessed (*vide* the *Esquire* piece) an ardor for Naples. But although longtime co-workers such as Sophia Loren portray Mastroianni as somebody with an indisputable Neapolitan complexion, the actor himself has given indications that he is not so sure. Enthusiastic as he was to work for many years with Loren and De Sica, he has alluded continually to "their" Neapolitan instincts and intuitions, much as one would to generous people who have made him an honorary member of their group. This hasn't stopped him from recommending Naples to a fantasy traveler, such as Barbra Streisand, but it has deterred him from presuming to be the one to welcome her and offer her the keys to the city.

As in the case of Rome, much of Mastroianni's relationship with Naples has been defined by work and artistic considerations—in this instance, however, by a *lack* of a vital connection other than that of the film of the moment. No Italian city has a richer theatrical tradition than Naples; twentieth-century playwrights such as Eduardo De Filippo and performers such as Totò have been among the most accomplished heirs to a recital style stretching back centuries that has not believed in dramatic parentheses or comic subordinate clauses but instead has delivered even the most refined wit and claustrophobic tragedy as direct variety entertainment. It is a school of theater intricately woven into the assumptions of brusque Neapolitan culture and has very little in common with the layered subtleties emphasized by Luchino Visconti and other director-teachers to whom Mastroianni was exposed in his formative years as a professional. Even when the actor has given a good accounting of himself (as he has several times) in the role of a Neapolitan, he has arrived at the character from his own histrionic premises, without an intimate knowledge of the perspectives and techniques of the Naples-trained performers around him; that is, he has arrived at it as an outsider. Indeed, it would not be much of an exaggeration to say that if he felt less like an outsider while working with Loren and De Sica, to the point that they saluted him as one of their own, it was partly because they, too, were somewhat removed from the bases of local dramatic tradition—Loren having made her way to films through beauty contests and De Sica having done his important studying with a Russian, not a Neapolitan, drama coach.

On the surface, feeling neither wholly Roman nor totally Neapolitan would seem perfectly of a piece with Mastroianni's sometimes boastful reminder that he was born in the rural Ciociaria between the two cities, that he is a peasant rather than an urbanite; or, in the words of Italian film writer Claudio Fava, that he identifies primarily with "an ancient and vaguely barbaric *ethnos.*" As romantic associations go, there have been worse, and Mastroianni has been the first to admit that he has spent "a good part of my adult life dreaming; it's so much better than what reality has to offer." But the practical deciphering of his dreaming where a sense of home is concerned has been problematic, to say the least. On the one hand, he has been effusive in his recollections of a 1954 film stint that permitted him to return to his native district for the first time since he was four and his family had moved to Turin; on the other hand, the same experience pitted him against a director also from the region who, by all accounts, seldom allowed him to forget that he might have been a *ciociaro* by birth and a *ciociaro* by café table yearning but little beyond that.

More significant, in talking about his career, Mastroianni has constantly portrayed himself as a city bourgeois who might as easily have gone into accounting or another kind of office employment as into acting. Furthermore, he has described his progress toward increasingly meaty film roles as having been measured by his abandonment of proletarian and peasant parts in favor of more fissured characters of an urban bourgeois stripe. Whether or not this has set up some exploitable psychological tensions for his rendering of such roles, it has left a substantial body of evidence that his most recurrent "dreams" (as he has habitually characterized his film acting) do not owe a great deal to some feeling of an atavistic relationship to the soil. What they are obligated to, on the other hand, and what the actor himself has acknowledged in reviewing the unparalleled number of films that he has made over the course of four decades, is *work*—and more work. If that does not necessarily mean that he has merely fanciful attachments to Naples and the Ciociaria, it at least suggests that Rome, the vital source of his work, has ignited more of his practical dreaming than the other places. Among modern film actors, in fact, Mastroianni's work load over the years has been the equivalent of somebody who, morning after morning, has had to report to a desk— or plant a seed.

3

Stage Doors

For many years, Mastroianni the film actor tended to disparage his theatrical beginnings, arguing that motion pictures had no equal as a medium for revealing character and taking a particular delight in sticking pins into Shakespeare as the deity of stage professionals. Although he later went to the opposite extreme, especially after theatrical triumphs in the 1980s, his sustained critical posture helped to obscure for some time the long years that he had put in as a stage performer for Italy's most prestigious drama company in the immediate postwar period.

Not counting the parish playlets that he had done for Virgilio Caselli, Mastroianni made his theatrical debut in February 1948, in the University of Rome troupe's production of Leo Ferrero's *Angelica*.

> I had never been particularly passionate about the theater. The only piece I had ever really seen was a work by Eduardo De Filippo called *La Fortuna con l'Effe Maiuscola* [Luck with a Capital L]. It entertained me, but I also couldn't understand what Shakespeare, for instance, had to do with Gary Cooper. What I really liked was just to get up there on the stage and *do* it, somewhat the way that I always liked kicking around a soccer ball but have never been a great one for going out to the stadium to watch a game as a spectator. Doing *Angelica* in front of an audience, meeting all the other people connected to the show that I might not have met otherwise, *that's* what the experience was really about for me. Of course, the other guys back in my neighborhood didn't understand that. I would go to the billiard parlor or the bar after performing, and they had nothing to say but, "Hey, fairy, is it true? You're now an actor?" Maybe I tried to explain to them at the beginning, but then I stopped. It was useless.

Angelica was an anti-Fascist satire that called for all the performers to don masks. Despite his mask and a review that characterized his performance as "enthusiastic inexperience," Mastroianni, playing the youthful male lead to Giulietta Masina's title role, impressed a representative of Luchino Visconti sufficiently to earn an invitation to join the director's theatrical company the following fall. Friendship with Masina (already established as a radio actress) also led to the opportunity to join a second drama group headed by Nino Besozzi. It was with the Besozzi company that, in April 1948, the actor uttered his first dialogue professionally.

It was an adaptation of Alberto Moravia's novel *Gli Indifferenti* (The Time of Indifference), and my part was practically nonexistent. In fact, I even said the handful of lines that I had from behind the curtain. But it was the start of a valuable experience, and I stayed with Besozzi through the summer, right up to when I began rehearsing with Visconti. All my parts were small—a manservant in *The Importance of Being Earnest*, a police detective, even an old man—but they helped me get my feet wet.

They also helped him get fired from his job as a bookkeeper for Eagle-Lion. After a series of unheeded warnings about arriving late and leaving early for his rehearsals with the university troupe and Besozzi's group, Mastroianni was shown the door.

I couldn't tell my mother for weeks. My father was sick with diabetes, his sight was about gone, and I didn't want to add to her problems. So every day I got up in the morning and pretended to go off to Eagle-Lion. I parceled out my severance and the little I picked up from Besozzi, letting her think it was my regular pay.

On the brighter side, there was the prospect of making more money with Visconti later that year.

They invited me to Visconti's office. Visconti looks at me and says, "They tell me you have some talent. We will see about that." I said, "Uh, excuse me, but we won't just *see* about anything. I have a job. I can't just walk out of it without being sure that I'm walking into something else." Then Visconti just waved his hand and said, "Talk to our business manager about that." The business manager, who was sitting there, immediately piped up with a figure that was practically double what I was making at Eagle-Lion. "Mastroianni ready to sign whenever you are," I said.

If Mastroianni viewed Fellini as a classmate and De Sica as his venerable uncle, his relationship with Visconti—a homosexual aristocrat who was one of the most impressive cultural emblems of the

Italian Communist party—was far more complex. On at least one occasion, he was attributed with claiming that the director's sexual leanings created a distance between them that he never fully overcame. In December 1985, he was quoted by the Italian-language American daily *Il Progresso* as asserting:

> To work with a recognized homosexual was regarded as a bad mark against you, earned you a reputation with some people in the industry. I always spoke to him using the polite third-person *Lei*, and I was the only one who did.

But while it was true that Visconti did draw whispers over the years about liaisons with his male stars (notably France's Alain Delon and Austria's Helmut Berger), it is likewise true that Mastroianni has always had a promotional instinct for directing his responses to the constituency of the interviewer in front of him—in the case of *Il Progresso*, a reporter for an obscurantist sheet aimed at elderly Italian immigrants in the United States. Asked specifically about the quote, he replied in October 1992:

> Newspapers are always publishing a lot of banalities. There was never any problem of the kind. In ten years of working in the theater with Visconti and making two films with him, I never had any such apprehension.

Mastroianni has also been known to joke about Visconti's sexual tendencies where he was concerned. Victor Cavallo, a character actor who has been in four of Mastroianni's films, recalled the star relating how, in the 1970s, he once approached Visconti and sardonically asked him why "you never showed any interest in me." Visconti's answer, according to what Mastroianni told Cavallo, was "I did, but you never realized it."

Certainly, far more of the actor's comments have made it clear that if he was intimidated by anything, it was by Visconti's patrician airs and often ruthless working methods. On several occasions, he has compared his place and that of the other young performers in the director's company to that of "stable boys on the count's estate." He told one interviewer:

> He was disrespectful to a lot of actors. He used to get a particular kick out of humiliating poor Marga Cella, an elderly actress. One time, he made her dance until she was exhausted. He treated her terribly, tried to provoke her any way that he could. He treated everyone badly.

But side by side with these recollections have been repeated references to his opportunity with the Visconti troupe as having been an equivalent of "entering the theater world through a golden door." After the director's death in 1976, the actor declared:

> He was a man who always wished me well. He always respected the work I did for him—if sometimes with the kind of sympathy that an aristocrat is bred to show for the so-called common people. I think he understood from the start that I wasn't one of those hangers-on that he always had around him and that he had to spend a great deal of time keeping an eye on. As far as I was concerned, he was like that rare teacher in school that you admire for teaching well, for being smart at what he does.

In the fall of 1948, however, Mastroianni was considerably less philosophical while sweating out rehearsals for his first play under the director. "We were working on Shakespeare's *As You Like It*. I was one of the members of the exiled duke's coterie. At one point, I had to sing, 'What shall he have that killed the deer?/His leather skin and horns to wear.' Visconti exploded in front of the whole company that I was playing it like a tram conductor. Another time he accused me of sounding like Johnny Weissmuller calling his baboons. It was very mortifying. I wasn't used to that kind of disapproval. The Maestro could be very cruel."

Retitled *Rosalinda* because of some ballet scenes that were mixed into the original Shakespearian text, Visconti's production of *As You Like It* found Mastroianni surrounded by a host of high-level theatrical personalities. The sets for the production were designed by Salvador Dalí, while the art director was Franco Zeffirelli. Among the other cast members were Vittorio Gassman, Paolo Stoppa, Rina Morelli, Gabriele Ferzetti, Luciano Salce, Franco Interlenghi, and Sergio Fantoni. Another member of the company was Ruggero Ruggeri, one of Italy's grand old men of the stage. Mastroianni recalled later:

> I had seen Ruggeri a couple of times before I joined Visconti, and I always thought: What a big bore these old-timers! Then I ended up working with him, and I understood right away that he knew everything there was to know about working on the stage, while I knew absolutely nothing. There was a magic to the way he said the simplest things. Naturally, I felt as guilty as a thief around him for what I had thought about him. I couldn't get myself to say more than a hello to him. He got even with me—he didn't even say that much.

Rosalinda opened at Rome's Teatro Eliseo on November 26, 1948, with scant critical attention paid to Mastroianni's minor role. But less than two months later, he drew very positive notices for a

Visconti production of Tennessee Williams's drama *A Streetcar Named Desire*, in which he played the part of Mitch to Gassman's Stanley Kowalski and Morelli's Blanche DuBois.

> It was a very big break for me. The characters of both Mitch and Kowalski had this very rough speech, a lot like the way my father always spoke, so I used that. But what I remember most about it was Morelli. She was mesmerizing. Morelli in that play was the only time that I ever really felt passion on the stage for a woman.

There were other passions offstage. Another member of Visconti's company was Flora Carabella, the nineteen-year-old daughter of Ezio Carabella, an established composer of ballets, operettas, and film music.

> Even with the money Visconti was giving me, every saving I could make was a help, so I skipped a lot of meals. Then one day Flora bought me a slice of pizza and invited me to a party. I was astonished to see the full refrigerator in her house. That's when I really became interested in her.

After dating for about a year and a half, Mastroianni and Carabella were married on August 12, 1950. The ceremony was attended by a future who's who of Italian show business, with Tino Buazzelli and Paolo Panelli, actors whom Mastroianni had met at the university theater, as official witnesses. As a wedding gift, Ezio Carabella gave his daughter and son-in-law the top floor of his spacious Rome residence—quarters they would keep for more than forty years. The couple's only child, Barbara, was born on December 2, 1951.

Less happy was the deteriorating condition of Mastroianni's father at the time.

> He came to the first few plays I was in. The diabetes had blinded him and made it difficult for him to travel, or even move around. My mother had a hearing problem of her own, so the two of them were like the Odd Couple—he could hear everything but see nothing, while she could see everything but couldn't hear very well. But since I was their son, that was all that mattered.

Or, almost.

> When my mother found out that I'd been fired as a bookkeeper and had been faking all those mornings about getting up and going off to the office, all she really said was, "How long do you think this acting thing will last?" In a way, it was something she never stopped asking me. Even years later, after I had made a little money, she would always tell me how quickly I was going to lose it all, that I would've been better off with a regular job of some kind. There

was something really obsessive about the way she would go from pampering me to scolding me. Deep down, I think she wanted me to have a job with the national railway, the way my uncle did, so that I could eventually get promoted to station master and get discount tickets for the family.

The actor might not have been exaggerating. Asked once by Italian television what she thought of her son's success in the movie world, Ida Mastrojanni said only: "He was doing well when he was working for the city, too."

Ottorino Mastrojanni finally succumbed to his illness in November 1950, just a few months after his son's marriage. Ida, on the other hand, lived another thirty years.

In April 1949, following his success in *Streetcar*, Mastroianni was tapped by Visconti for the role of Pylades in Vittorio Alfieri's *Oreste*.

Things got off to a bad start on that production. The idea for doing the play was Gassman's. Visconti made it pretty clear that he didn't think too much of the work, that he was willing to do it only because it gave him an excuse to mount some major theatrical opus, right down to the use of a Beethoven symphony as background music. That wasn't the way that Vittorio saw the play at all. He had much too much respect for Visconti to make a public issue of it, but we all had the impression that he was chomping at the bit and that he would be leaving the company soon, which in fact he did. Visconti also had his doubts that I could handle blank verse, and I know he was ready to replace me with Giancarlo Sbragia. But I kept at it, and he detected enough improvement as we went along to leave me in the role. Considering everything, it came out pretty well.

The starring roles given to Gassman in *A Streetcar Named Desire*, *Oreste*, and (immediately prior to his departure from the company) *Troilus and Cressida* fueled speculation that Mastroianni was haunted for some time by envy of his fellow actor. Shelley Winters, who was married to Gassman for several years, said that it was her impression that

they were a little jealous of one another. Kind of like the way that Dustin Hoffman and Al Pacino have absolutely nothing but respect for one another and are always wonderfully friendly to one another whenever they meet, but you always sense an edge. In Marcello's case, it might have been because Vittorio was such a grand name in the theater, but that's just my conjecture.

For his part, Mastroianni has denied any envy or jealousy. "Gassman and I were never in competition. Frankly, I never understood why producers didn't realize that he was the perfect movie star. There was nobody more handsome than he was. With his aquiline nose he had the air of a true aristocrat, someone larger than life." On the same subject, he told another interviewer in 1992 that he regarded Gassman as "the greatest actor in Europe right now."

According to Mastroianni, it was also Gassman who awakened him to the realities of the actor's life.

> There is all this talk about the glamour and mystique of the acting profession, as though actors are some kind of magical creatures around whom the world ought to turn. All you had to do was see Vittorio during a performance to disabuse yourself of that idea. He would be out on the stage saying "To be or not to be," or whatever his lines were, then he would run into the wings where an assistant was waiting and say, "Okay, let's put aside 150,000 lire for the phone because my wife has been using it a lot, 40,000 lire for gas. . . . Hold on, I'll be right back." And back on the stage he would go for more 'To be or not to be,' then once again back to the wings. "Okay, another 150,000 has to go for this. . . . " The only thing he ever worried about when he wasn't onstage was how to divide up his salary among all the wives and children and assistants he had. Watching him go through that every time he was paid, I told myself that any actor who gets to believe that he's some kind of nuclear scientist has to be avoided at all costs.

Gassman has also given short shrift to stories about any ill feelings between the actors.

> I think I can say we are very good friends, and always have been. In the many years that we've worked together or on parallel projects in the industry, not once have we ever gotten into any kind of squabble. I think one reason for this might be because we are so different. For instance, we have practically antipodal ideas about acting. What unites us and makes us friends is that we both have a sense of humor and irony about what we are doing.

Mastroianni continued to act with Visconti's company until 1956, by which time he had consolidated his reputation as one of Italy's most reliable stage performers. His most conspicuous efforts in the 1950s, abetted by Gassman's decision to leave the troupe and juicier roles to him, included playing the younger son of Willy Loman in Arthur Miller's *Death of a Salesman* in Rome in February 1951, with a cast that featured Stoppa, Morelli, Interlenghi, Carabella, and

Cesare Danova; a second version of *Streetcar* in Milan in April 1951, with Mastroianni taking on the Stanley Kowalski part opposite Morelli; a presentation at the International Theater Festival of Venice in October 1952 of Carlo Goldoni's *La Locandiera* (The Innkeeper), in which he appeared with Morelli, Aldo Giuffré, Stoppa, and Carabella; and a second production of *Death of a Salesman* in Rome in February 1956, in which he played the older son opposite Stoppa, Morelli, Interlenghi, and Carabella.

The actor also began to show a knack for the works of Anton Chekhov, appearing prominently for Visconti in *The Three Sisters* and *Uncle Vanya*. His performances in these plays in particular prompted Visconti to say that

> of all the young actors who came to work with us in the company, Mastroianni was by far the most interesting case. When he started, he was truly incapable even of delivering a line. He worked very hard for me, and I was very proud of the results.

Nikita Mikhalhov, who directed him in both the theater and films many years later, has traced some of Mastroianni's effectiveness before the camera to his grounding in Chekhovian drama.

> To me, he is quite a Chekhovian actor. Most of all, he knows the art of semitone—an essential for both performing something like *Uncle Vanya* on stage and working in cinema. With his talent for understatement, he is capable of conveying three pages of text with a single glance.

For many years after leaving the Visconti company to concentrate on films, however, Mastroianni showed little understatement in his evaluation of the theater medium. In a January 1965 interview with the American monthly *Holiday,* for instance, he declared:

> I really have no use for the stage. The plays I've seen are never about anything that I care about. They're never about life as we live it today. Maybe you'll think I'm an ignoramus for saying this, but . . . well, take Hamlet. They say it's a great play because we're all Hamlets. But we're *not* all Hamlets! I'm not, my friends aren't.

In April 1975, in another conversation with the Rome daily *Il Tempo,* he ridiculed the notion that he was still attached to his days with the Visconti troupe, asserting: "At bottom, the theater just amuses me. I consider movies much more advanced."

The actor maintained this attitude throughout the 1960s and 1970s. But then, with creativity stagnating in the Italian film industry and with his decision to return to the stage in Paris, he took the opposite tack. In December 1987, for example, he told *People* magazine:

"The stage—I love it! Film is bad for actors. We go soft. I do plays to cleanse myself, inside and out. It's like a cure."

He told another interviewer:

> There is no doubt that a good deal of what I have learned as an actor, I learned in my theater years with Visconti. He taught me to distinguish real theatrics from false theatrics, to throw away the tricks that a lazy actor gets to depend on to see himself through. Most of all, he taught me that the profession is a discipline. But it's also true that, in general, I've preferred using this experience in the cinema. What I was probably reacting to in those early interviews was the excitement that existed in the Italian film industry in the 1960s—the fresh subjects, the original way of dealing with them. I don't think anyone would argue that there was a similar excitement about the plays being done then.

Mastroianni has also laughed off the suggestion that his periodic sallies against Shakespearean roles stem at least in part from his exhausting experiences with Visconti during the rehearsals for *As You Like It* and *Troilus and Cressida*.

> Psychology! And who am I to say that there might not be a germ of truth in it? But the fact is, I *have* played Hamlet, I *have* done King Lear. It's just that they didn't have those names and were characters in a modern setting in front of a camera. You'd have to be an imbecile to contend that Shakespeare was without value. But that isn't the same thing as walking around in a cloud insisting that a Shakespearean role is the only reason for living. If I've said something about that in the past, I was talking about the actor, not Shakespeare. I've always thought we should have the opportunity to talk to our gods and ask them whether they really wanted to be gods. Someone like William Shakespeare, who always wrote for the people, I have a feeling that he wouldn't want to be one.

4

Close-up: The Body Not So Beautiful

In 1990, a somewhat weary looking Mastroianni starred in an equally tired film entitled *Stanno Tutti Bene* (Everybody's Fine). About midway through the film, however, there is a genuinely comic moment when the actor's elderly character comes upon a prostitute who flashes a thigh at him to drum up some business, whereupon Mastroianni promptly lifts a pant leg to show that he has some flesh there as well. Although fleeting, the scene was one of the most difficult ever done by the actor, who has never concealed his dislike for his own body, especially his disproportionately skinny legs.

In a 1984 interview with the Rome daily *La Repubblica*, he declared:

> I've never loved my body. I've even despised it. Look here, I have absolutely no muscles. As a kid, they called me all kinds of things— a midwife, a blob, you name it. That's what I've remained, too.

A couple of years later, after being reminded of a poll that cited him as the most handsome man in Italy, he told the *New York Times*:

> I've never been handsome, and have never thought so. Alain Delon, Tyrone Power, *they* were handsome. Vittorio Gassman is handsome, even aristocratic, with his aquiline nose; my nose is up-turned. What I suppose I have is a face that's likeable, pleasing. . . .

More so than for many actors, the physical impression that Mastroianni makes on the screen has been at the service of specific roles and costars, at times making him seem taller than his slightly less than five feet eleven inches (no actor has shared more film frames with women) and giving him a lissomeness that a progressive chunkiness from his former 170–180 pounds might not have promised. That

not too much has ever been made of his very average build is in part
a tribute to other, more prepossessing physical qualities; it is also a
by-product of the fact that his smooth screen style has usually had
the odd effect of diverting attention from his physical appearance
even as that presence has triggered dramatic action.

As with all effective film actors, the Mastroianni look begins
with eyes that never saw a camera they didn't like and that mirror
the camera's reciprocating affections. ("I don't need the stimulus of
an audience. I get all I want from the camera looking at me.") The
actor himself has always referred to his eyes as his main physical
asset and even credits his mastery of eye language for getting along
with foreign directors. Concerning his experiences on *Leo the Last* in
1970 with British filmmaker John Boorman, for instance, he told an
interviewer:

> I didn't speak English, and John Boorman didn't speak Italian. We
> had no interpreter, so I said to him in the two or three words of
> English that I knew, "Just look me in the eyes and tell me in your
> own language what it is you want and I'll understand." This was
> possible because in our profession there is true language based on
> eye contact. In that case, it worked perfectly well.

The secret to eye language, of course, is what it intimates the
eyes have seen and feel about what they are seeing. As a rule, the
eyes of Mastroianni's characters have seen a little more than they
have bargained for but have called a truce with memory, offering
irony and detachment in exchange for a lingering hope that they can
still be surprised. It is the hope more than the irony that threatens
anger on occasion and the irony more than the hope that already
foresees a futile outcome to the anger. Although some film writers
have characterized the basic Mastroianni expression as Italian (or
Roman) cynicism, it is, in fact, infinitely more suggestive and self-
critical than that: not mere cynicism but a profound resentment of
those (including himself) who claim to know enough to have earned
their cynicism. Of all the roles he has done on the stage and screen,
an Italian Sam Spade has never been one of them.

Mainly because of his parts in the early 1960s as a hollowed-out
writer or intellectual, particularly in *La Dolce Vita* and *La Notte*, the
Mastroianni Look has also been identified with a physical fatigue
alluding to an even deeper moral ennui. Indeed, for many years, it
was impossible to read anything about the actor that didn't insinuate
that he was something of a sober Dean Martin, only a rocking back
and forth or two away from falling on his face under existential tor-
ment. While male journalists had fun playing with this image to
debunk the actor for Latin Lover associations that they themselves

had done a great deal to propagate, female reporters were prone to promoting their impressions of this fatigue as some kind of an ultimate aphrodisiac. Symptomatic of such reporting in the 1960s was an article that appeared in the French weekly *L'Express* in which the woman journalist said in part:

> There is no doubt—he's very handsome. Soft hair, fleshy lips that part to reveal two rows of extremely white teeth, straight nose, and, to complete his charms, tiny lines around his eyes and a dimple on his chin that seems to grow bigger whenever he smiles. Nobody knows as well as he does how to carry the kind of sad and tired air that awakens immediately the desire to console him.

Adopting the more objective tone of a social scientist but operating from the same premise of the weary Mastroianni as the essential Mastroianni, a male British writer from the same period chimed in:

> What makes up for his deficiency [as the perpetually limp, tired male] is the wishful thinking of his mass public, in the main female and romantic, which is attracted by the sight of him as a suitable case for their care and at the same time aroused by the thought of him with all his powers restored.

That Mastroianni could arouse at least such gushings from the bedroom and the library argues for both the plausibility of his performances and the impressionability of the people exposed to them. No question, he *has* played characters who were past the point of even thinking about carrying the weight of the world on their shoulders. Moreover, he himself has abetted the perception of some fundamental weariness in his persona with a cascade of remarks over the years about his laziness, the overenergetic demands of the women in his life, and his disenchantment with this, that, and the other thing. But on the screen, the "tiredness" of the stereotypical Mastroianni character has never been quite the passive, consolable commodity that erotic fantasies and erudite analyses are made of. On the contrary, its very elusiveness within a labyrinth of earnestness, coldness, and anger make it the dramatic material out of which an actor with Mastroianni's creative skills has been able to fashion roles, indelible or not as they may be. Aside from his eyes, his most important physical asset in this effort has been his silken, at times even dainty, movements. At its best, the fluidity seems to come from nowhere, but only to be going somewhere: not the lighter being taken from the pocket but the light being ignited beneath the cigarette. At its worst, as when it arises from some cumbrous character, it calls attention only to itself for its precision, much in the way that a drunk displays too much meticulousness in performing feats to deny his condition. In either case, it seems to separate the screen action from the bodily Mastroianni, almost as though the actor has staked out for himself merely the first in a printed series of consecutive exposures, with the consequent development phases not his responsibility.

In contrast to the Experience implied by the Mastroianni Look, the Mastroianni Sound has retained a hint of callowness, the slightest edge of a determined balkiness within an otherwise deliberate modulation. Echoing the harsh resonances of the actor's Roman background, the edge has been to the fore usually when he has played Roman characters, such as in *Dramma della Gelosia: Tutti i Particolari in Cronaca* (The Pizza Triangle, 1970). Otherwise, what has generally been described as his "mellifluousness" owes its timbre and cadences to his theatrical training—a cultured neutrality that is not Roman, Neapolitan, nor Ciociarian, nor is even Italian except to the degree that "transatlantic" speakers of English might be American, British, or Canadian. By and large, this generic vocal base has left him free of embedded handicaps when called upon to do regional Italian dialects, although he has had occasional problems with the softer accents of Italy that have superficial similarities to his professional modulation but which, in fact, are not co-opted so easily.

For all the physical and vocal smoothness that often borders on the fugitive on the screen, Mastroianni has never encouraged the incorporeal in his private life, on several occasions irritating directors by showing up for a role ten to fifteen pounds heavier than expected and forced to diet in a hurry. He has few culinary peeves outside of spinach, and the stories are legion of his occupation of favorite restaurants in Italy and abroad when he is not actually before the cameras. Jack Lemmon, Gene Saks, and Lauren Hutton are only three of numerous American motion picture people who have voiced wonder and admiration at his capacity for eating, and eating well. Conversely, in a December 1992 interview in connection with the release of *Used People*, Shirley MacLaine giggled at the idea that she and Mastroianni might be attracted to one another offscreen along the lines of their middle-aged characters in the film. MacLaine told Jeanne Wolf of the *New York Times* Syndicate: "Marcello's idea of a big evening is to go to dinner at two o'clock in the morning and have a big bottle of red wine and a seven-course pasta dinner. All I would be thinking about is having to get up at six and start to film. So I think we have different life-styles."

Mastroianni has also had a couple of periods, most conspicuously after his breakup with Catherine Deneuve in the mid-1970s, when he liked wine and grappa more than they liked him. A chain smoker for most of his life, he was still going through three packs a day as he neared his seventies. Earlier, some of his friends had nodded knowingly, and for more than one reason, when he had an exchange with Simone Signoret in *Adua e le Compagne* in 1960 that went:

SIGNORET: You go from one cigarette to another and never stop. What are you trying to do, save matches?
MASTROIANNI: Look, I've heard it all before. If I smoke during the night. If a box of matches lasts me my whole life. If I put out a cigarette when I make love.
SIGNORET: Well, do you?
MASTROIANNI: No.

The actor's only concession to his attachment to tables, bars, and ashtrays is to check himself into a spa a couple of times a year for a ten-day detoxification therapy. More often than not, he schedules the treatments for periods immediately preceding a new film engagement. He has always made it clear that the health retreats were precisely that and that he never embarked upon them with the goal of altering his habits.

If any of this smacks of the self-abuse of the body that Mastroianni admits despising, it has also provided him, literally, with very physical material for the aging, if not despoiled, characters that he began playing with more consistency in the 1980s. In 1984, he went so far as to overcome a previous aversion to nude scenes because he was persuaded that disrobing entirely was crucial to the plot of an adaptation of Luigi Pirandello's *Enrico IV* (Henry IV). The scene was not one of the actor's happier experiences. Then sixty, he acknowledged embarrassment for a paunch that had been inflated further in preparing for his role as a heavy drinker in the French stage production of *Tchin-Tchin*. ("I had fit into the role and gained about twelve pounds.")

If all this sounds a long way from "handsome tiredness," it is. Needless to say, when the character in *Stanno Tutti Bene* finished lifting his pant leg for the prostitute, he looked at her without saying a word. She glanced at his skinny calf and thigh, then up into his eyes, and laughed. He laughed back at her.

5

Taxi Driver

As innovative as it was in the 1960s when Mastroianni became an international name, Italy's film industry was equally unadventurous in the late 1940s and early 1950s, when the actor snared his first conspicuous screen roles. After several years of attracting world attention for the neorealism movement spearheaded by De Sica and Rossellini, the industry found itself paying a stiff creative price for the onset of Cold War politics. Under heavy-handed pressures from the United States, and especially from the American Ambassador to Rome, Clare Boothe Luce, the government of Prime Minister Alcide De Gasperi made it clear that it would deny vital state subsidies to any film that even implied sympathy for the Italian Communist party or its positions on the social and political issues of the day. De Gasperi's point man was Giulio Andreotti, then in charge of entertainment and cultural affairs and destined to be one of the country's most prominent politicians over the next four decades. In a notorious but emblematic incident of the period, Andreotti sent shivers through the film industry in 1952 with an attack on De Sica's *Umberto D* for depicting some of the unpleasant realities of postwar Italy. Writing for the influential weekly *Libertas*, Andreotti declared in part:

> If it is true that evil can sometimes be combatted by showing some of its crudest forms, it is also true that some people will be misled into believing that the Italy of *Umberto D* is the real Italy of the 20th century. De Sica will thus have rendered a terrible service to his country . . . and its progressive social legislation.

Not too long after this warning, two Italian film critics were arrested and tried by a military (not civil) court for "defaming the armed forces"; their crime had been a public proposal that a motion picture be made about the Fascist regime's occupation of Greece in World War II.

Given such an atmosphere, it was hardly surprising that a

majority of the films turned out in the late 1940s and early 1950s recalled the safe, insipid melodramas, comedies, and costume spectaculars that had been popular during other repressive periods; equally predictable, the features had little export appeal, adding economic problems to the industry's political restrictions (and making state subsidies even more imperative). Concerning his screen roles of the time, Mastroianni once told an interviewer:

> They've all blurred for me. I'm always confusing what part I had in what picture. Of course, most of them were made with nothing more in mind than turning a fast profit, so maybe that's how they ought to be remembered, anyway.

In fact, however, it was the predominantly banal melodramas, watered-down neorealistic comedies, and B-budget mysteries that permitted Mastroianni to establish his film career. Between 1949 and 1952 alone, while working for Visconti's theater company in the evening, he spent his days shooting fifteen movies.

> At first, it was fairly easy. I'd work before the cameras in the day and onstage at night. Sometimes I'd be working on two films simultaneously. Half the time, I wasn't all that sure what the film as a whole was supposed to be about. The important thing was to get down my scenes and get paid.

The first one he got paid for was *Passaporto per l'Oriente*, a British-financed anthology film about an amnesiac RAF pilot's efforts to find the mother of his presumed child. With five different directors calling the shots on separate stories in five different cities (Rome, London, Paris, Berlin, and Vienna), the production ended up with a lot more titles and distribution problems than applauding critics or paying spectators. At one time or another, in Italian and English, it was known as *Passport for the East*, *A Tale of Five Cities*, *Five Women and a Crib*, and (the ultimately prevailing English title) *A Tale of Five Women*; begun in 1949, it became entangled in enough financial squabbles to postpone its distribution until 1952. In the Rome episode directed by Romolo Marcellini, the pilot (Bonar Colleano) looks up Maria (Gina Lollobrigida), a woman that he vaguely remembers from the war. Mastroianni played Maria's fiancé Aldo, a cabdriver who is so ecstatic over having apparently won the national lottery that he burns his taxi. While Maria is demonstrating to the pilot that she was not his lover but only someone who gave him language lessons, Aldo realizes to his chagrin that he has won only a minor lottery prize and will have to spend years paying off his company for the burned taxi. His consolation is Maria's love.

Highly visible as it was, Mastroianni's role in the Italian episode of *Passaporto per l'Oriente* got lost within the tepid reaction to the film as a whole and the thick slabs of anti-Communist propaganda that marked the story's perceptions of postwar Europe; for the most part, critics merely acknowledged his professional presence. To the actor himself, the film was mainly memorable for giving him the first of several taxi-driver parts that he ended up bemoaning. "I always seemed to be playing some awkward or clumsy young guy behind the wheel of a cab in Rome," he once reflected. "For some reason, the people making movies back then seemed to see that experience as the quintessential metaphor for getting through in postwar Italy."

His next stint before the cameras was in *Una Domenica d'Agosto* (Sunday in August; 1950), directed by Luciano Emmer, who until then had been known almost exclusively for his pioneer filming of art in such documentaries as *Goya, Giotto,* and *Leonardo da Vinci.* It started off as a very bumpy experience. Mastroianni:

> The very first day, I walked off the set and went home. There was just too much confusion and disorder, and I was disgusted by it. I was used to working in the theater, where everything was done according to a certain order. I also didn't like the way everybody was insulting one of the women, just to get a rise out of her. For a few hours, I really thought I was never going to make another film. But I went back the next day.

Una Domenica d'Agosto unwound several parallel stories in a light neorealistic vein to offer a somewhat melancholy look at Romans on a summer weekend in Ostia. Mastroianni played Ercole, a traffic cop who looks around frantically for a room for a girlfriend he has impregnated and who ends up with her moving in with him. The picture earned respectful attention in Italy, with Mastroianni among those singled out for contributing to its persuasive spontaneous air (with hardly any critic noticing that because of theater commitments the actor wasn't around for postproduction dubbing and spoke with Alberto Sordi's voice). Overall, however, it suffered from comparisons with its neorealistic sires and provoked considerable resentment from some quarters as typifying the diluted results of the Christian Democratic government's pressures on the industry. Mastroianni has never agreed with this evaluation.

> Without trying to compare it to the masterpieces made earlier by other directors or afterwards by the Fellinis and those people, I think Emmer sounded a new note with *Una Domenica d'Agosto*. In a way, it was a foretaste of the *commedia all'italiana* that would be so popular a few years later—a wry look at everyday problems. Emmer has probably never received the attention he deserved.

Sordi's voice or not, the actor also had a personal reason for remembering the film in a special way.

> I'd been working in the theater for a while, but after that film began circulating, it was as though I had never done anything else. To people on the street, I wasn't a member of Visconti's company, I was the actor who had played Ercole the traffic cop.

After *Una Domenica d'Agosto* came *Vita da Cani* (A Dog's Life), in which Mastroianni had the relatively minor role of the fiancé of a suicidal actress; it was principally noteworthy as the actor's first of many collaborations with director Mario Monicelli. In Giorgio Bianchi's *Cuori sul Mare* (Hearts at Sea), he was a naval cadet who rejects the military career planned for him by his father, gets involved with a gang of smugglers aboard a freighter, gets rescued by his best friend, then (typical of the paternal airs of many pictures of the period) realizes that his father was right all along and returns to the naval academy.

Although it was little better than *Vita da Cani* or *Cuori sul Mare*, Flavio Calzavara's *Contro la Legge* (Against the Law) assumed importance as Mastroianni's first real starring role on the screen, portraying a witness to a murder who is first suspected of the homicide and who then helps bring the real killer to justice. The production was a low-budget, cooperative effort involving Mastroianni and other members of the cast and crew, and because it fell outside normal industry channels, it went begging for a distributor for almost two years. When it was finally shown in 1952, it got generally favorable, if somewhat condescending, reviews. It would not be the last time that the actor became involved in production matters.

Murder and betrayal were also the dominant motifs of *Atto d'Accusa* (The Accusation), the first mainstream film in which Mastroianni starred. Directed by Giacomo Gentilomo, the actor was praised for his performance as a returning prisoner of war who gets framed for two murders, then hires the real killer as his defense attorney. In retrospect, however, he himself was less than impressed.

> None of these films was very credible. Every one of the characters was either all good or all bad. It was very hard to find a part where the characters had various sides to them, the way it is in real life. Almost always, I was the all-good one—ingenuous, paying the price for what some all-bad character did, but usually coming out all right in the end. It took me a number of years to get away from that kind of schematic role.

In 1951, he returned to Emmer for *Parigi È Sempre Parigi* (Paris Is Always Paris), a film sponsored in good part by French money but ballyhooed at the time as the first postwar Italian production shot completely abroad. In an attempt to repeat the parallel-stories formula of *Una Domenica d'Agosto, Parigi È Sempre Parigi* followed the adventures of a group of Italian soccer fans in the French capital for a big game. What the film did not follow, on the other hand, was Mastroianni's offscreen infatuation with costar Lucia Bosè. ("Just about every night, Franco Interlenghi and I would be in her room to talk about this or that.") Although the actress never returned the ardor, it was the first recorded instance of his more than professional feelings for a fellow film player.

Mastroianni's maiden experience in filming outside Italy also opened his eyes to the fact that foreigners didn't always look at Italian pictures in the same way that people at home did.

> It was surprising how popular Emmer was in France. While we were doing our film, there were cinema clubs that kept showing *Una Domenica d'Agosto*, treating it as an important thing. I didn't know if we were the provincials in not appreciating Emmer more or if they were exaggerating their attachment to something foreign.

But not even the French came to the rescue of *Parigi È Sempre Parigi:* The film was almost universally written off as a pale reflection of *Una Domenica d'Agosto*, which, outside of Paris, had itself not exactly bowled over anyone. In the part of the most guileless of the fans, Mastroianni emerged relatively unscathed, although theater commitments again forced another actor—this time Nino Manfredi—to dub his voice for the Italian version.

As feeble as *Parigi È Sempre Parigi* turned out, it was a masterpiece compared to the actor's next foray, Anton Giulio Majano's *L'Eterna Catena* (The Eternal Chain), an especially lugubrious soap opera that evoked memories of the worst Rossano Brazzi and Amedeo Nazzari melodramas. In *L'Eterna Catena*, Mastroianni played a merchant seaman who returns home after years at sea, is falsely accused of murder when he tries to protect his brother's wife from a suitor, and ends up having to join the French Foreign Legion; the real murderer this time turns out to be the brother, who is conveniently killed at the end, permitting Mastroianni to go off with his erstwhile sister-in-law. Because of its violently fratricidal feeling, the picture appalled many critics, and it died quickly at the box office. *L'Eterna Catena* also signaled an awareness that Mastroianni wasn't the only one who recognized the professional rut he was digging for himself. As the critic for *Corriere Lombardo* put it:

> Marcello Mastroianni is the eternal target of fate; the eternally disillusioned lover; the nice young man who has to win the love of a

woman at the price of going to jail, accepting exile abroad, tears, repressed desires, and various murders and betrayals of which he will always be guilty until his innocence is firmly established.

The actor's third venture with Emmer, *Le Ragazze di Piazza di Spagna* (Three Girls From Rome; 1952), was an even stronger concentrate of all the other films that he had made up to that point. Once again, Emmer sought to balance parallel stories, in this case of three co-workers who eat their lunch together every day on the Spanish Steps, where they talk about their shared dream of finding a husband and a home; once again, Mastroianni played a cabdriver who gets smitten with one of his passengers, ultimately having to rescue her from suicide and a cad of a boyfriend before going off with her into the sunset. Again as well, the picture was compared unfavorably to *Una Domenica d'Agosto*, while Mastroianni was patted on the back for "his usual effectiveness as a good-hearted young man."

Pier Luigi Faraldo's *Tragico Ritorno* (Tragic Return), produced soon after *Le Ragazze di Piazza di Spagna*, makes it clear why the actor would later have a problem distinguishing one of his roles in the early 1950s from another. Once again, his character arrives on the scene after years in a prisoner-of-war camp, in this instance to find that his wife has thought him dead and has remarried, while his son doesn't recognize him at all. One hapless choice after another leads to a bank robbery, a murder for which the Mastroianni character believes himself responsible, and his suicide in despair; only after his death does it emerge that he was not accountable for the murder. *Tragico Ritorno* left only the traces of an especially severe censure from the Catholic church, which banned it for all Catholics because of its alleged advocacy of adultery, murder, and suicide. The church stand was the final nail in the coffin for a feature that had already discouraged its distributor because of its relentlessly morose plot.

With Clemente Fracassi's *Sensualità* (Sensuality) later in 1952, Mastroianni had his first taste of star-powered tantrums on a movie set. In her first significant screen role, Eleanora Rossi Drago played a factory worker who tries to seduce her boss (Amedeo Nazzari), gets spurned, then marries his smitten brother (Mastroianni) out of spite. Before long, Nazzari has betrayed his brother with his sister-in-law, rejected her again, and gotten a fatal bullet for his indecisiveness; the film ends with Mastroianni killing his wife. Throughout the making of *Sensualità*, gossip columns were filled with behind-the-scenes stories of Rossi Drago's alleged caprices on the set—tantrums that, according to Mastroianni, never happened. But cameraman Aldo

Tonti was only one of several who recalled otherwise a few years later. Tonti:

> There was nothing subtle about the picture. It was Rossi Drago showing off her chest and legs whenever she had the opportunity. When she realized that she would be the only reason people would pay to see the picture, it went to her head. Nazzari finally had enough and took her aside one day. He really gave it to her. He'd been in the business forever, one of the most generous professionals there ever was, and he just wasn't used to her kind of behavior. After that, things got a little better, but not totally. What struck everyone was that she didn't have much more at risk in terms of starting a career than Mastroianni had, but he went to work every day giving it all he had, while she didn't.

Mastroianni's tactfulness about the actress ("She has always been very professional with me") is typical of his comments about fellow players in general and former Visconti troupe colleagues in particular. (Rossi Drago appeared with him in *Uncle Vanya*.) As for *Sensualità*, it was seen as a poor man's *Riso Amaro*, with only the actor attracting positive notices. Illustrative was the response of the reviewer for the Rome daily *Messaggero*, who, in the middle of a diatribe against the picture's "ridiculous artificiality," saluted Mastroianni for "moments of beautiful spontaneity."

There were no such compensations for the actor's next handful of screen appearances: Oreste Biancoli's *Penne Nere* (Black Feathers; 1952), Mario Camerini's *Gli Eroi della Domenica* (Sunday's Heroes; 1953), and Dino Risi's *Il Viale della Speranza* (The Boulevard of Hope; 1953). In *Penne Nere*, he played the native of an Alpine village who is drafted into the Italian army, is left to fend for himself in Albania when the Fascist regime collapses, and then returns home to join in the resistance against the Germans. Even the ruling Christian Democratic press, with an interest in lauding Biancoli's view of the resistance movement as a nationalistic instead of Communist-Socialist–led phenomenon, was hard put to commend the feature. In *Gli Eroi della Domenica*, Mastroianni played the second male lead to Raf Vallone as two soccer players who have to overcome bribery attempts, injuries, and personal disillusions to win the big game. A couple of critics suggested that Mastroianni might have been a better choice than the often declamatory Vallone for the role of the protagonist, but most attention was focused on the decline of the once-gifted director Camerini. The actor was once again largely a supporting presence in *Il Viale della Speranza*, a somewhat predictable look at three women and their aspirations to break into Italian movies;

Mastroianni had the part of a cameraman who helps his fiancée (Cosetta Greco), the only really talented one of the trio, realize her ambition. The film drew unfavorable comparisons to Emmer's *Le Ragazze di Piazza di Spagna*, just as the latter had to *Una Domenica d'Agosto*—in both instances, critics showing short memories of how the older film had been assailed when originally released.

According to Mastroianni, his subsequent project, Claudio Gora's *Febbre di Vivere* (Fever for Living; 1953), was the first film that allowed him to play the kind of complex character that he had been trying to play since appearing in *Les Misérables*. "I've always had a deep affection for Gora's film," he has said. "I've always believed that it was ahead of its time, that it was a sort of *La Dolce Vita ante litteram*." A similar claim has been made by director Gora himself.

On the surface, *Febbre di Vivere* told a fairly banal tale of a racetrack operator (Massimo Serato) who tries to con his way through life. Among his victims are an old friend (Mastroianni) who takes a minor criminal rap for him; a lover (Anna Maria Ferrero) whom he impregnates and betrays regularly; and another associate (Sandro Milani) who initially agrees to arrange an abortion for the girlfriend but who then changes his mind, with disastrous consequences. Although it hardly raised as many official hackles as *La Dolce Vita* did some years later, *Febbre di Vivere* had considerable troubles of its own, first in getting made at all, then with distribution. As Gora has recalled:

> We had to stop production twice because we ran out of money. The producer we had on the thing was a wonderful man, but also slightly touched. What other producer would have let almost the whole financing for the picture be burned up in a single sequence of a horse race that was the very first thing we shot?

Even when enough rescue capital had been found, other difficulties remained. Gora:

> The censors were watching us from the very start, and I was ready to quit more than once. A key element in the story is when Serato tries to set up an abortion. Well, we weren't allowed to use the word *abortion*. Then there were scenes with Ferraro in her underwear that had to be cut down or eliminated altogether. But most of all, they insisted on a happy ending. No happy ending and we wouldn't have gotten a distribution license. I suppose that was the biggest compromise of all that we were forced to make. Were we right to make it? We thought so at the time that that was the only way to get the film out to the public.

What appeared to bother officialdom as much as specific references to abortion and specific glimpses of Ferraro's bras was the ambience of *Febbre di Vivere*—not the working-class neighborhoods that usually served as backgrounds for melodramas of the kind but a decidedly middle-class Rome, with almost all of its young characters depicted as a postwar generation well on its way to being lost amid daily hustlings and nightly distractions. With its emphasis on atmosphere even more than on plot, Mastroianni's subordinate (in terms of story line) role as the most decent of the male characters hanging around Serato gained extra weight precisely to the extent that he played a satellite figure—another reason why he could subsequently compare the picture to *La Dolce Vita.*

Inevitably, the film divided critics along ideological lines, with left-wing reviewers congratulating Gora for going as far as he did but lamenting that he didn't resist censorship pressures to go further and right-wing writers scoring the director for his failure to give Mastroianni's character more dramatic leverage against Serato's basic bad guy. For example, the Communist party organ *L'Unità* declared in part:

> Weighing everything together, *Febbre di Vivere* is a courageous film, one that has announced a readiness to battle for a worthy Italian film industry. The survey of the fatuousness of the Roman bourgeoisie, the subtle shadings of marginal characters, the happy choice of faces and ambiences, the direct way of recounting what is essentially a complicated story, all of these things make it a work of value.

On the other hand, right-wing critic Giulio Cesare Castello missed the importance attributed by Gora to the ambience characters and warned his readers that Mastroianni's star billing did not make him the protagonist. Castello asserted:

> Given the priorities of the director in showing a young generation cynical and without scruples, it follows logically that the main character is [Serato] and not [Mastroianni]. . . . Negative characters in art always have the upper hand on positive ones, and [Mastroianni's character] is no exception, despite the solid performance of the actor himself.

If Mastroianni expressed satisfaction with the complexities of his character in *Febbre di Vivere,* he was anything but happy with his roles in two other films released around the same time. The first was Filippo Walter Ratti's *Non È Mai Troppo Tardi* (It's Never Too Late), a loose adaptation of Charles Dickens's *Christmas Carol* in which Paolo Stoppa played the Scrooge role and Mastroianni was a rival for the affections of a woman with whom the miser was deeply in love. This time around, there were no divisions along ideological lines, with critics of both the Left and Right blasting the film as "heavy-handed," "mechanical," and "without a scintilla of human feeling." One critic went so far as to mock Stoppa for playing Scrooge as though he were trying to repeat his stage success as Willy Loman in *Death of a Salesman*. For the first time, Mastroianni also came in for some knocks, his performance written off as "functional at best" and "replete with lazy mannerisms." The actor himself agreed, calling the experience "misguided."

A similar response was accorded *Lulu*, directed by Fernando Cerchio from Carlo Bertolazzi's 1903 play about a cabaret singer (Valentina Cortese) who drifts back and forth between an earnest student (Jacques Sernas) and a well-heeled protector (Mastroianni) before finally being accidentally killed by the former. Although *Lulu* gave Mastroianni a rare opportunity to play a man of the world rather than his usual young innocent, his role was trashed as "little more than a caricature," while the picture as a whole was dispatched as "laughable." As he was to comment later on, the film was noteworthy "only insofar as it taught me it would not be enough just to do the opposite of what I had been doing."

6

Close-up: The Workaholic

Of all the qualities that Mastroianni has ascribed to himself over years of public self-reflection, none of them has sounded more exaggerated than his recurring contention that he is lazy. Even without counting stage and television appearances, his 125 films since the 1950s have made him one of the world's busiest performers outside an Egyptian or Indian movie studio. Moreover, while the number itself might not flabbergast that small handful of Hollywood bit players (Dub Taylor, R. G. Armstrong, et al.), without whom theatrical features and TV movies seem unable to be made, Mastroianni has almost always had the starring role in his projects, committing him to months of shooting and postproduction dubbing every time around. Add to this the fact that the actor, despite his declared aversion to the obligation, has been scrupulous about making himself available for thousands of media interviews over the years to promote his ventures (on one day alone in Paris in 1984, he met separately with thirty-eight journalists) and the notion of being lazy seems absurd.

Longtime friend and frequent director Federico Fellini agrees:

> The legend that Marcello is indifferent and lazy is nonsense. He spends hours discussing his role until he understands it thoroughly, extracting the most extraordinary nuances.

To the question of why he has worked so much, Mastroianni has offered the elementary explanation that this is simply what he does. As he once told the Rome daily *La Repubblica*

> All I know is my work. By myself I don't even know how to get a ticket for a soccer match between Lazio and Roma. . . . I'm an actor because I couldn't exist otherwise, so I act.

Similarly, in another conversation with the Milan daily *Il Corriere della Sera*, he insisted: "If I'm not working, I'm bored." Wife Flora

Carabella has confirmed this attitude, adding the observation that Mastroianni's notions of work encompass far more than studying his lines or getting down his marks on a set.

> He's never without a telephone in his hand. As soon as he gets up in the morning, the first thing he does is to grab the phone and call up somebody to talk about what he's working on or is thinking of working on. If he can't get by without working, he can't get by without the telephone, either.

From the moment that he appeared as an extra in *Marionette* and had his first taste of a motion-picture set, Mastroianni has conceded, life elsewhere had a decidedly duller cast.

> Making a film is having a party, a happening. It's like the Sunday afternoons when the kids would go out dancing. Sometimes the day is a great success because somebody brings along the pizza and somebody else has the drinks and everybody is feeling good. Sometimes it can turn out to be a big bore, with nothing quite right. That's how I think of making a film. It's a sort of game. You have to approach it seriously, yes, but it still has to be entertaining if it's to be worth anything. A day on the set is a very long day, and if you don't bring a little irony to it, if you don't know how to laugh at the situations that arise, at yourself, at this wonderful way of making a living that, thank God, the Lumière brothers invented, then it becomes intolerable.

On another occasion, he noted that the French use the word *jouer* (to play) also for saying "to act."

> What is more beautiful than playing? You are with a gang. They wait for you in the morning. They're mostly nice people, if you don't count some of those who think of themselves as grand artists. You show up, and it's "Want some coffee? Have a seat. Relax." I don't know what the hell there is to relax from, but I relax, anyway. There are beautiful women everyplace you look. The world turns around you. What could be better?

"That's it exactly," according to one longtime associate. "Marcello's world is really the world of the set, of the continuous set. If he didn't keep working, he'd be a very lonely man. Making movies is his reality."

If this recalls some of the actor's admissions about growing up as a dreamer and seeing no good reason to stop dreaming just because of some gray hairs, it also misrepresents the many roles that he has taken on for reasons other than wish fulfillment. As he once told *Il Corriere della Sera:*

I have always been very available, maybe too available. I've agreed to do things abroad just to get abroad. I did other things just to get away from people or because some friend asked me to. And, too, I've made a number of films just because of money, because I go around spending and spending and spending and end up behind on taxes and other things.

In fact, Mastroianni's casual way with a checkbook in the 1960s and 1970s gave him a reputation as a profligate. Returning to his abandoned interest in architecture in the period, he spent the next couple of decades helping to design as many as eight houses for himself and Carabella in various parts of Italy, forgetting about most of them as soon as they were ready for occupancy and selling them off. He also bought a villa on the outskirts of Rome for his mother that included the ruins of an aqueduct and theater, a pre-Christian burial ground, and more rooms than the woman could cope with. Asked to explain his real-estate ventures, he has said only: "Obviously, I haven't needed all the houses that I worked on. It's a game, an expensive game, and much better than throwing away my money at the chemin de fer table in Monte Carlo."

Another passion for some time was sports cars, with Mastroianni and Fellini literally trading in Jaguars for BMWs and Porsches for Triumphs weekly in an attempt to outdo one another. The mania got so out of hand that his attorney colluded with his wife to sell off the cars behind his back. They intervened too late, however, to avert a call from Italian tax collectors. Aroused by the money splurged on the cars (and also, for a brief time, on classical Roman antiques), the tax men assessed Mastroianni millions in extra payments at the beginning of the 1970s. For the next decade or so, half his annual earnings went toward that debt.

Asked about some of these misadventures, the actor usually shrugs and agrees that it is better having his wife handle all his money.

I've made a lot of money in my time, but I've never really become rich in the head. Usually, somebody who's been poor knows how to manage his money. Not me. I'm always taking strides a lot longer than my legs. I've always handled my money like some parvenu who's afraid that he won't have enough time to spend everything that he's suddenly gotten his hands on.

In the view of some members of his circle, the houses, cars, and antiques have been signposts for a man who not only doesn't know how to spend his money but when not working doesn't know how to spend his time. Worse, it has been said, he gets little stimulation from those around him, because they are as lost as he is between one film and another, between one meal and another. Thus, as Fellini assistant Liliana Betti has said of the director: "He has no interests outside of moviemaking, he has no hobbies whatsoever, he doesn't like traveling, going to the movies or to plays. . . . " Although again in the face of other interviews in which he has affirmed precisely the opposite, Mastroianni has also boasted that the only films he sees are his own in a dubbing studio or during a festival where he has been called on to make a promotional appearance. ("Maybe I'm just afraid that I'll find someone who's a better actor than I am!") If he has had anything like a regular pastime, it has been traveling, though again, usually at the expense of a production company or a festival.

Even within his profession ("my whole life"), the actor has shown little inclination to be anything except that. His few excursions into producing found him largely fronting for others who did the real work. Periodic nudgings by friends to direct have been met with bafflement.

> Why should I want to be a director? Directors spend all their time having to *convince*. First of all, they have to convince themselves they have talent. Then they have to convince their wives, their lovers, their children, their landlords, their supers, their producers, the producers' wives and lovers, the banks, and, finally, the public. I could never do that. I feel safe and comfortable as an actor. Leave me alone.

But for all the emerging picture of what one friend has called "a big little boy" and what Mastroianni himself has typified as "a big butterfly," it still wouldn't seem to merit the title of laziness; killing time in the adult world, maybe, but not laziness. Even those who do not fully subscribe to Fellini's denial of the actor's indolence have been careful to distinguish it from his professional sense of obligation. "Of course he's lazy," Stefania Sandrelli, his costar in *Divorzio all'Italiana,* has said. "Not while he is working but between takes. I never saw anybody so capable of just falling asleep while everyone around him is running here and there and making an uproar in preparing for the next shot." For director Elio Petri, any work-related laziness stemmed more from his choice of roles than from actually doing them. Petri declared back in the 1970s to a writer:

> He has a Roman's faults, and sometimes he takes parts that aren't going to tax him. But that is not the same thing as not delivering what he's asked to by a script or a director. Just the opposite, most of the time he ends up giving *more* than he has been asked to give.

Some have said that the real foundation for Mastroianni's frequent self-deprecations of his industry is to be glimpsed in his reminders of his mother's attitude toward his career. As he has described it:

> She never really believed in my line of work as a serious thing. Even when I had a lot of money and some assistants around the house, she would warn me that it was all going to end. One time I offered her a car and a driver, and she told me that I was being ridiculous, that she had gotten around Rome all her life without such things and she wasn't going to start in with them at her age. Half of it was pride in her ability to get along by herself. But the other half was real apprehension that I was indeed going to end up on my ass, and she didn't want to get used to something that she was sure was going to be taken away from her in the end, anyway.

Such statements have encouraged interpretations that Mastroianni's mother wasn't the only one who never entirely accepted his career, that on some subterranean level the actor himself has never quite found peace with either his bourgeois upbringing or his fantasies regarding the peasant's way of life, that his self-perceived laziness was the underside of his attitude toward acting as an adult version of a boyhood game. One friend offers a different analysis, however.

> Marcello is no American obsessed with the Protestant work ethic. He's an Italian Catholic from the central-south who knows that he works very hard and has no reason to apologize for it. The problem isn't the work that other cultures consider the end-all for determining who is and who isn't doing his share. The lazy Marcello, the one that he recognizes as lazy, is the one who has been lazy about everything *except* work, *except* the fact that he's starred in more films than anyone else in the last thirty years.

7

Finding Direction

Aside from their script failings, most of Mastroianni's earliest films lacked the kind of imaginative director that he learned to insist on as a prerequisite for a screen project. The only arguable exceptions were Emmer, whose forte remained documentaries on art; Camerini, whose best days were behind him; and Monicelli and Risi, whose best days were still ahead of them. But then, with his dramatic talents on both the stage and the movie set established, the actor came to the attention of more endowed filmmakers. One of these was Alessandro Blasetti, the most gifted of Italy's directors during the long night of Fascism, for such seminal works as *Sole* (Sun; 1929), *1860* (1934), *La Corona di Ferro* (1940), and *Quattro Passi fra le Nuvole* (Four Steps in the Clouds; 1942). Mastroianni would recall:

> Blasetti was one of the greatest fans I had. He believed in me very much. He saw me doing *Oreste* for Visconti, and from that point on he was practically my personal handler and private talent scout. He was totally convinced that I could do well in films, and he began acting like a father to me, advising me what parts I should take and which ones were bad for me.

One that was good for him, according to Blasetti, was in an episode of the director's own *Tempi Nostri* (Anatomy of Love), an anthology film that sought to offer an overview of Italy at mid-century. The tale featuring Mastroianni, based on Alberto Moravia's short story "Il Pupo" (The Little One), teamed the actor with Lea Padovani as a desperately poor couple who decide to abandon their recently born child in a church in the hope that he will be adopted by someone with more material means. After finding fault with several churches, they leave the infant in the back of a taxi, but then have second thoughts, retrieve their son, and resolve to go on as a family as best they can. Although the film as a whole earned only tepid praise, "Il Pupo" was widely praised as Blasetti's most effective sequence, in no small part because of Mastroianni and Padovani. Among those offering that opinion was Moravia, who, as a movie critic for the weekly *Europeo*, cited the treatment as the best screen adaptation of his prose to that point. Mastroianni himself described the project as "an opportunity to do a profoundly human and dramatic character" and defended Blasetti from his critics (on the film in general) by defying them to name another director who had captured "the true melancholy of poverty" with equal clarity.

The actor next hooked up with Carlo Lizzani, one of Italy's most curious directors for his odd mixture of Marxist rhetoric and commercial fireworks. In *Cronache di Poveri Amanti* (Chronicles of Poor Lovers), based on a novel by Vasco Pratolini, Mastroianni had the role of an anti-Fascist fruit vendor who tries to stir up his neighbors against the Mussolini regime and local Blackshirts in 1920s Florence. In a contrast to much of his later work, Lizzani eschewed his ideological and Hollywood tendencies in favor of an intricate choral approach that calmly laid out the neighborhood tensions among anti-Fascist, pro-Fascist, and indifferent Florentines in the period treated. Despite that, however, the picture had enormous difficulties with officialdom, in part because of the director's noted political leanings, in part because of the story's less than endearing portrayal of some middle-class characters considered synonymous with a Christian Democratic constituency. (It didn't help, either, that one of the most stalwart anti-Fascist characters had the name Maciste, a direct Pratolini-Lizzani shot at the film establishment's buildup of that actor as the ultimate nationalistic strongman.) When *Cronache* was entered into the Cannes Film Festival, it prompted Rome officials to warn the show's organizers that Italy would boycott future festivals if the picture were given an award. Other efforts were made to persuade France and other Western European countries to ban it altogether. (The film didn't win any prizes, but it circulated freely abroad.)

Critically, *Cronache di Poveri Amanti* didn't stir as many ideological passions as, say, *Febbre di Vivere* had; even regime apologists acknowledged its cool approach to the material. This did not prevent some (unfounded) concern, however, that an attack in the weekly *L'Epoca*, a frequent forum for unofficial government attitudes, might signal an attempt by officials to decentralize the industry to weed out left-wing intellectuals in the capital; the thrust of a review by *L'Epoca* was that *Cronache* represented one example too many of characters supposedly from another zone of Italy falling into a Roman dialect. On the other hand, Moravia found the Lizzani production to be "a good, clear, serious film that has been well told, without propaganda, without experimental tricks, and without snobbisms." In spite of the ensemble approach to the material, Mastroianni, Antonella Lualdi, and Anna Maria Ferrero were cited by Moravia and other critics as particularly indispensable to the film's texture. As for Mastroianni, he has identified *Cronache* as "one of the best things I did back then" while also conceding that he had been surprised ("but probably should not have been") by the official reaction. "Obviously, what Lizzani and Pratolini had to say could still disturb a government that relied on the parliamentary support of neo-Fascists to stay in power."

Cronache di Poveri Amanti was one of six films that Mastroianni shot in 1954—a load that finally made it impossible for him to continue working on the stage. When it was announced that he wouldn't be part of the Visconti company's season, some colleagues began whispering that he had been bitten by the star bug, that he had never gotten over his increased popularity after the release of *Una Domenica d'Agosto*. There were other claims that he was again chasing after Gassman, who had gone to Hollywood a couple of years before. The actor has snorted at such interpretations of his decision to take a leave from Visconti.

> To begin with, I went back to the company as soon as I had fulfilled my film obligations. I also never understood why anybody was supposed to have wanted to emulate Vittorio's bad time in California. It wasn't a craze for popularity that drew me to films. Even less was it some dream of money, which never interested me and which I've never learned how to manage, anyway. Anybody who knows me can attest to that. Actors, as the old saying goes, are those who always die poor. I did movies because producers wanted me, because it was a way of realizing a boyhood dream, and because I enjoyed myself. That's all there was to it.

As he has made clear on several occasions, his "boyhood dream" of making movies was linked very closely to his notions about the United States.

> I wasn't the only one. Directors like Fellini and Scola were the same way. We all grew up with a mythology about American movies and American comic strips. These allowed us to use our imaginations in a way that, under a dictatorship like Mussolini's, isn't easy. One of the main enemies of dictatorship is imagination, and we felt almost like outlaws thinking about what we saw in American movies and then pretending that *we* were those American heroes. John Wayne and Gary Cooper—that was what America was to me as a boy, and I was always determined to do what I'd seen and imagined for myself.

Following *Cronache di Poveri Amanti*, Mastroianni found himself back in turgid territory with Raffaello Matarazzo's *Schiava del Peccato* (Slave of Sin), a four-handkerchief soap opera about a prostitute (Silvana Pampanini) who tries to adopt a child whom she has rescued from a train wreck but who must ultimately give her up for adoption to a former lover (Mastroianni). The actor was hardly noticed for what was essentially a garrulous supporting role, and he returned the favor some years later. "I don't even remember that one," he told an interviewer. "It must have been one of the things that I did between Saturday and Monday."

He fared better in his next assignment, *Giorni d'Amore* (Days of Love), directed by Giuseppe De Santis, then one of Italy's most sought after filmmakers because of the international attention generated by his *Riso Amaro* and *Roma Ore 11* (Rome Eleven O'Clock; 1952). *Giorni d'Amore* was a fable about two peasants (Mastroianni and Marina Vlady) who are stymied in their plans for a wedding by the fact that neither of their families can afford it. Taking matters into his own hands, the Mastroianni character persuades his fiancée and the two families to go along with his plan to abduct his love and "dishonor" her, thereby necessitating a hurried ceremony that will save both families from the embarrassment of admitting to the village that there isn't enough money for a proper wedding. Matters go awry when the supposedly fake tension between the families degenerates into a serious feud, but in the end the lovers are united in church.

For Mastroianni, *Giorni d'Amore* was more than an opportunity to work with De Santis.

> The film was shot in the Ciociaria, not far from where I was born, so the entire project for me was a sentimental return to my roots. I enjoyed every bit of it. It was probably the most delightful time that I'd had making a film, and the character of the *simpatico* peasant I was playing made it more so.

But De Santis, who was born in the same region, would have a somewhat different memory of the filming.

> Trouble started even before we began shooting because the producers didn't want Mastroianni; they wanted Gérard Philipe. I was the one who held out for Marcello because I just couldn't see Philipe in that part. Once we began shooting, Marcello got me very angry. He was one of those overgrown boys—Gassman was another one—who had theater or academy training and who never let you forget that they regarded themselves as independent spirits. They had what I considered a real arrogance. So the tactic I had devised in working with Gassman in *Riso Amaro* was to tire them out, the way a torero does to the bull. I put Mastroianni through so many

setups, takes, and tests that he had other things to worry about besides being independent. Only when he was exhausted, when he couldn't think about anything but finishing with some shot, was he ready to give me what I wanted.

While Mastroianni has denied any significant conflicts during the making of the picture, Elio Petri, the future director who was then working as De Santis's assistant, acknowledged some "missed connections" between the actor and the filmmaker. According to Petri,

Marcello wasn't arrogant. He just had his way of doing things that had been tried with the best and the worst and that had never really been challenged before. And when it comes to arrogance, De Santis was no model of humility, either. Marcello was really excited to be in the area where he had been born. Maybe De Santis, who hadn't moved away at an early age as Marcello had, decided that there was only one real *ciociaro* on the set. In any case, the film turned out all right.

For Mastroianni, in fact, *Giorni d'Amore* reaped a Nastro d'Argento (Silver Ribbon), a prestigious Italian-industry prize and the first he received for his film work. The part also led more than one critic to observe that the actor had become both physically and emotionally more mature on the screen, suggesting that his days as the ingenuous cabdriver were behind him.

But it wasn't quite that easy. Although he would have reason to remember his next three films—Carmine Gallone's *Casa Ricordi* (House of Ricordi), Blasetti's *Peccato Che Sia una Canaglia* (Too Bad She's Bad), and Paolo Moffa's *La Principessa della Canarie* (The Island Princess)—only the Blasetti project would be recalled with any artistic pride.

In *Casa Ricordi*, Mastroianni played the prominent role of composer Gaetano Donizetti in a story that mainly concerned the founding of the Ricordi music publishing company and that came across as a high-toned M-G-M musical, with its cavalcade of opera and concert performances. Aside from Mastroianni as Donizetti, the cast included Paolo Stoppa as the publisher, Gabriele Ferzetti as Puccini, Roland Alexandre as Rossini, and Fosco Giachetti as Verdi; among those drafted for the musical interludes were Mario del Monaco, Tito Gobbi, and Renata Tebaldi. Critical reaction to the film was totally negative, with the Milan weekly *Oggi* summing up the general response by declaring: "*Casa Ricordi* brings no honor to the Italian film industry. Probably never before on our screens has there ever been such an accumulation of banalities and historical errors."

But if Mastroianni wrote off the film as fast as did Italian critics, one member of his family took an opposing view. The actor revealed:

> As far as my mother was concerned, doing Donizetti in *Casa Ricordi* was the best performance I ever gave. She was mad for certain kinds of film musicals. Nelson Eddy had been a favorite, and the thing she was proudest of when I got my first work as an extra in *Marionette* was that I was in a scene with Beniamino Gigli. I think she must have seen *Casa Ricordi* two hundred times, even traveling sometimes out to the rerun houses on the outskirts of the city to catch it. She never seemed to get tired of watching it. "There," she'd say to me, "there you're finally playing a serious person!"

For Mastroianni himself, Blasetti's *Peccato Che Sia Una Canaglia* proved far more gratifying. Aside from reuniting him with the director of the "Il Pupo" episode from *Tempi Nostri,* the comedy about a family of con artists and a Roman cabdriver (guess who?) also represented the actor's first important work experience with his "uncle," De Sica. Moreover, it teamed him for the first time with the most frequent screen partner of his career—Sophia Loren. Blasetti would say later:

> A lot of people have taken credit for bringing them together, but I think it really was me. I already had the idea for doing *Canaglia* with Marcello while I was shooting another picture with Sophia and Totò. She was very untried, to say the least, and I was apprehensive about a couple of scenes that she had to do with Totò, who was notorious for improvising dialogue and adding his own little flights of fancy not in the script. Suddenly, we're shooting one of these scenes, and he's doing exactly what I was afraid of. But there was Sophia, giving as good as she got, daring Totò to go along even further. There was an instinctive Neapolitan rapport between the two of them, and I decided right then and there that she'd work fine with Mastroianni and De Sica in *Canaglia.*

As far as Loren was concerned, the key to her instant rapport with Mastroianni was that the two of them came from the Naples vicinity.

> A lot of people think that Marcello is Roman because of that redistricting that happened after he was born, but to me he's always been a lot more Neapolitan. As soon as we met on the set of *Canaglia,* there was a spark between us. And with De Sica also from the same area, the three of us were united in a kind of complicity that the Neapolitans always have among themselves. The same sense of humor, the same rhythms, the same philosophies of life, the same natural cynicism. All three of us did our roles instinc-

tively. It worked so well that when the film came out, there weren't too many people who remembered that it was really the first time Marcello had done comedy on the screen.

Mastroianni, who has habitually referred to Loren as "a sister," shared the actress's enthusiasm, and then some.

For once, I wasn't bothered by doing the Roman taxi driver. In fact, I got so immersed in the part that during breaks I'd get into the cab that we were using and go for long drives around the city. I was very proud when somebody whistled for me to pick him up.

Mastroianni picked up more acting prizes for *Peccato Che Sia una Canaglia* as well as some of the most glowing reviews of his career. One critic went so far as to address an appeal to the Italian film industry that "it show its awareness that Mastroianni is one of the most precious assets of our cinema" and find him good roles with more consistency. But there were also comedowns. Only a few days after receiving them, the actor and his mother had to walk his prizes over to the state-run pawn shop.

In those days, you often got paid with promissory notes that you couldn't collect on for months. When the man behind the counter recognized me and saw how embarrassed I was, he said, "Hey, look, Mastroianni, there's no reason to be ashamed about coming in here. I could give you a list of names of famous people who practically live in here." He gave us 100,000 lire for the awards.

The appeals of critics notwithstanding, *Peccato Che Sia una Canaglia* also did little for the way producers viewed the actor.

The Blasetti film almost ended my career. It was so successful that all I got sent were a lot of comedies about a Rome cabdriver. At least when I had done a part like that before, the picture had just gone away after a couple of months. But with the film taking in so much money and everybody saying how good Sophia and I were together, I really had to fight producers to do something better.

The fight was temporarily lost, but not because he agreed to do more cabbies. "Maybe I got impatient to do *anything* different," he has said of his decision to appear in *La Principessa della Canarie* (The Island Princess). "Well, I certainly did anything different."

In *La Principessa della Canarie*, Mastroianni played a Spanish officer sent to the Canaries at the head of an army in the fifteenth century to colonize the archipelago for Madrid. Inevitably, he falls in love with the daughter (Silvana Pampanini) of the local ruler, and they must combat enemies on both sides before bringing themselves and their peoples together. An Italian-Spanish coproduction, the picture was held up for a long time because of financial problems before being released and was scarcely noticed by the critics. Mastroianni has never had any hesitation about calling his role as the Spanish officer "the most ludicrous" of his career, even more embarrassing than his character some years later of a pregnant man.

> Every once in a while, I think to myself I'd like to see *La Principessa della Canarie* again, to see if I really looked as ridiculous as I felt I did. What I remember most was the atrocious heat down on the islands and how every morning I had to put on these long stockings and armor and god knows what else. To make it worse, I have terrible legs, so they decided I had to wear extra pairs of stockings to make my legs look like their idea of a Spanish officer's. I didn't know how to ride a horse; I didn't know how to use a sword. I never felt so unhappy or ridiculous in my life. That's why I'd like to see it again one of these days. Maybe invite a couple of close friends, go into a theater, and laugh at this imbecile up on the screen doing who the hell knows what.

Unfortunately for the actor, *La Principessa della Canarie* wasn't his only experience in feeling ridiculous while on an exotic location; two pictures later, he had the starring role in Gian Gaspare Napolitano's *Tam-Tam Mayumbe* (Mayumbe Drums). Set in the Belgian Congo, *Tam-Tam Mayumbe* cast Mastroianni as a medical officer sent to a remote jungle outpost to investigate reports that the natives were buying contraband liquor instead of taking the medicine they were given to combat sleeping sickness. The Italian-French-British co-production was largely written off as an excuse to show the African wilds and supporting player Pedro Armendariz's ability to outham anyone else on the screen.

> The whole thing was absurd, senseless. The film cost a mint to make. It was filled with all the usual European condescension toward Africans. My only excuse for agreeing to do it was that it seemed like an opportunity to see a place I might never have seen otherwise. What a disaster! We were in the middle of the jungle, completely cut off from everything. Wherever you looked, there were poisonous snakes. Half the company came down with malaria or something else. It was hell.

Between *La Principessa della Canarie* and *Tam-Tam Mayumbe*, he agreed to another teaming with Loren and De Sica. The project was *La Bella Mugnaia* (The Miller's Beautiful Wife)—the second time that director Mario Camerini had brought Pedro de Alarcón's *Three-Cornered Hat* to the screen. Set during Spain's seventeenth-century occupation of Naples, *La Bella Mugnaia* featured Mastroianni as a wily miller who uses the flirtatious beauty of his wife (Loren) to win favors from the Spanish administration. When he clouts a Spanish officer for being more forward with his spouse than he is willing to tolerate, he is thrown into jail, thereby precipitating a series of comic misunderstandings involving the wife, a skirt-chasing governor (De Sica), and the latter's wife. Despite Camerini's familiarity with the material, *La Bella Mugnaia* sagged under pressures from producers Carlo Ponti and Dino De Laurentiis to embroider the film with some of the comic elements that had made *Peccato Che Sia una Canaglia* so popular at the box office. The result was a half satire, half farce that left De Sica seeking hammy solutions to the film's lack of direction, pleased few critics, and did a barely respectable business. On the other hand, Mastroianni and Loren escaped unscathed, the consensus being that the move from twentieth-century Rome to seventeenth-century Naples had not affected their chemistry together.

Back from the jungles of the Congo, Mastroianni wasted little time in agreeing to a third go-around with Loren: Blasetti's *La Fortuna di Essere Donna* (Lucky to Be a Woman). A comedy still again aimed at repeating the success of *Peccato Che Sia una Canaglia*, *La Fortuna di Essera Donna* saw Mastroianni as a fast-talking photographer who promises to launch an acting-modeling career for Loren in order to bed her down, then realizes that he is in love as soon as she tries to heal her emotional bruises by going out with an older Lothario who can also help her career. Any chance that the picture had of trumping *Peccato Che Sia una Canaglia* was lost when the French coproducers demanded that the role of the older Don Giovanni go to Charles Boyer rather than to the originally projected De Sica. As Loren put it: "Boyer was a wonderful actor, but he was not the one for this picture. Marcello and I went around feeling like two sides of a triangle missing its base."

Most critics agreed with Loren, but some of them also called for an end to the knee-jerk attempts by Italian producers to seek endless variations on a film (*Peccato Che Sia una Canaglia*) that had not been a masterpiece to begin with. Once again, there were calls for Mastroianni, who received just about the only positive notices in *La Fortuna di Essere Donna*, to make better use of his talent. As it turned out, any temptation to pair the actor with Loren yet again was foiled by her decision to go to Hollywood for several years. According to Mastroianni:

> They wanted me to go, too. But I couldn't imagine for what. What was I supposed to do there? Play a Hollywood cabdriver? Maybe play a miller in Los Angeles? Sophia was right to go. It was what

made her the international star she became. But I couldn't even speak English. I had no desire to make a fool of myself.

Instead, he returned to Visconti for *Uncle Vanya* in December 1955 and *Death of a Salesman* a few months later while maintaining a steady series of film commitments. For Emmer, he starred in a French-Italian coproduction entitled *Il Bigamo* (The Bigamist), a somewhat noisy story that moved uneasily between comedy and drama in depicting the plight of a happily married salesman (Mastroianni) who is accused of having marched to the altar with another woman a few years before. Unlike a low-budgeted American film of the same title with Edmond O'Brien that was then circulating in Europe, *Il Bigamo* ultimately skipped away from its own premise by having everything resolved by a second character who had the same name as Mastroianni's and by presenting the alleged first wife as a liar. Critical reaction to the film was predominantly negative, with the Milan weekly *Oggi* declaring in part:

> *Il Bigamo* is a barometer of the present crisis of the Italian cinema. It is a crisis that extends to the need to go abroad for the capital for a wholly Italian subject, to the moral ambiguities and ambivalences of our writers and directors, and to the choice of subjects in the first place. The film rests entirely on the strong shoulders of Mastroianni, who, however, is far too *simpatico* for audiences to believe for a moment that he is guilty of what he has been accused of.

For the actor himself, the film was worth remembering only because it gave him another opportunity to work with De Sica, who played the part of a windy lawyer who only makes the problems of the Mastroianni character worse.

For his work in Monicelli's episodic *Padri e Figli* (The Tailor's Maid), Mastroianni collected some of the best notices of his career as a husband who has become embittered because he and his wife cannot have children but who then spends an afternoon with a nephew who convinces him that there is no shame in adopting a child. After noting that the film as a whole sagged under its device of a home nurse visiting various patients, *Il Corriere della Sera* pointed to the Mastroianni story as "easily the most tasteful" in the film. *Il Giornale dello Spettacolo* congratulated the actor "for being able to give an extremely human and concrete face" to his character, while the Communist organ *L'Unità* said that the performance "reconfirms Mastroianni's status as our surest and most confident young actor."

A couple of months later, however, the same *L'Unità* reviewer saw Frantisek Cap's *La Ragazza della Salina* (The Girl of the Salt Works) and suggested that Mastroianni exercise more discretion in his choice of film roles. Another laughable daughter of *Riso Amaro*,

La Ragazza della Salina cast Mastroianni as a fisherman who is so captivated by Isabelle Corey that he follows her to a job in a salt works. There, amid scenes that strongly recall Silvana Mangano's tensions with Gassman in *Riso Amaro*, he convinces her of his love while battling a cruel foreman (Peter Carsten). As with *Tam-Tam Mayumbe*, Mastroianni's explanation for doing the picture was that it gave him the chance to get out of Italy, in this case across the Adriatic to Yugoslavia.

> It started off as a West German-Yugoslav coproduction, and I kind of liked the idea of working with foreigners. But then Rizzoli got involved, and it became an Italian coproduction. It just seemed like something to do—and to forget.

What the actor would admit subsequently, however, was that *La Ragazza della Salina*, and the opportunity to get off to Yugoslavia, coincided with a growing personal crisis. For one thing, his marriage had entered choppy waters, not least because of his roving eye and his reluctance to spend more time at home. Even when he was at home, according to Carabella, it was as much as a host as a husband. "I never felt that this man belonged to me alone," she would admit sometime later. "Maybe once a year we would be alone together. He always invited people to the house; people were always around. Or he was flitting here and there, aimlessly, except perhaps to look for himself." Given his widely noted affairs to come with Jeanne Moreau, Faye Dunaway, Ursula Andress, Catherine Deneuve, and others, Mastroianni has hardly been in a position to deny such an appraisal. "The record speaks for itself, I suppose. I've agreed to do several films abroad just to get out of some love mess that I had at home."

But the mess wasn't just marital, and Yugoslavia didn't offer all the solutions.

> That was not a very good period for looking at myself in the mirror. What the hell had I accomplished? On the screen I was always some kind of imbecile being saved from prison by the great lawyer De Sica or bouncing on mattresses with Sophia. I was already past thirty and getting absolutely nowhere.

Despite good personal notices, matters didn't improve much when he agreed to make still another film with Emmer, *Il Momento Più Bello* (The Most Wonderful Moment), a melodrama midway between a soap opera and a documentary about an obstetrician (Mastroianni) who pioneers a new childbirth method but who has problems delivering his own commitment when his fiancée (Giovanna Ralli) announces that she is pregnant. But at least in retrospect, *Il Momento Più Bello* was a significant undertaking in that it persuaded him that if he were ever to escape from his rut as a personable young hero, he was going to have to take matters into his own hands.

8

Close-up: The Reactor

In keeping with his view of filmmaking as a serious game, Mastroianni has tended to play down the difficulties involved in creating a character for the cameras. More than once he has voiced skepticism about Method acting ("nonsense"), about the physical and research efforts made by performers such as Jack Nicholson and Robert De Niro to get into roles and about the importance of the actor to begin with. At the same time, however, he has reacted angrily to suggestions that his own labors consist of little more than placing himself in front of a director and improvising additions to a script that he has usually memorized after a couple of readings. As he told one interviewer:

> I'm no imbecile out there with nothing on my mind but to follow orders and throw in whatever occurs to me. I learned a lot of things with Visconti and have learned a few others with other directors since then.

Commenting once on his habit of jumping immediately from one film into another, the actor dismissed it as anything exceptional, asserting that only American performers restricted themselves to a single film every year or so "because they're always chewing themselves up and need the time to recuperate before they go back to doing the same thing." As an example, he cited Nicholson's reported stay for several weeks in a mental institution prior to the shooting of the Oscar-winning *One Flew Over the Cuckoo's Nest*, calling it "useless" and insisting that the madness of the American actor's character in the film "had to come from within and not from some imitation of how disturbed people are supposed to behave." Time and again in interviews over the years to the drastic weight gains and losses endured by De Niro while making *Raging Bull*, variously branding it "senseless," "laughable," and "dangerous." He told the monthly magazine *Attenzione* in 1981:

To me that's going overboard, being far more serious about acting than acting deserves. . . . There's seriousness and there's seriousness. No need to be grave about what you're doing. . . . It's fine to be a great actor, to apply yourself to your task. But up to a certain point, no? Movies aren't life. Be a helluva thing if we ruined our health just to make a movie.

He has been equally iconoclastic about acting theories that call for some physical trigger for emotional expressivity. In 1985, he told the Italian magazine *L'Espresso:*

Why should you have to bang your head on the wall to show that you know how to cry? If it was that simple, I'd give you a kick in the balls, and you would do an astonishing crying scene.

To another writer, he dismissed the importance of actors who suffered during preparations for a role:

Every time I read about actors suffering, I don't know what the hell they're talking about. I suffer if I have to get up early in the morning. All this grander kind of suffering they're supposed to be enduring is totally alien to me. The only truly painful thing for an actor is not getting hired.

Another frequent target has been the Method—even if some people think that he doth protest too much on the subject. Shelley Winters, for example, insists that Mastroianni has

always been a Method actor. What he is embarrassed about is any conscious approach that endangers his notions of a private life. But, objectively, he is as much of a Method actor as anybody working at the Actors Studio.

Mastroianni is willing to concede that he shares the Method's approach "unconsciously," but not much more. At his most benevolent, he has portrayed the teachings of Konstantin Stanislavski as "something far more attuned to the nature and psychology of American actors than to Italians because Americans seem to like to disembowel themselves when they go about things." Less philosophically, he has been quoted as saying that

I can't abide a place like the Actors Studio in New York as an institution. I don't know what its purpose is aside from providing a place where one maniac can meet a whole lot of maniacs just like him.

In the same vein, he has spoken often of a visit to New York in 1962 during which he met Lee Strasberg, creative director of the Actors Studio.

At one point Strasberg turns to me and says, "The actor is everything." No, Strasberg. *You* think the actor is everything because
training actors happens to be your profession. But there is nothing
special about an actor. The actor is someone who goes out to
recite "To be or not to be" while he's thinking about his lawyer
or worrying about the money that he has to send to his first
wife.

Glib or not, this latter remark echoes the impression made on
Mastroianni back in his days with Visconti's theater company when
he witnessed Gassman dividing up his salary among wives and children. It is also the frequently present Gassman who comes up in conversation when Mastroianni tries to distinguish his manner of
approaching a role from that of other performers. Typical was a 1987
interview that he gave to the New York daily *Newsday*, in which he
said:

I always try not to disturb, but to remain on the side. I'm a bit passive and reactive—unlike Gassman, who's a lot more aggressive.
That's why I have such good chemistry in working with somebody
like Loren. We complement each other like Laurel and Hardy. She
acts, while I react. Once, I refused a role with her, and it ended up
going to Gassman. My mother predicted that it would be a disaster,
and she was right. They're both actors, not reactors.

As Mastroianni sees it, there is nothing mysterious or alchemi-
cal in the makeup of an actor.

Assume that you have some basic training, that your diction is
intelligible, that you can walk across a room and not fall over your
feet, that you're not up there to make a personal spectacle of yourself and that you're dedicated to doing your part, not some clown
show for your friends. From that point on, all an actor really has to
do is to develop his intelligence, to cultivate it as he needs it for his
work. For me, I don't think actors should dwell on their roles while
sitting by themselves in some dark room. You can work on a character anywhere; while you're eating spaghetti in a restaurant, for
instance. The real test is being able to feel what our lives are like in
their best and most difficult moments, to recall the suffering that
we may sometimes feel in the middle of the night, to summon up
the joy that we may feel on seeing somebody we love. If I'm considered a good actor, it's because I've lived a full enough life to have
material to draw upon with the help of what I've succeeded in
learning from good teachers and directors. I'm not saying it's the
simplest thing in the world, but it is hardly a religion worthy of a
cult following, either.

According to the actor, the investment process was probably as close as a man ever got to being pregnant. As he once described it for the *New York Times Magazine:*

> This character, this person that I am to become, starts to grow inside me, little by little. He begins to talk to me, and I listen like a primitive naïf. If I don't listen, he will die in me. So I'm eating a plate of spaghetti, and I hear him. Then I stop somewhere, say, at a traffic light—and there he is in the car next to me. In a flash, I know all about him—his wife, his children, his mistresses, his fantasies, all of it. . . . So when I come onto the set, I ask, "What happens to me today?" They tell me, and this character inside me takes over. But since he is filtered by a sensibility through the intelligence, I have to also take one eye out of my head and keep looking at what's going on, to control it.

The process doesn't always start with a script.

> I have rarely gotten a script with Fellini. What happens with him is that we talk for several weeks before actual shooting, and I gradually get to know the character he is proposing.

And with a script?

> It's a different process. I read the whole thing through maybe twice or three times; then I put it aside. From that point on, I am usually thinking of my character whatever else I am doing. I begin to creep up on him. I'm not worried about memorizing things. The lines I've read are settled in. I let it all drift. That way, when the director changes the script—and almost all of them do—I'm still able to reach my character, whatever line changes there have been. My job is the character, not the lines per se. They always seem to come to me when we get down to shooting.

Mario Monicelli, who has directed the actor in a number of films, has confirmed his working method.

> He'll go over a script, then put it aside, thinking about the role. He doesn't mark pages, memorize lines. When he comes onto the set, he feels fresh and free for whatever the scene calls for, and he draws it out of a tremendous reservoir.

Mauro Bolognini, director of two Mastroianni films, says that the key to his performances is "an incredible capacity for concentration. Before going into a scene, he stops and, in an instant, is transformed into that role."

As for Mastroianni, he says that once he steps in front of the

camera, most of his real work is done and that it is then completely
up to the director.

> As soon as you are confident about your character and are ready
> every way you can be, it's no longer your show; it's the director's. I
> let a director use me any way that he sees me, to express his own
> view of the story that we happen to be doing.

Or: "I go along with the idea of the actor as a blotter. We're all a bit
amorphous, nonexistent, useful for what only the director is able to
make out of us." And again:

> In most of my better films, especially those that brought me some
> success in the 1960s, the character doesn't do life; life does to him.
> As someone trained in the theater, I feel that my knowledge is
> always at my command. But I also feel that I belong to the director,
> and while I can give, he's the one who does the creating.

Is there a link between such an attitude toward his function and
the criticism that he has been less than energetic about his life off the
screen?

> For a long time, I felt particularly close to the roles I did in things
> like *La Dolce Vita* and *8½*—characters who were essentially incom-
> plete. I believe doing them was part of my development as a man,
> as a human being. In any case, actors are always incomplete people
> who regard acting as a way of making them feel a little more com-
> plete as human beings.

Not surprisingly, he has named Fellini, the maker of *La Dolce Vita*
and *8½*, as his favorite director for an "enormous ability to see inside
people and their faults. Actors are always good in his films because
they don't play roles; they play themselves."

While Fellini has skirted around this contention as well as
around the rival argument that Mastroianni has usually served him
as an alter ego on the screen, other filmmakers have shaken their
heads at the actor's oversimplifications, cautioning listeners not to
accept them seriously. Petri, who directed Mastroianni in three films,
told an interviewer shortly before his death in 1982:

> The man is an artist in every sense of the word. He's also sweet,
> sensitive, and one of the most intelligent people in the industry.
> Maybe he talks about "being himself," but the fact is that he's one
> of the least naturalistic actors in Italy. If there has been a compa-
> rable performer in the United States, it hasn't been the Bogarts and
> Gables and Coopers he's always referring to, but John Barrymore,
> the greatest of all American actors. Barrymore was hardly natural-
> istic, and neither is Marcello.

Petri also took issue with filmmakers who prized Mastroianni mainly for his minimalism.

I'm a Roman like he is, and sometimes I've seen him fall into what I recognize as a Roman kind of passivity. I understand where it comes from, and I've been the first one to exploit it in him as I've used it in myself. But there's much more to Mastroianni than that. On the surface, you get this calm, phlegmatic man, looking sensible and maybe exuding a degree of cynicism. But there's also a great self-destruction within him that leads him to do some of the risky and bizarre characters he's done. As far as I'm concerned, the Mastroianni of the understatement is my least favorite Marcello because I think it's the easiest and least taxing one for him to do. The Mastroianni I prefer is the one who has great moments of fury—the character who explodes, who scratches away at bourgeois reality to see what's behind it, who wouldn't be content looking at a John Cassavetes movie, at all that flatness, and saying, "Oh, yes, how true, just like our flat, boring lives."

Mastroianni insists, however, that there is no genuine and less genuine levels for measuring his performances by, that his ability to understate or explode are products of the same training and always at the service of a specific role and a specific director. Moreover, there is the even greater common denominator of personality.

The best film actors are those with strong personalities—the James Cagneys, Henry Fondas, Gary Coopers, Humphrey Bogarts. They weren't character actors, and I don't want to be a character actor, working constantly with heavy makeup and pretending to be somebody other than myself. I'm content to be myself on the screen— the myself who can get into the feelings and emotions of a given character but who remains Marcello Mastroianni. If a director doesn't want that, he doesn't hire me for the part. If he does hire me, he knows that he will not get an impersonator, a mimic. It is the actor *acting* as a character that makes for what some people call art in this business, not the actor *becoming* a character, which probably means that he belongs in a loony bin. I suppose that is what has always bothered me about De Niro doing all that weight stuff for *Raging Bull.* Isn't the man sure enough of his own personality? Isn't the director sure enough of it to prevent De Niro from putting himself through all that torture? In any case, if you can keep separated the obligation to act and the temptation to ape and are competent at it, then you're the kind of strong personality they call an actor and, even in some cases, a star.

But even with all these distinctions, Mastroianni the reactor has never been ready to concede that his profession is an art. As he told *Attenzione* magazine in 1981:

In their origins, actors are as much miserable beggars as they are special craftsmen. An actor is still basically somebody who does cartwheels in the town square to attract attention and make a living. Why should somebody like this suddenly be expected to be a saint or make only great, brilliant films? An actor isn't a physicist or a mathematician. He has to do a lot of rotten stuff to get by. In fact, the whole excitement of being an actor is in being able to do something good after being bogged down with a lot of roles that are garbage.

In an interview three years later with the *New York Times*, he put it another way:

The actor is a liar, the most ancient seller of smoke who finds satisfaction in stimulation. Acting is a pleasure, like making love. . . . Correction: Lovemaking can be an ordeal.

9

Big Deals

D espite his experiences with *Contro la Legge* in 1950, Mastroianni took another gamble as a producer in 1957. By his own account, it wasn't too much of a gamble.

> I knew that I couldn't keep doing the *bravo ragazzo* if I wanted my career to get anywhere. And there was nobody who was going to walk up to me, drop a script in my lap, and announce, "Here, Mastroianni, here's the character that's going to change everything for you." So the only thing was to form another production partnership and sink my own money into it.

His partners were Visconti, producer Franco Cristaldi, and producer-screenwriter Suso Cecchi d'Amico. It was Mastroianni who came up with the idea of making their project a Dostoyevski story entitled *Le Notti Bianche* (White Nights) and who persuaded Visconti, his theatrical mentor, that it would make a good film. Then the complications started.

Cecchi d'Amico:

> Marcello and Luchino said they wanted to do a small, small thing. I wrote the adaptation with Luchino, and then I happened to be in Livorno, where I was struck immediately by the canals there as the perfect setting for the film. Marcello and Luchino agreed. But then one day Visconti announces that the more he's been thinking about the script, the more convinced he is that it should not be done realistically, that we should reconstruct the canals of Livorno at Cinecittà in Rome to give everything more of a fictitious look. So much for the small, small. Then Visconti decides that the woman should be played by Maria Schell, who was very much in demand in those days. I had nothing against Schell as an actress, but she wasn't part of the cooperative we'd set up, so she expected to be paid.

And, according to Cecchi d'Amico, it didn't stop there.

The script had a small but critical role that we kept trying to cast without luck. Then Visconti went to Paris and signed Jean Marais, an old friend of his, for it. Naturally, Marais had to be paid as well. It was pointless to make a scene with Luchino over unexpected expenses. It wasn't that he was some kind of wastrel, eager to squander other people's money. What he was was an aristocrat, an extremely rich man who never considered the possibility that other people might have money concerns.

For his part, Mastroianni also kept his eyes averted from the production's mounting financial weight, concentrating instead on the role he had given himself an opportunity to play.

It was the first film that I did where my usual ingenuous, good-hearted character had more of an intellectual slant. Instead of a simple worker or driver, my character was clearly bourgeois, opening up many more possibilities that, in the end, led to the character that I did in *La Dolce Vita*.

Moreover, the actor was distracted by the different Visconti whom he encountered on the Cinecittà set.

Visconti the film director was not Visconti the theater director. He was much less coercive than he had been with our stage company. In the theater, he had been terribly dictatorial, demanded that the actors perform according to rigid formulas. He would even insist that we say words with exactly the intonation he gave to them. It's not that with *Le Notti Bianche* he was any less meticulous. Hardly. We decided to shoot in sequence, and every morning he would sit Schell and me in a room and go over every little detail of what we were supposed to do that day. Then we'd go on the set, and he'd go over it again. But once the cameras started rolling, he gave us much more room to maneuver because he understood that film acting had to be much more naturalistic than theater acting. I always thought that his appreciation for the difference showed how much of an "instructor-director" he really was.

Le Notti Bianche was a melancholy story of a lonely man (Mastroianni) who meets an equally isolated woman (Schell) one night on a bridge. She eventually confesses to him that she has been going to the spot regularly in the hope that her lover, gone from the city for more than a year, will return there to meet her as promised. Little by little, the man falls in love with the woman, and she seems to return his feeling. But just when the two of them appear to have overcome all the emotional and practical obstacles to their love, the lover (Marais) returns, and the woman goes off with him. The Mastroianni character is left even lonelier than he had been.

Reaction to the film was wildly mixed. Visconti, who had established himself as one of the fathers of neorealism with *Ossessione* and *La Terra Trema* (The Earth Trembles, 1948), was blasted for betraying his origins. The director himself acted uncomfortable with the results of his deliberate theatricalization of the script, telling one interviewer that "the film was shot in seven weeks, and I'm afraid it sometimes looks it." On the other hand, a nucleus of critics and filmmakers who ignored the expectations raised by Visconti's background awarded the picture a Silver Lion at the 1957 Venice Festival. As the director admitted subsequently, it was principally because of this prize that he was able to put together the financing to make *Rocco e i Suoi Fratelli* (Rocco and His Brothers) some months later.

As far as Mastroianni was concerned, the film delivered all the artistic rewards that he had hoped. Whatever their ideological agendas (and the Communist Visconti made it an issue), almost every critic in the country pointed to the actor as the feature's chief asset. For *Il Corriere della Sera*, he demonstrated "a prodigious spontaneity." For the weekly *Oggi*, he "towered over the material and the other performers." For *L'Unità* he contributed "the best performance of his already illustrious career." There was little surprise when he won another Nastro D'Argento and little contradiction when the critic from *Il Messaggero* observed that *Le Notti Bianche* was evidence that "Mastroianni is capable of taking on the most mature roles that our filmmakers have to offer."

But satisfied as he was artistically, Mastroianni went into a funk over the film's scant commercial success.

> It was a "head" film—very romantic but also very intellectual. We shot everything with a special photographic process, and a lot of people who went to it said, "Hey, everything is so black, I can't see a damn thing!"

Nor, despite the Silver Lion from the Venice Festival, was there any immediate relief from foreign art circuits in other countries. On the contrary, because of the fierce competition from the British and then the French industries, *Le Notti Bianche* didn't even arrive in New York for six years, by which time (after the release of *La Dolce Vita*, *Rocco e i Suoi Fratelli*, and Antonioni's *L'Avventura*) it was dismissed as dated. (Among other things, there was a crucial rock-and-roll dancing scene between the principal characters that looked as ancient in the 1960s as it would today.) At one point, the actor was so dispirited by the picture's commercial failure that he told an interviewer: "I have no more hope. I am resigned. I'll be playing taxi drivers until the end of my days."

Stretched financially by *Le Notti Bianche*, Mastroianni hurried into Monicelli's *Il Medico e lo Stregone* (The Doctor and the Witch Doctor) to make some money. The modest comedy cast him as a doctor sent to a country village who finds himself up against a charlatan (De Sica) who has held sway over the villagers with a dollop of superstition and a timely dose or two of his own patent medicine. The Mastroianni character wins the day for modern science by saving the life of the charlatan's own daughter. For most critics, the film was largely an excuse to see Mastroianni, De Sica, and Alberto Sordi show off their different acting styles.

With *Un Ettaro di Cielo* (A Piece of the Sky), the actor was back on less solid financial ground but in a part that he viewed as one of his best in the pre–*La Dolce Vita* days. Directed by Aglauco Casadio, a former art critic and documentary filmmaker, *Un Ettaro di Cielo* spun the fable of a flimflam man (Mastroianni) who persuades a village of largely elderly eelers that he can sell them pieces of the sky where they can live comfortably after death. Once the villagers have paid for their "land," one of them goes down to a swamp to end his earthly existence and take immediate possession of what he has paid for but lands atop a school of eels. Everybody takes time out to have one last grand feast, and then one villager after another tries to drown himself, figuring that the least he will end up with is a bounty of eels at the bottom of the swamp. Matters are resolved only when government bulldozers move in with the intention of covering over the swamp with farmland that will be apportioned among all the would-be suicides. Petrified by what he has almost caused, the flimflam man resolves (sort of) to reform his ways and wins the love of one of the village girls (Rosanna Schiaffino).

For the most part, *Un Ettaro di Cielo* struck critics as the genial fable it sought to be, with Mastroianni again praised for his versatility. Commercially, however, the film died quickly—a fact that did not bother the actor as much as it had with *Le Notti Bianche*.

> I was very enthusiastic about doing that picture, and I still like it very much. It probably didn't succeed at the box office because it was pure fantasy, and maybe the public has become accustomed only to what is real and tangible. I've always thought it a work of great imagination.

If *Un Ettaro di Cielo* was a work of artistic imagination, *I Soliti Ignoti* (literally, "Persons Unknown," also its British release title—but shown in the U.S. under the more salable: Big Deal on Madonna Street), Mastroianni's follow-up project for Monicelli and his single biggest triumph in the 1950s, was to an appreciable extent the product of an accountant's imagination. Screenwriter Cecchi d'Amico recalled:

Mastroianni and Deneuve enjoying Paris night life in 1974. (*Globe Photos*)

The actor with his wife Flora Carabella and then-teenage daughter Barbara in 1967. (*AP/Wide World Photos*)

Mastroianni has called his relationship with Faye Dunaway the "most devastating" of his life. (*UPI/Bettmann*)

Mastroianni and Catherine Deneuve on a vacation in Venice in 1972. The actress is holding their daughter Chiara, then less than two. (*AP/Wide World Photos*)

The 1954 comedy *Peccato Che Sia una Canaglia* (Too Bad She's Bad) marked the start of Mastroianni's long starring partnership with Sophia Loren.

Il Bell'Antonio in 1960 was one of Mastroianni's earliest attempts at countering a Latin Lover image. Also pictured, Claudia Cardinale.

Adua e le compagne (Love à la Carte), costarring Sandra Milo (center) and Simone Signoret, prompted some of the worst notices of the actor's career.

Aside from their personal relationship, Mastroianni and Jeanne Moreau had few positive memories of Michelangelo Antonioni's *La Notte* (The Night).

Cronaca Familiare (Family Diary), costarring Jacques Perrin, is one of Mastroianni's few films in which he played off a man rather than a woman.

Divorzio all'Italiana (Divorce—Italian Style), even more than *La Dolce Vita*, established Mastroianni as one of the world's most gifted screen actors. His costar was the emotion-wracked Daniela Rocca.

8½ consolidated Mastroianni's reputation as a screen alter ego for director Federico Fellini. Here he is shown with Anouk Aimée.

I Compagni (The Organizer) allowed Mastroianni to portray the "romantic socialist" he thinks of himself as politically. Flanking him are Folco Lulli and Bernard Blier.

Cinecittà was about to strike the sets that had been built for *Le Notti Bianche*, and there was a lot of hand wringing about how much it had cost to build them for a picture that had been a commercial failure. Then somebody had the bright idea of using the sets for another film before they were torn down so that at least some of the money might have been recouped. The picture we ended up doing there was *I Soliti Ignoti*.

Mastroianni's involvement in the film was belated, and only because of the presence in the cast of his former theater-company colleague Gassman. Although one of the most familiar performers in Italian films, Gassman had until that point built up his career doing haughty characters that had little in common with the genial satire that was at the heart of *I Soliti Ignoti*. In the face of Monicelli's insistence that Gassman be signed for the leading role, producer Franco Cristaldi agreed only on the condition that Mastroianni and the veteran comic Totò be added to the cast as insurance policies. Recalled Mastroianni:

> Vittorio wanted to do the part very badly, and he had the full support of Monicelli. The things they did with Gassman! The makeup people widened his ears, lowered his forehead, and a dozen other things. By the time they were finished, there was nothing of the aristocratic Gassman to be seen.

I Soliti Ignoti was a takeoff on the *Rififi* heist pictures that were popular in the 1950s. Instead of the violent, cold-blooded burglars of the prototypical French film, the band in the Italian story was a quintet of bumblers who, despite a calvary of preparations for the Big Job, break into a kitchen rather than into a vault and have to be satisfied with filling their stomachs rather than their pockets. Over and above its immediate intent as parody, *I Soliti Ignoti* sought to throw a light on the star-crossed scufflers populating Rome's underworld, with Monicelli going so far as to say that he wanted the picture to come off as "a modern version of *Oliver Twist*." While it did not succeed at that lofty goal, it contained at least one scene that stunned other filmmakers and that would exert a considerable influence on Italian screen comedy. As director Ettore Scola recalled:

> Before *I Soliti Ignoti*, there were certain implicit rules about comedy, one of the biggest being that if anybody died or got killed in the course of a story, it happened in a very humorous way. In the middle of all the comedy in Monicelli's film, however, there is a scene where a purse snatcher gets run over by a tram and there is absolutely nothing comical about it. What that scene does have, on the other hand, is a logical relevance to the rest of the story. From the

moment I saw it, I knew there were going to be no more shibboleths about what a film comedy could and could not contain.

Italian critics were somewhat divided on *I Soliti Ignoti*, with the stodgiest opinion finding nothing at all funny about the film's insinuations that the gang led by Gassman and Mastroianni was merely more unsuccessful than some Establishment thieves. On the other hand, reviewers, then obsessed with the Italian industry's devastated position vis-à-vis the United States and France, pointed to the picture as one of the few signs of artistic health in the period. Even those who were unenthusiastic singled out Mastroianni ("the only member of the cast from whom one might have expected a measured performance and from whom one gets it, as usual") and Gassman ("playing a slightly punch-drunk boxer as exactly that and not as the Great Vittorio"). For his part, Mastroianni has tended to play down his role as a small-time photographer who is always available for the big chance but has always had praise for both the film as a whole and Gassman in particular.

> I had really done characters like that before, for instance in *Peccato Che Sia una Canaglia*. It was the usual well-meaning innocent who at bottom isn't really comic but who reacts to situations in a way that brings smiles to other people. But over and above that, I think the film is a comedy classic—a fact recognized not only in Italy but abroad. The most striking thing about it was Gassman's extraordinary revelation as a comic actor, and that launched him on a totally unexpected career as a comedy lead.

Even with *Le Notti Bianche* and *I Soliti Ignoti* establishing broad parameters for Mastroianni's range, he went in and out of another half-dozen films in 1958 and 1959 that did little to advance his career further. Most of the projects were simply for making money, as was an initial foray into an Italian television variety show. "It was another period of trying to figure out what to do next. I got so tired of some of the scripts I was sent that I thought about going back to the theater, and this time with my own company."

The theater-company idea was born during the filming of Angelo Dorigo's *Amore e Guai* (Love and Troubles), one of two parallel-tales films that Mastroianni made immediately after *I Soliti Ignoti*. In the picture, he portrays a club-car waiter who, because of last-minute railroad-schedule changes, can never quite get together with his fiancée (Eloisa Cianni). As uninspired as the film was, the actor's interest in it evaporated altogether when Dorigo brought in another voice to dub him, prompting several critics to question whether the director's ear was as bad as his sense of visuals. Other members of the cast included the married couple Richard Basehart and Valentina Cortese, and it was with Cortese that Mastroianni planned to launch his drama company with a production of Chekhov's *Platonov* under the direction of Visconti. The project came to nothing, however, when *La Dolce Vita* intervened.

Prior to *Amore e Guai*, Mastroianni had merely been waiting for a train in *Racconti d'Estate* (Love on the Riviera), playing the role of a police detective who must escort a prisoner (Michèle Morgan) to the French border but who, because of train delays, ends up spending a night with her and falling in love. The film, which contained several other stories set in and around the Italian Riviera, was based on an idea by Alberto Moravia and directed by Gianni Franciolini. Mainly because of the actors, the Mastroianni-Morgan episode was the only one that escaped critical wrath, more than one reviewer suggesting that the relationship between the detective and his prisoner should have been expanded into a film by itself.

With the French-Italian coproduction of *La Loi* (Where the Hot Wind Blows), Mastroianni had his first experience in working for a foreign director—the American Jules Dassin, who had moved to Europe to avoid becoming entangled in the anti-Communist witch hunts then going on in the United States. The picture also matched him up against such other big continental names as Greece's Melina Mercouri and France's Yves Montand and Pierre Brasseur. As it turned out, the mixture (which also included Italy's Gina Lollobrigida and Paolo Stoppa) was the first problem for a film that was based on Roger Vailland's French novel *The Law* but that was so vague in its Mediterranean setting that dubbing in some countries rendered the venue as Corsica and in others as southern Italy. That Mastroianni had the relatively small role of an agricultural engineer who gets caught up in a village's power struggles and romantic complications did not exempt him from some of the worst notices of his career. "Forced," "petulant," and "insupportable" were just three of the adjectives applied to his performance in a film that, according to one periodical, wasn't so much Italian, French, or something in between as it was "some absurd concoction from Mexico."

For all that, the actor found some consolations in the experience, particularly in the opportunity to work with Dassin.

> I really think there were a few beautiful things in it. But I suppose it's always hard for a foreign director to deal with subjects that he doesn't really know intimately. On top of all his other problems with the actual text, Dassin had a lot of difficulties with the money people in just getting the thing going. I didn't know all the details,

but he was forced to make compromises left and right to please this one and that one. All that said, I thought he was a wonderful director. Having been an actor himself, he knew exactly what we could all do and knew how to get his directions across. It's too bad that my only chance to work with him was in this unfortunate film.

Mastroianni's next three films were the last three that he would make in the relative anonymity of being one of Italy's most reliable screen performers. The first of the three was Gianni Puccini's mild comedy *Il Nemico di Mia Moglie* (My Wife's Enemy), which was dismissed as a piece of fluff by most critics and attacked more vigorously by left-wing reviewers as a betrayal of the director's earlier promise to tackle more demanding subject matter. *Il Nemico di Mia Moglie* cast Mastroianni as a soccer referee whose laziness about his marriage precipitates a walkout by his wife (Giovanna Ralli), a flirtation with a woman (Luciana Paluzzi) who really only wants him to make some favorable calls during the Big Game, and a deus ex machina beating by some soccer fans that leads him back to his marriage. Both the actor and De Sica, who plays the referee's bearish father, acknowledged later that their only interest in the film was to make money to pay off some pressing debts.

Equally forgettable was Giuseppe Orlandini's *Tutti Innamorati* (All the Lovers), in which the electrician Mastroianni, a widower and father of an eight-year-old boy, is pursued by Jacqueline Sassard but doesn't give in until he has brought together his two oldest friends, played by Gabriele Ferzetti and Marisa Merlini. A typical review called the actor's performance "diligent and detached—extremely appropriate given the circumstances."

With Franciolini's *Ferdinando I Re di Napoli* (Ferdinand I, King of Naples), Mastroianni concluded what was in effect the first part of his screen career. In *Ferdinando,* he got to work with the cream of the Neapolitan theater (brothers Eduardo and Peppino De Filippo and their sister Titina) but had little else to show for a nineteenth-century costumer about the civil unrest under the eponymous monarch. Among the many problems with the picture was its refusal to choose between being a straight drama and a farce, ultimately leaving one and all stranded. Mastroianni had the role of a young lawyer enamored of the king daughter's (Rossana Schiaffino). In the nineteenth or any other century, in Naples or any other city, he would never play such a role again.

Part Two

The Other MM

10

La Dolce Vita

Against the background of the Christian Democratic party's need to strike ruling alliances with political forces less indebted to the Holy See, official censorship in the Italian film industry started to weaken near the end of the 1950s (and was practically gutted altogether by legislation passed in 1962). Right up to the end of the decade, however, government functionaries were warning filmmakers to watch their step. Typical was a 1958 declaration by future Italian president Oscar Scalfaro, who was then serving as the country's top cop in the role of interior minister:

> The cinema must entertain, relax, offer a sense of optimism and a more serene vision of life to citizens who suffer through the stresses and discomforts of the working day. . . . It is appropriate to ask that all films respect the spiritual needs of individuals and the population as a whole. It is not permissible that the cinema nullify or humiliate the ideal of the fatherland. It would be bad taste, negative, and uncivil to tolerate offenses to religious principles. It is not possible to allow some public spectacle to make a mockery of religious principles. It is necessary to respect family values.

And then Federico Fellini made *La Dolce Vita*.
Mastroianni got involved in the project through a phone call.

When Fellini telephoned, I gave myself some airs and went off for a meeting with my lawyer. We got together at a beach in Fregene. I will always remember that the first thing Fellini said to me was, "I telephoned you because I need a face with no personality—like yours." That humiliated me, but I asked to see the script, anyway. He turned to the writer, Ennio Flaiano, who was sitting under a beach umbrella a short distance away, and asked him if he had "the stuff" for me. I didn't say anything while Flaiano got up, went into the house, and then came out again with a batch of papers. Except for one sheet, they were all absolutely blank. That one sheet was a drawing of a man in the sea with a prick that reached all the way down to the sea floor. All around his prick were sirens swimming and smiling. I turned red and green and a lot of other colors in my embarrassment. I was sure that Fellini was teasing me, that he thought he had this twit of an actor who had come along with his lawyer and that he wanted to make it very clear to me that he didn't do things that way. Mainly to get myself out of that corner, I said, "Okay, it's interesting. I'll do it."

But many months passed between the day that Mastroianni was won over by Fellini's unorthodox explanation of his role and the start of shooting. First, according to screenwriter Brunello Rondi, there was the problem of finding a producer.

Dino De Laurentiis was supposed to produce it, but he didn't like the screenplay at all. In addition, he didn't want Mastroianni or any other Italian actor. He thought that the lead had to be played by some big foreign name to guarantee international distribution. One of the people he kept mentioning whenever we'd get together was Paul Newman—something that Fellini didn't want to hear about. But the real problem was the script. De Laurentiis even sent it to three Italian film critics so they could second his opinion that it was all a piece of shit. Sure enough, they told De Laurentiis what he wanted to hear. That was all he needed. He threw the script back at us and said he wasn't interested. Fellini went around for almost a year trying to find another producer.

The director finally found one in Angelo Rizzoli, a member of the wealthy Milan publishing family who prided himself on undertaking projects that had nothing to do with his father's money. Famous for his less than sparkling erudition and his relentless flattering of directors until he read the first reports on their box-office results, Rizzoli was largely talked into the venture by Giuseppe Amato, who ended up with the actual producer credit for the picture. Veteran Italian screenwriter Leo Benvenuti once recounted the initial reaction of the two money men to the project.

I was in Rizzoli's office one day, and Amato suddenly walks in without knocking, a copy of *La Dolce Vita* in his hand. "I just read this thing," Amato says to Rizzoli. "If you read it, you'll throw up because you won't understand a damn thing about it. In fact, know what I'm going to do? I'm going to throw this damn thing up against a wall." And with that, Amato takes the script and fires it across the office against a wall. For the longest moment, Rizzoli just sat there, terrorized. Then Amato turns to him and says in this very icy voice, "And you absolutely *have* to make that film."

Despite their backing of the project, both Rizzoli and Amato went through the shooting in a state of continuous anxiety—the former because he basically found the script immoral and knew that there would be a firestorm of protests from critics, industry people, and politicians dedicated to preserving the spiritual health of the nation; the latter because he was pessimistic that he would ever recoup his investment. (The final cost of the film was $1.6 million.) At one point, Amato, known for an ambiguous relationship with language in the Sam Goldwyn mold, told an aide: "I think there's a great deal of sporadic interest in what will come out of this." For his part, Rizzoli adopted his usual tactic of praising Fellini at every opportunity, such as at a dinner when he told his guests: "Fellini is great, like that mountain. . . . " "Everest," whispered an assistant. "Right, like Everest," Rizzoli continued. A couple of days later, at another function, the producer took the occasion to proclaim: "Fellini is great, great like that mountain . . . that my assistant knows."

Mastroianni aside, Fellini's first problem in mounting the film was casting, since most of the performers that he had gotten commitments from back when De Laurentiis had been in charge were no longer available. Mauro de Vecchi, an associate of the director's, recalled:

> All the actors he had lined up . . . had either taken other jobs or were in some way indisposed. . . . A few of them had moved away, two were in jail, several lost interest, and one actor's father reported that he had changed his sex and disappeared.

According to de Vecchi, another problem that was to become more serious down the road was the nonchalant way that Rizzoli, Amato, and Fellini were all making vague promises to different distributors in the United States that the film would be theirs.

> Everyone seemed to have some kind of agreement that had been reached in a bar or restaurant, and nobody bothered telling anybody else what he had just said okay to. By the time the film was ready to be distributed in America, there must have been fifteen different claimants. The reason for all the confusion, I think, is that everyone was a little nervous about the picture paying off, and so there was this rush by everyone concerned to commit a distributor.

The origins of *La Dolce Vita* were in Fellini's long-postponed intentions of shooting a film that he had tentatively called *Moraldo in Città* (Moraldo in the City), an autobiographical account of a Rimini native's first experiences in Rome. The more the project got put off, however, the more the Rome that the younger Fellini had known disappeared, to the point that the director had become resigned to the possibility of never realizing his plan. Then, in 1958, he began frequenting the Via Veneto in the company of paparazzi, the news photographers who made their living by provoking celebrities and rich Italians in the bars and restaurants of the area; in the best of cases, the paparazzi got their prey to take swings at them, this producing photographs that could be sold around the world and enriching accompanying stories that only every once in a while contained a fact. It was in the course of these nightly expeditions that Fellini gradually changed the character of Moraldo to the journalist named Marcello played by Mastroianni.

The plot of *La Dolce Vita* was summed up by Mira Liehm in her book *Passion and Defiance: Film in Italy from 1942 to the Present*:

> *La Dolce Vita*, a gigantic fresco of certain segments of European society in the sixties, is a series of episodes held together by two picaresque heroes, a journalist who is a chronicler of scandals and a "paparazzo," his photographer. They travel through the cynical "world without love." They are first shown symbolically descending from a helicopter that is carrying an enormous statue of Christ the Redeemer above the roofs and terraces of Rome. Twelve more episodes/stations follow: Marcello meets with Maddalena, a rich industrialist's man-hungry daughter who wishes to make love with him in the bed of a prostitute; he finds out that his girlfriend Emma, an insecure, possessive woman, has attempted suicide; he rushes her to a hospital and then is off to cover a Hollywood sex bomb's visit to Rome; after a hectic day and night, culminating with the famous wading scene in the Fontana di Trevi, Marcello meets his friend Steiner, a writer, who seeks calm by playing the organ in a church; Marcello makes a short trip to the seashore where he chats with Paola, a young waitress, whose profile reminds him of little cherubs; then he is back on assignment, this time covering scenes of religious hysteria following the false appearance of the Virgin Mary to two children who are being exploited by their parents; after a visit to Steiner's snobbish literary salon, Marcello is unexpectedly visited by his father; the evening ends almost tragically when the old man follows a nightclub dancer home to her apartment, suddenly feels sick, and leaves hastily to return to his quiet hometown where people grow old prematurely because of boredom; the Via Veneto's merry-go-round catapults Marcello into a castle outside the city where he finds Maddalena amidst the aristocratic decadence; when he becomes convinced that she is willing to marry him, she disappears with another man; next morning he learns that Steiner has killed his children and himself; he rushes to Steiner's apartment, which had seemed to him almost a refuge from the horrors of the outside world; and a moment later he finds him-

self in the street waiting for Steiner's wife, who is surrounded by a cloud of "paparazzi" trying by fair means or foul to photograph her bewildered face. The final sequence shows an orgy in a luxurious villa at the seashore in Fregene; in the morning Marcello walks to the beach where some fishermen have just dragged a hideous fish out of the ocean; a transvestite tells Marcello: "I think we shall all be like that in 1965, completely rotten. It will be worse than the apocalypse. God, what an abomination it will be. . . . " The little waitress Paola appears on the other side of the beach, shouting and waving at Marcello; he cannot understand what she is saying; one of the women from the previous night's party grabs his hand and leads him back to the group. No more redemption, no more hope. The spiritual annihilation is complete.*

In a film of numerous memorable episodes, undoubtedly the most emblematic of all was the Trevi Fountain scene between Mastroianni and Anita Ekberg, in the role of a Hollywood actress. Like a good many other moments in *La Dolce Vita*, according to photographer Pier Luigi, the scene grew out of an actual event.

I had known Ekberg a long time before *La Dolce Vita* . . . and we used to go out often together, dancing away a lot of nights. One night, it must have been near four o'clock in the morning, we were on our way home and she scratched her foot and wanted to wash it off in the Trevi Fountain. As she was doing that, I looked around at this perfectly deserted piazza and started shooting pictures. They were published by a magazine in September 1958, and not too long after that Fellini called to tell me about his film.

But there were also differences between the real event and what ended up on film. For one thing, Ekberg's original dip took place on a warm August evening, while Fellini staged his scene in a winter passing itself off as summer, driving both the actress and Mastroianni to frequent nips of liquor just to get through the experience. As well, Ekberg's chemistry with Mastroianni was not as automatic as it had been with Luigi; on the contrary, they got off on as chilly a note as the temperatures during the Trevi Fountain filming. According to Fellini, the trouble started when, despite his own protestations, Mastroianni insisted on breaking the ice with the Swedish actress prior to working together. The venue was a dinner hosted by the director at which Ekberg greeted the actor with the aloofness of a "female cardinal" and then spent the rest of the evening totally ignoring him. The irate Mastroianni complained later that he hadn't been treated

---

*University of California Press, 1984.

so rudely since a German soldier had shoved him into a truck during the Nazi occupation of Italy. For Fellini, however, the incident was only grist for the mill of the initial antagonism that he wanted to establish between the characters in the film. As he was to put it with typical extravagant style: "He [Mastroianni] felt offended by that glory of elemental divinity, that health, that reflection of a sun force which, instead of exalting him, nauseated him."

Another private evening hosted by Fellini and involving another actress also contributed to the nuances of the character played by Mastroianni in the picture. According to actress Laura Betti, she got it into her head one night at dinner with Mastroianni and Fellini to bait the actor and "shake that usual calm of his." It took some doing, but "Mastroianni finally erupted like a volcano, tearing into me the way I was doing to him. The only difference was that he had a reason for going after me, while I'd had none except a few too many glasses of wine." After peace was restored, by Betti's account, Fellini sidled up to Mastroianni and suggested that they use some of the dialogue in the fight for the picture.

In spite of such bumpy beginnings, the actual shooting of *La Dolce Vita* turned out to be the most galvanizing experience of Mastroianni's career to that point.

> I went into that film completely trained in the way Visconti did things—every little particular in its place, everything researched thoroughly. But then I did something that I'd never done before—I went to work one morning without the coat that I'd been wearing in the scenes we had done. When Federico found out, he didn't hesitate a second. He didn't want to lose any time by sending someone to my house to get the coat; he just grabbed the first coat he found, threw it on me, and began the day's work. To see the way he moved around the set like a friend who wasn't going to be distracted by small things was stunning. That's why I've always bored people to death telling them that we worked together like classmates. But that's exactly what the atmosphere on the set was like. He never stopped making cracks about me, himself, the technicians. The man *enjoyed* what he was doing, and that feeling was communicated to everybody.

Not that Fellini improvised everything; on the contrary, according to Mastroianni, the director just had a more relaxed approach toward what he considered being professional.

> Visconti had always stood to the side, like the Maestro watching his pupils recite the lessons that he had taught them. Fellini was in the middle of everything. Whenever we'd run through a scene before shooting, he'd play all the parts, making all these atrocious faces

and pretending to be Anouk Aimée or somebody else. I thought, "This is great! It's all a game as far as he's concerned!" That didn't mean he didn't take his work seriously. He just wanted us to share *his* vision of things, since that was going to be the only way that he succeeded in making *his* film.

Because of both international distribution calculations and the numerous foreign roles in the picture, *La Dolce Vita* was shot primarily in English, with only Mastroianni doing his lines in Italian. "But the words were the least of it," according to the actor. "What was important was the language of the film itself."

For the Trevi Fountain sequence, the director required three full nights in frigid January temperatures. His first solution for protecting Mastroianni and Ekberg from the gelid waters was to outfit them with big rubber boots not seen in the shots. But the actress discarded them almost immediately. "She didn't feel anything," according to Mastroianni.

> She was Swedish, and as a child she had gotten used to diving into icy water. She liked telling everybody that. I think it was meant as sort of a challenge to me, but what the hell did I care about how she had grown up in Sweden? The only concessions she made were to take a little cognac and agree to the rubdowns that Fellini insisted we get between takes. I was half-drunk with vodka by the time we got finished with a night's shooting.

One of the more curious production footnotes to *La Dolce Vita* was that unlike the Trevi Fountain sequence, all the action centered around the Via Veneto actually took place in Cinecittà, on a set facsimile ordered by Fellini. For Mastroianni, this was a telltale sign of Fellini's intention of being more than realistic. Referring to his earlier experience with Visconti in re-creating the canals of Livorno in the studio for *Le Notti Bianche*, the actor detected at least one point of contact between the otherwise diverse directors:

> Neither was a documentarian. Reality could always be improved upon. With Visconti, it was a question of driving the reality to some logical extreme; with Fellini, the approach was to go off from the reality into fantasies and dreams.

Fellini's rough cut of *La Dolce Vita* did nothing to calm Rizzoli's anxieties. As screenwriter Rondi recalled some years later to an Italian interviewer:

> There were only a couple of minutes to go before the end of the screening that we had in Rome, when Rizzoli suddenly stood up and marched out. He was beside himself. He understood absolutely

nothing of what he had seen and was petrified that he not only had a financial disaster on his hands but that he would be accused of making something that denigrated Italian men and women. Then Amato got to him and started screaming at the top of his lungs, "Angelo, you don't understand shit! Fellini has done a great and magnificent thing!" And for weeks afterward, while Rizzoli refused to see Fellini, Amato would keep telling Federico, "You've done a great and magnificent thing, absolutely great and magnificent!"

But even Amato's cheerleading was practically drowned out about a month later by the response at a Milan screening set for industry people. According to Rondi:

> It was a nightmare. Nothing but hoots and whistles from the beginning to the end. After it was over, somebody went over to Rizzoli and accused him of being a Communist and of letting himself be used by an anarchist like Fellini. Needless to say, Rizzoli was shaken up.

Some of the initial negative industry reaction was predictable; for instance, one of those blasting the film was Gualtiero Jacopetti, the crypto-Fascist director of such sex-and-gore "documentaries" as *Mondo Cane*. Whenever he got the chance, Jacopetti proclaimed *La Dolce Vita* as "nothing but left-wing shit." But there was also disfavor from some unexpected film quarters. Roberto Rossellini, for example, called the film "the lowest point in Italian cinema since neorealism" and chided Fellini for having made a "sad mess."

Italian film critic Tullio Kezich, who was then close to Fellini, recalled that the initial critical reaction began to get to the director.

> We were in Milan the day the film was to open at the Capitol theater. It was the beginning of February 1960. Around lunchtime, we were in the foyer of the theater, counting the minutes on the clock. The doors weren't scheduled to be opened until two forty-five, so the place was deserted except for us and the manager. Fellini was very restless, kept tapping his foot nervously. Finally, we decided to go to lunch at a restaurant nearby. The atmosphere around the table was like the condemned man having his last meal. We started back to the theater and couldn't believe what was in front of our eyes. It was still only two-thirty, fifteen minutes before the doors were supposed to open, but the street was a mob scene. They had completely surrounded the box office and were demanding that the manager begin selling tickets. It was the same scene every day for weeks afterward, even for the afternoon shows.

The public's appetite for *La Dolce Vita* had been whetted significantly by an unusual editorial attack from the official Holy See newspaper *L'Osservatore Romano*, which denounced the film's alleged immorality and warned Catholics that their souls would be at risk by going near it. Publications close to the Christian Democratic party turned over editorial space for similar condemnations, often in language that characterized Fellini as some kind of diabolical force that had been loosed on the country. In parliament, Christian Democrats, neo-Fascists, and monarchists demanded that the government bar the film's release or at the very least hold back the refunds to producers on entertainment taxes that had been Italy's way of encouraging domestic production. Although tourism and entertainment minister Umberto Tupini was not about to endanger the Christian Democratic coalition with more centrist parties by agreeing to the ban, he, too, denounced the film as "conducive to national decadence."

For the most part, however, Catholic Italy was not listening, and the picture became the hottest ticket in the country. Even members of the church hierarchy disagreed publicly with the official line espoused by *L'Osservatore Romano:* Following a widely reported meeting with a Jesuit theologian, for instance, the archbishop of Genoa, Cardinal Siri, praised the film's fundamental morality. Nor was it only cultural contrariness or a heightened curiosity for scandal that led to the unprecedented box-office triumph. Even many conservative Catholics had begun to question the Vatican's suffocating views on what was and was not acceptable on the screen; in 1959, for example, the church's most influential reviewing board had found a mere five films out of the hundreds produced in Italy acceptable for children. It was this growing sense that the papacy had gotten out of touch with reality that made it easier for even the most conscientious Catholics to ignore the Holy See's condemnation. (On the other hand, the church could still be intimidating enough in the United States that, even fifteen years later, American television was showing the film with all the key sequences involving religion—the opening helicopter scene, to name one—cut out.)

If sometimes for the wrong reasons, other segments of Italian society were still quicker to embrace Fellini and his work. As the director recalled later:

> A half-hour after the film came out, and I mean literally a half-hour, somebody from the Communist party telephoned to say that they were going to give me this award of theirs called the Golden Chaplin. Getting awards is always nice, even if in this case I was astonished by so much haste. In any case, I went to the presentation, and during a question-and-answer period, somebody asked me if I considered *La Dolce Vita* a snapshot of Italy. "No," I said. "Italy has nothing to do with it; it's about Rome." "But Fellini," the

man protested, "Rome was only an excuse. What you had in mind was the entire political situation in Italy, and that's what you were attacking." I thought it was kind of ingenious of him to know so well what had been in my mind. "No," I said again, "not for a second. It's a film about Rome, just as I might have made one about New York, London, or Baghdad." They didn't seem to like that answer.

Among the daily newspaper reviewers, *La Dolce Vita* was saluted enthusiastically. Gian Luigi Rondi of Rome's *Il Tempo* praised its "immense chorality" in offering "a shocking picture" of the capital and, like just about everyone else, singled out Mastroianni for what he called "a vivid, human, natural performance." For *L'Espresso's* Moravia, "Mastroianni has rendered one of his best performances—walking a tight line between disenchanted irony and a passing hope of a better world." Mario Gromo of the Turin daily *La Stampa* went further, citing the actor's effort as the key to the film's achievement:

> He could have been just a dramatic device to get us from one episode to another, but his skilled half-tones suggest reactions very much beyond those of a mere witness. . . . It is a job of marvelous subtlety and elegance and gives the film form.

The complexity of *La Dolce Vita*—not to mention the controversy it stirred and its enormous drawing power (it was the first Italian film to gross more than 2 billion lire domestically)—generated a tidal wave of heady analyses and round-table discussions in Italy and abroad. The written dissertations ran the gamut from the learned to the impenetrable, with the picture and/or its characters compared to everything from Greek tragedies and biblical allegories to animals in heat; the public debates asked whether it was Rome, Italy, or Western civilization that was under indictment. Fellini alone became a regular source of erudite conjecture as to whether he was the most moral or most immoral artist in Italy, with clerics of all persuasions having an opinion one way or the other. As soon as the film repeated its critical and financial success in other countries, it was hailed for not only rescuing the Italian film industry but also for putting Italy in a position to rival the influence of the United States cinematically; or, in the words of Peter Bondanella in his *Italian Cinema: From Neorealism to the Present,* "For a brief and exciting moment, it appeared that Cinecittà and Via Veneto would challenge Hollywood and Beverly Hills."

The film's popularity also had other ramifications. Its very title entered dictionaries around the world to describe a life of indolence and self-indulgence, "a sweet life." (American distributors had briefly played with the idea of releasing it under that title.) Just about

everything connected with the Mastroianni character in the picture—his sunglasses, striped shirts, and automobile—became fash-
ionable. Still further, *La Dolce Vita* made the Via Veneto a cardinal
selling point for Rome among tourist agents, despite the fact that the
paparazzi activities depicted by the film had peaked before Fellini
had completed shooting—at Cinecittà.

For Mastroianni, the consequences of the picture were markedly less abstract and evanescent. To start with, he won yet another
Nastro d'Argento for the year's best male performance and picked up
similar awards in other countries. No longer was there any discussion about whether assigning him some role other than that of an
earnest young husband or cabdriver would be risky. By winning
acclaim in New York, London, and Tokyo as well as in Rome, he
became the suavest symbol of the Italian cinema's renascence (neither Visconti's *Rocco e i Suoi Fratelli* nor Antonioni's *L'Avventura*,
the contemporary breakthrough pictures in the eyes of foreign critics, sported comparably striking male leads), and this was translated
immediately into the offers associated with an international star.

But the fallout from *La Dolce Vita* had as many personal as
professional implications. Most of all, there was the international
blessing on his newfound friendship with Fellini—a fact that he proclaimed at every opportunity and that was interpreted by associates
as a psychological liberation from his years-long subservience to
Uncle De Sica, Maestro Visconti, and even Godfather Blasetti; as one
friend put it: "It was really the first time he realized that he wasn't
the only one who thought of making films as an adult dream and that
it could be the kind of joyous thing that he had privately yearned for
it to be." In addition, he was on record even prior to the completion
of the film stating that he had a lot more tied up in the project than
some vindication as a new box-office power. As Kezich noted in a
book on the events surrounding the making of *La Dolce Vita*:

> "I have the impression," Mastroianni confides to me one day, "that
> this film is changing something in my personality as a man. I know
> it's a little ridiculous to say it, but I feel already that it will be a key
> episode in my life, whether or not the thing is a success." When he
> says things like that, Mastroianni is not in the least ridiculous.
> Nobody is less prone to striking a pose as some kind of an
> intellectual. . . .

In another interview many years later, Mastroianni again
emphasized that his primary gratifications from *La Dolce Vita* were
personal rather than professional, asserting:

> Look, there's no doubt that better parts came my way after that
> film, that I was even regarded as something of a star. But what was
> really important to me was the beginning of my friendship with

Fellini. While we were shooting, he kept saying that we were moving along like a couple of shipwrecked sailors on a raft, absolutely at the mercy of wherever the wind pushed us, proceeding in complete abandon. I found that image very exciting. It was an experience that went well beyond that of a professional actor; it was an experience lived more as a man than as an actor.

After reiterating similar sentiments to still another interviewer and being challenged that the international success of *La Dolce Vita* *had* to be of great moment to him, he replied:

Success has never meant that much to me for the simple reason that I don't believe it is ever the result of particularly noble reasons. Federico put it best in one of his films when he had a character say, "I have too many qualities to be an amateur but not enough to be a professional." I recognize myself in that line . . . Fellini is exactly like me. That's why I like working with him and why working with him makes you think about more than the results of a specific film. How can I help loving the man? He has the same flaws that I do, including an awful tendency to tell lies. Where I think that comes from in both of us is in some deep fragility. We both lack courage to say no when we should, to disappoint others in the image that they have of us.

It was in relation to one such image, according to the actor, that *La Dolce Vita's* success also posed some old problems in a new form.

There's no question that it was because of that film that I suddenly started being thought of as a Latin Lover—something absolutely ridiculous that had nothing at all to do with me. Suddenly, after all those years of being the ingenuous cabdriver or the ingenuous proletarian, I started getting all these offers to play people who were, yes, more complex intellectually, but who were always also part of this Latin Lover image—men who had bookcases but who were somehow always slithering across the rug toward some beautiful woman. I can't tell you how many times I had to say to these producers: "I beg your pardon, but have you really seen *La Dolce Vita*? The character in that film doesn't conquer anyone; if anything, he's the one who gets conquered, the one whom all these women use and who, naive idiot that he is, allows himself to go along." Even more than the Italians, the Americans had this fixation on me as a Latin Lover. No matter how many times I tried to get through to Hollywood producers who wanted me to go to California to play that kind of role, it was like talking to a wall. To be a Latin Lover in their eyes, obviously, all you had to do was to put on a dark jacket and mingle with some women.

As an international star created by *La Dolce Vita*, Mastroianni continued to fence with the numerous offers he received from the United States and from around Europe, even his regular rejections hiking his price to still higher levels undreamed of when he first discovered the world of the film set on *Marionette*. As an actor, his response was to jump into *Il Bell'Antonio*, in which he indeed played the role of a lover—an impotent one.

11

Close-up: The Promoter

If motion pictures were baseball and publicity interviews home runs, Mastroianni would be Hank Aaron. No actor in modern times has had more to say about his work to more media representatives; on one day in Paris in 1984 alone, following the end of a lengthy run on the French stage, he was estimated as having met separately with thirty-eight journalists. As accessible as he has been, however, he has also made it clear that he regards his promotional efforts as merely a part of the film "game" and as such a license to say whatever pops into his head at the moment, contradictions be damned. And, even allowing for inevitable changes in opinion and behavior over the years, the contradictions have been plentiful.

Depending on the interviewer, Mastroianni has both embraced architecture as a profound passion and dismissed it as a curiosity that engaged him only as a young man. With some, he has "confessed" a total ignorance of films other than his own, saying that the only thing he knows about them is what he has heard or read secondhand; with others, he has claimed that he sneaks off to cinemas whenever he gets the chance. While he has mocked American actors, such as Jack Nicholson, for painstakingly preparing for parts, he has also sometimes referred to his own trailing after paparazzi as research for his role in *La Dolce Vita*. In the early 1980s, he had chapter-and-verse arguments about why European film-industry unions were blowing out of all proportion the threat posed by shooting big continental productions in English; shortly afterward, he emerged as an especially visible spokesman against the use of English in European films.

Mastroianni has found nothing grave or even illogical about such incompatible contentions. As he told *Attenzione* magazine in September 1981:

> I'll give you an answer according to how I feel that particular day. Ask me something an hour before I'm due to go to the dentist and

I'll give you one kind of answer; ask me the same thing after I've found out that I've won the football pool and I'll give you a different answer. It's beautiful, it's part of life, but just as long as the people reading the quotes realize it, too!

In the same vein, he once admitted to being proud of the fact that a French periodical, annoyed at all the contradictions, took the unusual step of publishing side by side his replies to different journalists working for the same magazine. "They contradicted each other at every point!" he boasted.

Some of the contradictions have had a simpler name—lies. Repeatedly over the years, in fact, Mastroianni has identified lying as his greatest fault and then, in the same breath, pointed to his ability to fantasize as his sturdiest resource. While he has sometimes voiced regrets for the lies he has told in his private life, he has never expressed similar misgivings about something false told to the media; on the contrary, he has stood behind the rationalization that even in the most outlandish of cases, he was only giving as good as he got. ("Sometimes they don't just make up quotes; they invent the fact that there was even an interview!")

None of this, of course, has weighed very heavily on the media that have continued to seek interviews with the actor. Whether he has said left or right, black or white, up or down, Mastroianni has always been copy—not just because of his professional status and offscreen involvements with other celebrity names but also because he has usually been good for repeatable quotes in humorous and often epigrammatical evaluations of himself, his work, and others. Even his recycling of familiar anecdotes has normally included an added particular or two that has seemed, whether true, fictitious, or in contradiction to another telling, fine-tuned for the interviewer on the scene at the time. An inane fan-magazine–type question, such as his attitude toward topless bathing suits, will prompt a rumination on his hatred of the beach and a rueful recollection that "the last time I went to the sea, I was bitten by a fish." Mention of a recently deceased colleague will lead him to the conclusion that the man made a mistake in turning down a film because "actors never die when they are shooting—it is in their animal nature."

Italian embassies around the world have cringed when, during tours abroad, he has been asked his thoughts on the political situation in his country. Reporters expecting a ritual condemnation of the terrorist violence attributed to the Red Brigades in the 1970s heard, instead, how the "clowns and charlatans" running Italy since the late 1940s "helped create the terrorism with their scandals and corruption." Official propaganda about its economic recovery notwithstanding, Italy was "a South American country at the beginning of the twentieth century." A question out of left field on why the zoo in Rome contains alley cats in cages will not faze him for a second:

> Because they are cute. Because children like to see alley cats as much as zebras and giraffes and lions. Besides, it opens up all kinds of other possibilities. You could also put members of the Italian government in cages, for instance. You could take your son or daughter to the zoo and point out a tiger, a minister for public works, an elephant, a minister of labor, a buffalo, a minister for state industries, a kangaroo. . . . I think it's a wonderful idea!

In short, despite occasional moans over having to make promotional tours, Mastroianni has shown himself to be very much in his element with such undertakings. Moreover, his encounters with the press have allowed him simply to talk, and although there is little doubt that he would have preferred the company of friends in a favorite restaurant to that of probing strangers with recorders or notebooks in a hotel room, he has never been an exception to the garrulousness of the average Roman or to the habit of extroverted artists of spinning out ideas verbally to see if they make any sense. But even more important, he has given every indication of considering his meetings with the media as a delayed extension of the experience of filmmaking—certainly not as intimate or, in the best of cases, as joyful as the "adult playground" of the set but still a reverberation from it, right down to his self-discipline in going over the same terrain again and again. In discussing his most recent character and its relation to previous roles, he seems to draw his professional listeners into the same kind of conspiracy that the part usually entails with his female costar on the screen, coming across not merely as enthusiastic about something that he wants people to line up at the box office for but as equal to some emotional and intellectual challenge that everybody would be better off in life confronting. It is the skill of an expert publicist but also of an actor with his widely attested facility for moving in and out of characters at will once he has them down.

Naturally, there have been exceptions to the largely favorable impression he has made on media people over the years. In a 1987 interview with *People* magazine reporter Brad Darrach, for example, he was quoted as exploding at one point:

> I don't give a damn about the American public. America means nothing to me. My career is here in Italy. I'm not some kid actor with only four cents to his name. I'm an established star. For thirty-nine years, I have been answering the same stupid questions. Enough!

By Darrach's account, the tantrum was precipitated by Mastroianni's realization that the writer intended to stay with him for several days during the rehearsal of a play rather than simply ask his questions and go on his way an hour later. According to the *People* reporter, Mastroianni was also furious at discovering that other interviews had been completed with the actor's friends and professional associates. "He seemed to expect that I would be content talking to him."

There had been a far more serious clash between the actor and the Italian press during the 1970 shooting of *La Moglie del Prete* (The Priest's Wife). Triggering the conflict were a slew of scandal sheet charges originating with the American magazine *Confidential* and picked up by Italian gossip publications. A pioneer in *National Enquirer*–type fiction, *Confidential* had emblazoned one of its covers with the headline "I Married a Son of a Bitch" and then proceeded to have Carabella recount lurid stories of Mastroianni's alleged sex life, as well as her own. Although dissuaded from suing the Ameican periodical and its Italian cousins because such a move would have played into their hands, Mastroianni banned all photographers from the set of *La Moglie del Prete* and refused requests for interviews from his countrymen. When he then granted an interview to the *New York Times*, a segment of the Italian press charged that international stardom had gone to his head and refused to mention his name or his films for some months. The actor's normal public graciousness was also in short supply in 1975, when he was pressed to attend the Turin premiere of *La Donna della Domenica* (The Sunday Woman) with costar Jacqueline Bisset; at the time, he was winding down more of a fling than a flirtation with the actress.

In at least one sense, the *Confidential* episode was only an extreme example of the fiction that has been published about Mastroianni, his lovers, and his family. Even so-called reputable publications have never hesitated to attribute direct quotations to him that, upon investigation, have turned out to be either uncredited (and very approximately translated) borrowings from ancient Italian interviews or total inventions. ("It's happened more than once that I've opened a newspaper to read that I love or hate this person, then realize that it was something that I might have said in 1952 before I even knew who the person in question was. I pay for my sins that way, but who pays for them in the newspaper or the magazine that's presenting this stuff as new news?") In one recent example of journalistic license, the actor was stunned to pick up the Italian daily *La Repubblica* around Christmas 1992 to find the headline "A Mastroianni-Loren Romance."

Right there on the front page, next to all the horrors of the war in

Bosnia, was a story about how my daughter Chiara and one of Sophia's sons were having an affair. Chiara has never even met the boy! I called up the editor-in-chief and said, "Where the hell do you get this stuff? I thought you were a serious newspaper." All he did was mumble something about how he hadn't seen it. Swell! An editor who doesn't read his own front page.

For the most part, however, the shooting and release of a Mastroianni film have provided cordial media forums for pronouncements about love and life that, after obligatory promotional ablutions, have often made the picture itself seem incidental. Rare, in fact, has been the meeting with an interviewer in which the dominant themes were not his self-deprecating stance toward being regarded as a star, his iconoclasm about the art of motion pictures (as opposed to working in them), or his attitude toward women at the age of forty (or fifty or sixty). What this has done for the film being ballyhooed has varied and has been only one influential element along with such other factors as critical reception and distribution scope. What has seldom varied, on the other hand, has been a presupposition on the part of questioners on both sides of the Atlantic that whether saying something pithy, contradicting himself, or just lying, Mastroianni spoke with an authority that emanated from more than his latest character. If it has been the interviewers themselves who have conferred much of that authority with preconceived images of him, Mastroianni has habitually seized the opening—even to rebut them—as a part of the "game." Indeed, if he has always been an actor, and only that on a movie set, he has never been more of an intimate and reassuring star than when crooning into a tape recorder that he is no such thing. By his own lights, he has always been first and last the reactor. Asked once why Americans in particular seemed fixated on him as a Latin Lover, he replied: "Simple. Because *they* are the romantics."

12

Il Bel Marcello

Whatever might have been expected of Mastroianni after *La Dolce Vita*, it wasn't *Il Bell'Antonio*. Based on a widely read postwar novel by Vitaliano Brancati, *Il Bell'Antonio* was a tragicomedy set in Sicily that drew a straight line from the southern Italian male's sexual pompousness *(gallismo)* to the Fascist mentality that had brought the country to ruin. In the title role, Mastroianni played the son of an influential Catania businessman (Pierre Brasseur) who agrees to an arranged marriage with a local beauty (Claudia Cardinale), only to discover that he is too overwhelmed emotionally by his love for her to consummate their marriage. When the wife's parents find out about Antonio's impotence, they press successfully for an annulment and remarry their daughter to an aged nobleman. The disgrace drives the businessman to a local brothel where he is intent on demonstrating to his neighbors that his son's problems are not because of some genetic failing; the old man ends up dying in the arms of a prostitute. Antonio's own troubles are "resolved" when he is passed off as the lover of a pregnant servant. Although he knows that the real father is his cousin (Tomas Milian), he accepts marriage to the maid in the interests of restoring honor to his family.

Critically, *Il Bell'Antonio* drew more respectful than enthusiastic notices. Some of the reservations stemmed from the greater emphasis given by director Mauro Bolognini and cowriter Pier Paolo Pasolini to the personal drama of Antonio rather than to the sociopolitical context suggested by Brancati; other reviewers detected a smug Roman condescension toward Sicilians on a problem that applied to Italians in general. Although there were also some cavils that Mastroianni was not the "beautiful young man" described by Brancati in the book, the actor came off with reviews as favorable as those that he had received for *La Dolce Vita*. For the Milan daily *Il Giorno*, he gave "a performance of extremely moving bravura ... built up from inside with intelligence and without any false fireworks." In the words of the Turin newspaper *La Stampa*, his effort was "yet another piece of evidence that he is the richest, most pliable actor in the Italian cinema."

As might have been expected from the subject matter, *Il Bell'Antonio* irritated some Rome officials for whom impotence was strictly an affliction in other countries. Producer Alfredo Bini recalled:

> The idea of making a film about an impotent man in Italy was impossible. A couple of years before, there had been the American film *The Barefoot Contessa*, and the scene in which Rossano Brazzi tells Ava Gardner that he is impotent caused eruptions in theaters. . . . Before we even started shooting, I received a letter from some government official telling me to think again about the film because it would dishonor the morale and good name of the country. He even threatened to block our licensing. I pretended I never got the letter and made the film, but there were a lot of bureaucratic problems later.

For Bolognini, the film might never have been made, anyway, if not for Mastroianni.

> At the beginning, we were going after somebody who was considered "beautiful" in the pretty-boy sense. Somebody like Alain Delon. Then the Frenchman Jacques Charrier said yes, only to change his mind again. When I suggested Mastroianni, people had the same reaction: "You must be crazy! What does Mastroianni have to do with a character like that?" As it turned out, he had a lot to do with it.

As for the actor, he was amused by the eleventh-hour withdrawal of Charrier.

> A week before shooting was scheduled to start, he [Charrier] suddenly had a thousand scruples about playing an impotent man while he was in the tabloids every day as the ideal French lover for being married to Brigitte Bardot. So Bolognini called me on a Thursday and said, "I'm in trouble. Charrier has backed out, and we're due to start on Monday. Yell at me all you want for not having called you before this, but please do me a favor and read the script." In fact, I had already read the Brancati novel and liked it. I always thought it was a little ridiculous of Charrier to be so concerned about what image he had in the tabloids as Bardot's husband. In any case, we started shooting the following Monday.

For somebody who has always prided himself on his ability to play characters without becoming them, however, *Il Bell'Antonio* had at least one big drawback for Mastroianni. Bolognini: "One day, he came to me saying, '*Disgraziato!* Thanks to you, I can't make love anymore!'"

Mastroianni has admitted this (temporary) condition, but also insisted that even this was a small price to pay for the career implications of his decision to play the troubled Sicilian husband.

> The period immediately after *La Dolce Vita* was a period of some torment for me. The film was so successful that I was inundated with roles of bedroom conquerors, somebody who walked around wearing blue jackets with gold buttons. My private life became totally identified with that character. My theatrical instincts told me not to fall into that trap, not to accept some label that others wanted to stick on me. That's why I jumped at the chance to do a character so different and said yes to Bolognini.

The actor didn't have too many doubts about the authenticity of his character, either.

> It was the first time I'd been to Sicily. You didn't need very long antennae to sense what the predicament of an impotent man in that atmosphere might have been. There was a feeling about it everywhere: in the environment, in the sun, in the pride of the Sicilians, in their closedmouthedness. . . . A year or so later, when I went down to make *Divorzio all'Italiana* in Ragusa, there was a big story about this young bride who had castrated her husband with a razor because she had felt dishonored by this wretch who really was a "bell'Antonio."

Mastroianni's next project, Antonio Pietrangeli's *Adua e le Compagne* (Love à la Carte), was one of his less happy film experiences. Although top billed, he had little more than a supporting role in a soap opera about four prostitutes (Simone Signoret, Emmanuelle Riva, Sandra Milo, Gina Rovere) who try to make a go of it as restaurateurs after the Italian Parliament passes legislation shuttering the country's bordellos. For one of the few times in his career, reviewers attacked him for mailing in his performance as Signoret's shiftless and cowardly lover. By the actor's own account, he mainly got involved in the project because he felt he had to say yes to Pietrangeli after having turned down numerous other proposals from the director. Others on the film said that it was doomed by a combination of Pietrangeli's constant indecisiveness and bitterness among several cast members, especially between Signoret and Milo. Among other things, Milo accused Signoret, who had just won an Oscar for *Room at the Top*, of making the petulant demands of somebody who took her stardom too seriously and of intimidating Pietrangeli into heeding her every whim. (It emerged subsequently that husband Yves

Montand was carrying on his noted affair with Marilyn Monroe in Hollywood while Signoret was in Italy.)

Ironically, Mastroianni was to defend *Adua e le Compagne* more ardently than he did his next venture, Michelangelo Antonioni's *La Notte* (The Night), which drove critics around the world into paroxysms of praise. Told in the spare, depersonalized style that marked Antonioni's work of that period, *La Notte* followed a successful writer (Mastroianni) and his wife (Jeanne Moreau) through the good part of a day and evening in Milan during which it becomes only too evident that their desensitized marriage is merely the centerpiece for a broader emotional and intellectual desolation. The film ends with a last-gasp try at reconciliation that seems to be too little too late.

Mastroianni has never disguised his disillusion with Antonioni or *La Notte*. Declaring that it was "not Antonioni's best work," he told one interviewer: "He hates actors, and I understand that. For the kind of films he makes, he doesn't need actors." To another interviewer, he compared the maker of *La Notte* to two other filmmakers with whom he was familiar thusly: "Visconti was the Maestro, the professor. Fellini is like a classmate. Antonioni is like a surgeon: He can save your life, but you're better off not getting sick to begin with."

The actor also dropped more than one hint that the film was undermined by Antonioni's affair at the time with Monica Vitti and the director's desire to give the third prominent member of the cast additional screen time.

> I didn't like the script of *La Notte*. I never believed in the crises of my character. And it was a very tense set. It was useless to try to talk to Antonioni, so I ended up bringing all my complaints to Tonino Guerra, the screenwriter. We got into so many arguments that we didn't talk for two years afterward even though we have always been friends. Moreau and I felt shipwrecked together. The whole thing was shifted because of the Vitti character. It really came out as just a romance with some great images.

So why had he agreed to do the film?

> Because at the beginning I had the impression that the writer character was someone at the very edge of the conventional. He reminded me of my writer friend Ennio Flaiano. But that wasn't Antonioni's idea at all. Little by little, all my eagerness and enthusiasm seeped away. Maybe some actors would have fought with Antonioni, but I'm not like that. To use a term from boxing, when I find myself in that kind of situation, I tend to withdraw to a neutral corner until the bell sounds.

His one comfort during the filming was Moreau. What began as mutual consolation between the costars eventually grew into a decades-long friendship. In 1992, the French actress told an interviewer:

> We have not been together all that often over the years, but Marcello's life has been important for me. I have seen all his films, all his photos in the magazines. During the making of *La Notte,* we were very much in love. After so many years of not seeing each other, it is still as though we never parted when we do run into one another. Very cheerful; or maybe a mixture of earnestness and cheerfulness. You're both different, but you still understand one another.

Like Mastroianni, however, Moreau would have preferred to meet her costar under circumstances other than the filming of *La Notte.* The actress, who was a last-minute substitution for Giulietta Masina, once told a Swiss magazine:

> The shooting went on forever. We worked at night, even on Sundays, and sleep became a problem for everybody. We started feeling like fish in a tank. I was physically prostrated by the experience. I began to feel as exhausted as any of the characters in the film. That's why I've never been able to watch *La Notte.*

Antonioni has never been drawn into debates about difficulties with Mastroianni or Moreau during *La Notte;* on the contrary, his few comments have tended to reinforce the notion that "withdrawing to a neutral corner" and "feeling like fish in a tank" were exactly what he had sought from his players. "I see the actor as part of the composition," he has said. "I do not want the actor to become his own director. I never explain to the actors the characters they play. I want them to be passive." In another remark reminiscent of Fellini's desire to have a "face with no personality" for the lead in *La Dolce Vita,* he later insisted that Mastroianni was ideal for the role of "a doubting hero . . . or better, someone for a world in which there are no heroes." According to the director, however, there was a great deal more involved in this than in just standing Mastroianni before a camera and photographing him. Concerning the actor's abilities, Antonioni told Curtis Bill Pepper in the *New York Times Magazine* in 1987:

> It's easier for Clark Gable, say, to pull out a gun and shoot a man through the heart than to have Marcello enter a man's heart or mind. That's where his great talent lies and where he has pioneered as the first star of his kind in Italian cinema.

La Notte's high visibility with international critics, if not audiences, only reinforced Mastroianni's screen image as somebody who wore well-tailored jackets and who had no equal working a gold cigarette lighter in an upper-middle-class setting. As with *Il Bell'Antonio*, he seized upon the first contrasting role that he came upon—in this case, in Elio Petri's *L'Assassino* (The Lady Killer of Rome). Originally pegged for Nino Manfredi, the project, again like *Il Bell'Antonio*, was on the verge of being shelved until the actor stepped in.

Mastroianni:

> Elio had been a writer and assistant director on a couple of other things I had done, and it was obvious that he had all the necessary talent to direct his own films. I had absolutely no hesitation about working with him, and I'm glad that I didn't, because *L'Assassino* was very well made and had considerable success.

According to Petri, however, it wasn't quite that easy; both Titanus studio chief Goffredo Lombardo and producer Franco Cristaldi had to be won over to the idea. Petri:

> Marcello had an old contract with Lombardo that went back some years and that would have paid him only a relatively modest amount to do a film. When Lombardo heard he wanted to do *L'Assassino*, he didn't think twice. "Fine," he said to Marcello. "Now let's find a director." Marcello just sat there in his office and shook his head and said, "No. Petri does it or I won't do it." That's how I began directing.

In *L'Assassino*, Mastroianni played the decidedly unsympathetic role of an antique dealer who is hauled in for questioning about the murder of a former lover. Although innocent of that particular crime, he is shown to be guilty of a hundred others in his pursuit of the quick buck and the quick chance. Even his harrowing experiences as a murder suspect fail to change his life, and he is seen at the end of the film returning to the habits that landed him in trouble. Numerous Italian critics found the actor's performance the equal of those that he gave in *La Dolce Vita* and *Il Bell'Antonio*; others expressed relief that he had returned to roles that had nothing to do with what one called "the pretentious intellectualism" of Antonioni's *La Notte*. The consensus was summed up by the critic for the Milan magazine *Oggi*, who concluded his review by asserting: "If anyone still has doubts about the identity of the best Italian film actor of our day, these doubts should be erased by the end of *L'Assassino*."

Mastroianni's subsequent undertaking, Pietrangeli's *Fantasmi a Roma* (Ghosts of Rome), appealed to him for several reasons. For one thing, it was a fable—a form that had fascinated him since doing the part of the con man among the eelers in *Un Ettaro di Cielo* several years before and that was the furthest thing possible from Latin Lovers, Latin Clothes Horses, and Latin Smokers. Second, it allowed him to work with some of his closest friends (actor Tino Buazzelli and screenwriter Ennio Flaiano) and oldest professional colleagues (among them, Gassman and Claudio Gora, the actor-director who had put him through his paces in *Febbre di Vivere*). Third, it gave him the opportunity to play two roles in the same film. These prospects notwithstanding, however, the main thing that he took away from the project was a resolve never to work with director Pietrangeli again.

Fantasmi a Roma revolved around four ghosts (Mastroianni, Sandra Milo, Buazzelli, Claudio Catania) who have been living without too much disturbance in a Rome palazzo for centuries, most recently with an aged prince (Eduardo De Filippo) who has gotten used to their company. When the prince gets killed in a household accident, a no-good nephew (also played by Mastroianni) takes over the premises, immediately announcing his intention of selling out to a developer who plans to tear down the property and build a luxury hotel. To avoid being evicted, the ghosts go to a sixteenth-century painter (Gassman), who assures them that he can save their abode by painting a giant fresco that will force the city to anoint the building a national monument. When the painter turns out to be little more than a hack, the ghosts resort to more direct action by stealing the down payment paid to the nephew by the developer and use it to bribe a celebrated art critic. The critic not only praises the trashy work of the painter as a masterpiece but suggests that it is a newly discovered Caravaggio. The house is saved, and the ghosts return to their haunting.

Fantasmi a Roma won over most Italian critics as a light fable directed masterfully by Pietrangeli. Most notices also stressed the appropriate ensemble playing of the cast rather than singling out a particular actor. For Mastroianni, however, the bounciness of the finished product on the screen had nothing in common with the arduousness of working for Pietrangeli, whose reputation as a perfectionist (some said an obsessive) had driven many actors off his sets in protests after dozens of takes of the same scene. As Mastroianni put it:

> He was a very good director, and I think I made two fine films with him—*Adua e le Compagne* and *Fantasmi a Roma*. But it became impossible for me to work with him after *Fantasmi* because I get tired when I work. I like doing a scene right away, in the best of

cases in one take. Antonio was nothing like that. He would build this very elaborate scene, go through rehearsals, and then suddenly, just as we're ready to shoot, would say something like "Now wait a minute. Suppose, instead of doing it this way, we were to put the camera over there and do it that way?" This was part of his anxiety to do everything to absolute perfection. Nothing would ever convince him that the first thing to occur to him might be the best thing. Any actor will tell you that the most boring part of shooting a film is all the standing around and waiting for setups and that the second most boring thing is having to do everything over and over because maybe the sound wasn't right or maybe the lighting wasn't right or maybe an actor didn't give what the director wanted. With Antonio, you never seemed to get beyond these obstacles. *Nothing* was ever right for him. That's why I couldn't agree to work with him again, no matter the script. What can I say? That's the kind of person I am, and I'm very sorry it ended that way between us because Pietrangeli went about his craft with immense passion.

Ugo Tognazzi, who appeared in other pictures for Pietrangeli, once laughed off the idea that it was Mastroianni's laziness that kept him away from the director after *Fantasmi a Roma*. Tognazzi told an interviewer:

Marcello makes it sound like it was his fault. But there wasn't anybody who ever appeared in a film for that mad and saintly Pietrangeli who didn't feel exactly the same way. One time, I was doing something for him, and I had told him ahead of time that I had to catch a plane to Paris in the evening. Well, over and over again, we spend the whole afternoon on the same damn scene. Finally, I realized that if I didn't leave right away, I'd miss my plane. So I waited until the end of the take, then just walked calmly over to my car, got in, drove out to the airport, and got my plane to Paris. I came back the next day, and Pietrangeli never said anything. But of course we then did another scene a hundred times!

(Pietrangeli drowned a number of years after the completion of *Fantasmi a Roma*. Bone weary after a full day of shooting, he had still insisted on checking out a setup for the following day that called for a beach to be shown from the water.)

Although it was *La Dolce Vita* that won Mastroianni world recognition, it was Pietro Germi's *Divorzio all'Italiana* that netted him the wagonload of critical raves and awards that cemented his international standing. Like *Il Bell'Antonio*, the plot of *Divorzio* took wing from an Italian reality (the lack of a divorce law) that fed off medieval notions of honor to produce morally and socially gnarled solutions for those affected by it; also like the Bolognini film, the Germi picture was laid in Sicily. According to the director, the original intention had been to do a straight drama. "The deeper we got into the subject, though, we simply couldn't ignore the grotesquely comic aspects to the so-called crime of honor."

For one of the only times in his career, Mastroianni openly campaigned for a role, going so far as to submit to a screen test and to have special photographs made up showing him with ridiculously slicked down hair in the manner of an eccentric Sicilian nobleman.

> I had heard all about all the other actors that Germi had interviewed for the role and how he had almost signed Anthony Quinn. Unfortunately for me, he was one of the people who had an image of me strictly connected to what I had done for Fellini in *La Dolce Vita*, and it was very hard to get him to change his mind. He was a strange one, anyway. He was very reserved, something of a bear, very misanthropic. I often had the impression that he despised anyone who had anything to do with filmmaking. But then, after he had failed to sign anyone else, he became a little more vulnerable to that idiot law of the cinema that says find somebody with "box office" in his name, so he agreed to see me. I brought along slews of photos of me with various hairstyles, mustaches, everything. I thought I was too close to say no when he asked me to do a test, so I went along, just like somebody starting out. It was only then that he agreed I might be right for the part.

Divorzio all'Italiana cast Mastroianni as the comically absurd Baron Cefalù, who is enamored of his beautiful sixteen-year-old cousin (Stefania Sandrelli) but is in no position to do anything about it because of his ugly, petulant wife (Daniela Rocca). His apparent salvation arrives in the person of a painter (Leopoldo Trieste) who was once in love with his wife, and from that point on the film moves between the baron's real attempts to put his wife into compromising situations with the painter and his ludicrous reveries about catching them *in flagrante* so that he can kill his mate and be absolved as a dishonored husband in a Sicilian court. He finally achieves his purpose and, as he had imagined, is indeed let off with little more than a slap on the wrist. But no sooner has he married his beautiful cousin to the celebration of all his friends and relatives than she starts playing around with her own boyfriend.

One of the most memorable nuances brought to the character of Baron Cefalù by Mastroianni was a mouth tic that he copied directly from his director.

> Germi was having a lot of problems with his gums, and he would keep distorting his mouth and making this sucking-clicking sound. Tics like that are infectious, and suddenly one day I did the same

thing in the middle of a scene. Germi didn't think it was at all funny
and asked me if I was mocking him. I apologized to him as sincerely
as I could, then suggested that maybe we could use that tic for the
character of the Baron; say, for instance, that he had a cavity that
was bothering him. Germi thought it over, ordered another take of
the scene with the tic, then let me do it for the rest of the film wherever I thought it was appropriate. We more or less agreed to do it as
a kind of counterpoint for the tensest, most dramatic junctures of
the story. Ever since *Divorzio all'Italiana* was released, I have been
approached by people all over the world who make that sucking
sound as a way of telling me that they've seen the film.

Despite Germi's initial hesitations about taking on the actor for
the role of the baron, Mastroianni eventually had nothing except
praise for his working relationship with the director. On the other
hand, the production was jeopardized by the behavior of Rocca, who
acted increasingly unstable as the filming went on and who ultimately tried to kill herself.
Mastroianni:

I don't think any of us realized how ill she had become. But I do
remember one incident that at the time annoyed me a great deal
and that, now in retrospect, makes me very sad. We were in the
middle of a scene in which the baron's family is seated at a table
eating fish. Suddenly, Daniela, without my having said or done
anything and without any warning from her, suddenly she gives
me a whack in the face that almost took my head off. I was stunned.
Then, just as I was getting my bile back up and was about to say,
"You idiot! What the hell's wrong with you?," I saw something in
her face that made me stop. From that moment on, I don't think I
or anybody else in the troupe could think of her as just another
working colleague.

Rocca's problems appeared to stem from a combination of inse-
curities about her role in the film and unavailing attempts to get
Germi, with whom she was rumored to have had an affair, to give her
more attention than he was giving Mastroianni, Sandrelli, and other
members of the cast. As regards the part of the baron's wife, the
actress was not only the whining heavy in the story but also had to
be made up to look as ugly as possible, an objective achieved in part
by painting on upper lip hairs. In the words of Sandrelli: "She had
won all these beauty contests and was being compared to Sophia
Loren and Gina Lollobrigida. It was very important for her to be beautiful and admired, and she would go into hysterics whenever she had
to put on her wig and the other things that made her ugly."
Both Mastroianni and Sandrelli have denied any direct knowl-

edge of an affair between Rocca and Germi, but the actor has admitted that the director's behavior was strange in the aftermath of the dinner-table slap.

> I never noticed any particular tie between the two of them, although some people said later that this was exactly the problem, that Daniela wanted more of a show from Germi. What struck me as odd was that he did absolutely nothing after she had hit me. His behavior that day was really embarrassing. A couple of days later, in her hotel room in Ragusa, she slashed her wrists.

Equally strange, in the actor's view, was Germi's reaction on that occasion.

> There was this tremendous scream from her room. We all had rooms on the same floor, and we all ran out into the corridor. All except Germi, that is. I don't know. There had been gossip about the two of them having a fight earlier in the day, and maybe he was thinking, She's just trying to shake me up. There was nothing at all theatrical about that screaming, though.

However aloof Germi was directly with Rocca, her hospitalization and absence from the set for a couple of weeks began to weigh on the director. Supporting player Lando Buzzanca was to recall:

> They decided to fake it with Daniela, just get a local Sicilian girl who resembled her physically and shoot her from the back until Daniela could come back. That's when Germi got his first taste of real Sicilian life. Up until then, he had been able to accept the fact that any woman doing a walk-on would show up for the day's shooting with her entire family, just to make sure these "northerners" weren't up to no good. But when he picked a woman to stand in for Daniela, all hell broke loose. The day that he was supposed to do the first setup with her, a relative showed up instead and said that the girl wasn't coming because an uncle had threatened to evict her and then kill her if she allowed herself to be used for a dishonorable purpose like making a film. None of this did anything for the tic that Germi had on one side of his face, and he was forced to shut down everything for a couple of weeks.

All these off-the-set dramas notwithstanding, Mastroianni later looked back on *Divorzio all'Italiana* as one of his most gratifying experiences.

> Germi was absolutely great with actors. He never talked for the sake of talking, but when the moment came for action, he was incredibly clear about what he wanted. He was an enormous director. He wasn't somebody taken by some idea that he was a great

artist or that everything he had to say was being said for the first time under the sun. He was the ultimate professional who knew that he had a series of little daily problems to work out and who then proceeded to work them out. If we had more directors like him, there would be no talk of a film-industry crisis.

As in the case of *Il Bell'Antonio*, *Divorzio all'Italiana* proved popular just about everywhere except in the Sicilian areas where it was shot. Critically, however, the film's subject matter touched on a volatile national issue that ultimately produced a more problematic and polemical response in Italy than abroad. While some Italian critics saw it as an entertaining broadside against Italy's lack of a divorce law and against the Vatican's pressures on Parliament to keep it that way, others argued that the picture's farcical emphases and storytelling adroitness would have just the opposite effect of ridiculing into insignificance an urgent issue. Among those taking the latter view was novelist Mario Soldati, who, reviewing the film for the Milan daily *Il Giorno*, declared:

> One walks out of the theater without any desire to see a divorce law or the abolition (of the present laws prohibiting it). Everything is just fine, audiences think: We live in the best of all possible worlds. Such an attitude is known as nurtured indifference. A real shame because the film is technically, and maybe artistically, the best ever made by Germi.

For Alberto Moravia of *L'Espresso*, the film also backed off from drawing real blood:

> The only way of presenting the *problem* raised by the film would have been to introduce a lot more black humor, to have the character of the husband, for instance, just shoot his wife with all the coldness (of the way these things usually happen).

Such reservations were in sharp contrast to the reactions of foreign reviewers, who, outside the immediate heat of the divorce issue in Italy, embraced *Divorzio all'Italiana* as the best Italian comedy since *I Soliti Ignoti* and decidedly more ambitious than the Monicelli picture. Evidence of this came when the screenplay by Germi, Ennio de Concini, and Alfredo Giannetti won a 1962 Oscar for best original work for the screen—the first time that a full-length feature from the European Continent had been so honored by Hollywood. What there was no argument about between Italian and foreign critics, on the other hand, was Mastroianni's performance. For the Genoa daily *Il Lavoro Nuovo*, his contribution was nothing less than "stupendous." Soldati called his effort a "masterpiece"; Moravia, "an example of a great actor in great form." Britain and West Germany, among others, awarded him their Oscar equivalents for best performance by a for-

awarded him their Oscar equivalents for best performance by a foreign actor. In Hollywood, he became the first male performer ever to be Oscar-nominated for a picture not shot in the English-speaking world (and was later saluted at the Academy Award ceremonies by recipient Gregory Peck as having been the most deserving winner). In Italy, his performance as Baron Cefalù not only gained him another Nastro d'Argento but resonated in the work of some of his peers for many years; Giancarlo Giannini, in particular, admitted that he consciously patterned some of his Sicilian characters for Lina Wertmuller on the cut given to the nobleman in the Germi picture.

With his prizes for *Divorzio all'Italiana* still in the offing, Mastroianni went immediately from the somewhat hysterical Baron Cefalù to a distracted director in *La Vie Privée* (A Very Private Affair), a French-Italian coproduction made by Louis Malle and costarring Brigitte Bardot as an ambitious actress who suffers a nervous breakdown, tries to show her love for the aloof director, but ends up toppling off a roof when she is blinded by a photographer's flashbulb. The picture was a disaster, with the stars clashing more than once on the set around his charges that Bardot was not being professional and hers that Mastroianni was not showing her enough respect as an actress. "She's no Moreau or Aimée," the actor was quoted as complaining to Malle at one point.

According to Mastroianni, *Le Vie Privée* should have never happened, and wouldn't have if Malle had been more honest with him.

> I had seen his work in *Les Amants* and liked it very much. He came to see me in Rome and told me about this idea he had for a film about a married couple. I thought it was a great idea because up to then there really hadn't been a good film that examined a marital relationship in the depth that he was talking about. So I said let's do it without even asking for a script. A couple of months later, I showed up for work and Malle handed me a script that had absolutely nothing to do with what we had discussed. Now it's all about Bardot playing Bardot and her obsession with the press and photographers. I looked at Malle and said, "This isn't what we agreed to," and he just shrugs and says to me, "Well, do what you want, but don't forget that MGM is behind this." I really felt deceived. I also couldn't understand why a talented director would want to get into a picture with an actor who hated what he was doing. The damned picture almost killed me. It was all so pointless. Then they got it into the editing room and made it even worse. It was terrible, a real atrocity.

Italian critics agreed with Mastroianni's overall evaluation of *La Vie Privée*, and they also hammered the actor for what one termed "his indifferent presence." He agreed. "I deserved everything they said."

Once again propelled by the need for a radical change of pace, the actor next took on Valerio Zurlini's *Cronaca Familiare* (Family Diary). Based on a novel by Vasco Pratolini, *Cronaca Familiare* was the most heavily literary film of Mastroianni's career, requiring him to deliver reams of dialogue in lengthy scenes. The story of the film was simplicity: a journalist (Mastroianni) reviewing the strong emotional ties that he had to a younger brother (Jacques Perrin) following the latter's death. Although Mastroianni has tended to classify *Cronaca Familiare* on the B list of his favorite films, frequently joking that his memory powers had never been so tested, many critics viewed his openly emotional performance as one of the jewels of his career, evidence of still another facet of his dramatic abilities. In the words of Tullio Kezich:

> Mastroianni seems totally committed to forcing every limit of his personality. But it is perhaps in *Cronaca Familiare* that he shows his most secret face and uses all his formidable means as an actor to get to the heart of a character.

Another critic cited the performance as "the greatest evidence to date of the maturity this actor has brought to the Italian screen."

Lost on nobody was the fact that *Cronaca Familiare* represented one of the few times that Mastroianni's costar was a man, not a woman.

13

Close-up: The Costar

As much as any of the specific characters that he has played in films such as *La Dolce Vita*, it has been Mastroianni's record of costarring with prominent actresses that has kept alive his image as the Latin Lover. Even a summary list of Italian and foreign screen partners over the years would have to include Sophia Loren, Gina Lollobrigida, Silvana Mangano, Claudia Cardinale, Virna Lisi, Jeanne Moreau, Simone Signoret, Anouk Aimée, Brigitte Bardot, Ursula Andress, Catherine Deneuve, Romy Schneider, Jacqueline Bisset, Faye Dunaway, Natassia Kinski, Hanna Schygulla, Sonia Braga, and Shirley MacLaine. In fact, with the conspicuous exceptions of Jacques Perrin in *Cronaca Familiare* in 1962, Michel Piccoli and Ugo Tognazzi in *La Grande Bouffe* (Blowout) in 1973, Jack Lemmon in *Maccheroni* (Macaroni) in 1985, and a couple of pictures with Massimo Troisi in the late 1980s, the actor has rarely shared a marquee only with other male performers. He hasn't appeared in too many films, either, in which he was the only one to merit a star's above-the-title billing, the most notable exceptions being Fellini productions partnering him with the director's visual orgies.

On occasion, the actor has denied that there was any grand design behind the roles that have matched him with the foremost actresses of the last two generations; as he has said, "Any role is okay as long as it contains a basic truth—something in which I can believe." At other times, however, he has indicated otherwise: "Women are an extraordinary engine. I need a woman to work, to think, to live." Certainly, even allowing for his other strictures about requiring a recognized director in whom he can place his confidence and about disliking characters that must be rendered from behind gobs of makeup, the record argues for more than coincidence in his usual pairing with a strong leading lady. No other modern screen name—in Italy, the United States, or elsewhere—has so few credits where so-called male bonding or tour de force roles are concerned.

Aside from the exceptions already noted, Mastroianni has seldom been available at the local cinema as a military man used to the company of his superiors or fellow officers, as a soldier of fortune most comfortable with his own taste for adventure, or as a masculine Thelma out on the open road with a masculine Louise. Gassman, Yves Montand, and Gérard Depardieu, to cite only three fellow stars from the Romance countries in recent decades, have occasionally distinguished themselves in such stories; save for his pre–*La Dolce Vita* appearances in the likes of *Tam-Tam Mayumbe*, not Mastroianni. In addition, he has not only avoided the matador roles that once defined "a Gassman film" or "a Sordi film" for Italian audiences; he has also generally steered clear of dramas powered by a single star, such as those made by Gian Maria Volonté. For Mastroianni, even the star vehicle has always been a two-seater, with the other passenger preferably a woman.

The readiest complement to this pattern would seem to be the actor's description of himself as being primarily a reactor; that is, a performer who is most at home when he is playing off other people, creating his character by filling in *their* characters. That this has most often been a woman suggests far more than the reductive psychobabble a number of film critics have been content to view it as. Most immediately, it points to the fact that producers and directors both in Italy and abroad have been at least equally amenable to accepting him in such a way by offering him the scripts that they have over the years. Second, it argues that whatever his private complexes and personal turmoils happen to be, he does not share the feelings of so many male actors who, along with animals and children, are threatened by women professionally and are loath to share the screen with them. On the contrary, Mastroianni's professional self-confidence has been such that his women costars are apt to be written as the dominant figures. The most obvious example of this has been his measurably secondary status, at least in terms of dialogue and time spent on the screen, to Loren in almost all the pictures they have made together since *Peccato Che Sia una Canaglia* in 1954. (In the actress's words: "When I perform with Marcello, I am the full moon, and he is the ring around me.") But even without a Loren, with lesser costars, such as Laura Antonelli, Sydne Rome, and Agostina Belli, there have not been too many instances when he was caught overtly competing for an audience's attention.

The biggest trap for somebody trying to fashion a reactor's presence on the screen is an impression of passivity—a charge that has been leveled against Mastroianni more than once, and not merely for films (e.g., *La Notte*) in which all the characters, male and female, were deployed as a director's objects more than as flesh-and-blood

people. The actor himself has encouraged critiques of the kind with
a series of remarks about being nothing more than putty in the hands
of his directors and by declaring, in alternate moods of pride and melancholy, that his characters, in the 1960s especially, were men who
did not do things so much as had things done to them. To the extent
that the things were done customarily by his female costar of the
moment, the larger stereotype of Mastroianni the Latin Lover was
filled in with the Latin Lover as Emotional Coward, the Mama's Boy,
and similar epithets denoting a weak man who craved to rest his head
on the nearest breast and who could count on an orgasmic reward for
his docility.

The trouble with most of these perceptions is that they have
usually had a lot more to do with projections—knowledgeable or
not—from the actor's private life than with the specific films in question. Over the years, especially in the United States, the journalist
named Marcello in *La Dolce Vita* has been run into the Marcello of
Mastroianni and out again to elucidate both his most recent film role
and his latest offscreen romance, with the crossover verdict being
that he is a master of inadequacy. Typical was an "anonymous journalist" quoted by *People* magazine in 1987 as expressing bafflement
(not to say indignation) at Mastroianni's popularity for so long:

> Marcello is just an overgrown mother's boy. He has no capacity to
> decide anything. With directors, he behaves like a little boy with
> the strong father he never had. He also depends on women—he
> expects the woman to be the strong one. When women get to know
> him, they find him boring.

Protestations to the contrary by the actor's numerous costars who
have found nothing mysterious about his appeal personally or professionally have done little to change such views; if anything, they
have been cataloged as confirmations that the actresses are vulnerable to the benefits accruing from Mastroianni's supposed psychological disposition.

More to the point, however, have been the dynamics of the films
in which Mastroianni has been teamed with a strong actress in a
highly visible role. Even those skeptical of the value of motion-
picture-industry prizes, for example, would have to be struck by the
fact that none of the actor's screen partners has ever walked off a
stage brandishing a piece of metal as the result of their work with
him, while he himself has decorated his mantelpieces and walls with
most of the honors that Europe and North America have to confer.
This applies not merely to the awards presented annually by the
motion-picture academy associations of the United States, Britain,
Germany, France, and other countries but also to those given by met-

ropolitan critics circles and by such international festivals as Cannes, Venice, and Berlin. Short of proposing a critical myopia on a transcontinental scale, in other words, Mastroianni has provided little evidence, within the framework of his individual roles, of having been dominated emotively by his costars; on the contrary, he has impressed a multitude of judging panels as having very much held the reins with (to cite only some of the films for which he has received industry awards) Maria Schell in *Le Notti Bianche*, Anouk Aimée and Anita Ekberg in *La Dolce Vita*, Micheline Presle in *L'Assassino*, Daniela Rocca and Stefania Sandrelli in *Divorzio all'Italiana*, and Loren in both *Ieri Oggi Domani* (Yesterday, Today, and Tomorrow) and *Una Giornata Particolare* (A Special Day). Put another way, whatever the specific character and whatever his own comments about being a reactor intent on doing only what a director wants from him, there has not been any appreciable *professional* passivity from Mastroianni vis-à-vis the actresses with whom he has costarred.

For most other film stars, it would be superfluous to point out that there has been a decided calculation behind many of these roles, that they appealed to the actor precisely because he discerned within them fertile terrain for his gifts. But with Mastroianni, the normal deliberations about career moves have sometimes been obscured by his own offhand statements about what led him to particular parts, by the frequently fortuitous matchings of scripts with actors in Italy, and by the usually intricate negotiations involved in casting the multinational coproductions that have accounted for a substantial percentage of his screen appearances since the 1960s. The impression of casualness has also been abetted, in the view of veteran screenwriter Age (Agenore Incrocci), by the actor's "love of risk—so that a few of his most ill advised roles seem to have arisen from a dare or from some table late at night where too much grappa was consumed." Finally, there is the anti-star factor, Mastroianni not known for rejecting parts only because of who his costar might be or because of some other tantrum common to performers with his marquee clout.

Nevertheless, all that said, the calculations have been there. If he has not objected to roles because of another contracted or proposed player, he has said no to a great many because of the director involved, with the consequence that, broadly speaking, he has lent his talents to only two categories of filmmakers: Italian directors with whom he has shared artistic and cultural assumptions (including an appreciation of his reactive abilities and an intuition about which performers he would work best with) and laureled foreign directors who have been able to satisfy his taste for risk, right down to the unknown (for him) quality of his fellow actors in a number of cases. Moreover, if scripts have landed in his lap after rejections elsewhere, he has hardly seized on them in gratitude for having been acknowledged; in fact, notwithstanding his willingness to jump into *Il Bell'Antonio* on short notice and his eagerness to do *Divorzio all'Italiana* after so many other actors had passed on it, Mastroianni has always had a reputation as something of a hard sell. Among those who could attest to this are Marco Ferreri and Ettore Scola, the directors with whom the actor has worked most often over the last twenty years. Back in the late 1960s, however, both Ferreri and Scola were mainly getting by as screenwriters, with one of their favorite ploys being to march in on producer Carlo Ponti with some vague idea for a new project for Mastroianni. As Ferreri tells it,

> Ponti would then give us enough money to go to London or New York to work out the idea in this foreign setting so the whole thing would have an international look and be easier to interest distributors in. Scola and I would go abroad, write the film, and then submit it to Mastroianni. Not once would he say yes. After a while, we used up our credit with Ponti, and Marcello ended up having to feed me.

Then there have been the projects that he has agreed to do. If there could be said to be a common denominator to the roles that passed the actor's other tests, especially in the 1960s and early 1970s, it was that they were decidedly antiheroic, even when, as in the instance of *I Compagni* (The Organizer) in 1963, a mere reading of the script could have made it appear otherwise. Although Mastroianni himself has always been ambiguous about his criteria for determining an antihero, it has emerged more clearly from the screen record that his antihero is considerably more than a nonhero or villain. Whereas the nonhero would be only a negation of what is expected customarily from a protagonist, the antihero is a declared antagonist to these expectations, combining in one character both the traditional hero and the foe who, dramatically and emotionally, will get the best of him by the end. However Antonioni might have described the writer in *La Notte,* it was the lack of such a distinction between the nonhero and the antihero in the film that, in Mastroianni's estimation, made his rendering of Giovanni Pontano such an unrewarding experience.

The arena for the antihero's struggles has seldom had room for (or interest in) the character as villain, so that Mastroianni, unlike Gassman, Tognazzi, and Volonté, rejected such parts except for one brief period in the mid-1970s. By the same token, his most insightful roles have avoided the temptation to lay the villainous burden elsewhere; for the most part, in a Mastroianni film, his character and that of his costars have been *accomplices,* wittingly or not, in struggle.

More often than not, the key accomplice has been a woman—a state of affairs that has evidently given the actor a greater sense of artistic purchase than hitting the open road with Mel Gibson, doing a Sordi turn, or abusing the female character as pure nemesis would have. If there is a fault in this, it is not in the self as glimpsed by tabloids but in the star who has shrewdly identified his success as a reactor with being a costar.

14

In America

The year 1962 was a signal one for Mastroianni. On the filming front, he followed up *Cronaca Familiare* with *8½*, one of the most important pictures of his career. Between assignments, he appeared on an Italian television variety show in the unlikely guise of a singer performing one of his own tunes ("a small indiscretion of youth!"). Finally, in the fall of the year, he made his first trip to the United States.

The visit to New York and Los Angeles was a promotional tour organized by distributor Joseph E. Levine on behalf of *Divorzio all'Italiana*. For Levine, it paid off in more than one way: The extensive coverage given to Mastroianni on both coasts (including a major article in *Time* magazine) produced not only unprecedented business for a foreign film but also the Academy Award nominations that broadened the producer-distributor's reputation from someone who had made a silk purse out of the sow's ear of Steve Reeves as Hercules. Mastroianni, on the other hand, confessed to being stunned, confused, appalled, and many other things by the reception accorded him and by the testing of his own preconceptions about America.

> I couldn't help thinking the whole time I was there, What's going on here? Why is everyone picking on me? Is something behind all this? It was absolutely incredible the way everybody welcomed me. It was like the first time that Marlon Brando had come to Rome; even bigger than that—and I say it with all modesty—because maybe the Americans are more prone than the Italians to glorifying somebody who has reached a certain fame or position in life. . . .
> Largely thanks to *La Dolce Vita*, they regarded me as a star, as one of those golden people who lived in a plush Hollywood mansion.

Mastroianni himself had been a little star struck in traveling over the Atlantic for the first time. To begin with, there had been his fascination since childhood with the heroic screen figures that had been cut by the Gary Coopers, James Cagneys, Humphrey Bogarts, and John Waynes.

But maybe the two who meant as much to me as any of them were Fred Astaire and Clark Gable. Astaire was always elegant in those musicals he made with Ginger Rogers, and that always struck me, even when I was very young, as a style that went beyond merely his dancing. And as for Gable, he may have been the only exception, at least to my mind, to the actor as an amorphous entity waiting to be shaped by a director. He had so much personality that he had no need to do characters in the way that we normally say an actor does a character.

Mastroianni met Gable only once, during the American actor's sojourn in Italy to make *It Started in Naples* with Loren in 1959. "It was something that Sophia knew that I wanted to do, but it was only for a few minutes. In cases like that, you have too much to say, so you end up saying practically nothing." He had even less luck with Astaire, never running into the dancer during his visits to America and having to satisfy himself some years later with a brief telephone call.

In the same vein of the fan, Mastroianni has admitted, one of his saddest moments came shortly before leaving Italy for the United States, with the news that the other MM—Marilyn Monroe—had died of an overdose of barbiturates.

One of my greatest unfulfilled dreams was to work with her. I even had a film in mind that we could do together. It was going to be about Marilyn coming to Rome to shoot some colossal epic and meeting this two-bit actor who was scheduled to play a Roman soldier in the film. I was going to call it *Quo Vadis, Marilyn?* There was a time that I spent hours dreaming about her and the film. Of course, I was too embarrassed to mention it to anybody else, let alone write to her and suggest it as a project. What a woman she was! She had so much sweetness about her: maternal and yet provocative. You felt that she needed protection. She was, or so it seemed to me, everything that a woman needs to be for a man.

But with Monroe and many of his earliest screen idols deceased, Mastroianni's most memorable moments during the visit were with the long-retired Greta Garbo.

To tell the truth, it wasn't a meeting that I had panted after. I had never been very struck by her as an actress. I thought that in most of her films she looked a little like Snow White's stepmother. When I dreamed of Hollywood actresses, I dreamed of Rogers and Turner and Stanwyck and Sylvia Sidney.

As the actor usually recounts the story, he was informed during his stay in New York that Garbo wanted to meet him, but behind the appearance of an accidental encounter. To this end, he was taken by limousine to an East Side antique shop one afternoon. Inside the store, the manager ("who looked like Jean Gabin") directed him to a second floor, where Garbo was sitting with two other women. Because he didn't speak English, Mastroianni introduced himself by uttering only his own name and that of the actress. Garbo's reply was to eye his feet and declare, "Beautiful shoes. Italian shoes are very beautiful." After resisting the temptation to tell her that they were English shoes, he thanked her for the compliment, drawing from her something like "Italy beautiful, Rome, the pope." According to the actor, Garbo then jumped up from her chair and began dancing around the room amid all the antiques. The pirouetting came to an abrupt end, however, when one of the other women sighed too loudly: "How beautiful you were as Camille!" With that, Garbo grabbed her bag and, not saying another word, marched down the stairs and out of the shop. A few hours later, Mastroianni was at a party hosted by Actors Studio director Lee Strasberg when somebody shouted out that Garbo was on the phone for him. Under the frozen attention of everyone present, the actor's interpreter went to the telephone and then reported back the Swedish star's words as "Tell Mr. Mastroianni that I'm sorry. That I admire him very much, but cannot stand stupid women." That message delivered, Garbo just hung up the phone.

His impression of her? "She seemed to me old and tired, with the face of a wolf. But she was still very beautiful. I don't think I'll ever meet any sacred monster more sacred monster than she was."

Even without the standard of his New York meeting with the sacred monster Garbo, the actor's subsequent trip to Los Angeles did not stand much of a chance. Months before leaving Italy, he had reiterated to the *Herald Tribune* his frequently stated aversion to working in Hollywood, asserting in part:

> Where would I go during the day? Is there a Piazza del Popolo where I can sit down to talk to friends and waiters? I belong with the old buildings of Rome and its streets under my feet. I would die of sadness in Hollywood. I think part of living is knowing where you can live best.

He also joked during several of his New York interviews that he was more than willing to take on a role in Hollywood—as long as the part was of a deaf-and-dumb sheriff in a western parody.

Actually being in Hollywood managed to persuade him only that visiting the place wasn't much better than working in it.

For all the things that I had said before getting there, I still had a notion that it would have been just enough to drop in at a bar or a café to meet Fred Astaire, just to sit down and chat with him the way you do in Rome. But the place was hallucinating, a desert. When I stepped out of my hotel, all I saw were these monstrous cars speeding back and forth. The streets weren't clean; they were spotless. You couldn't find a scrap of newspaper or a trace of old, dried shit anywhere on the sidewalk.

Aside from two encounters, the itinerary that Levine had planned didn't please him particularly, either. One exception was a visit to the home of the retired Harold Lloyd.

There was one cocktail party after another, so when Levine's people said there was a chance to visit Lloyd, I jumped at it. The house he had was the only thing I saw there that had a human dimension, although it, too, was furnished horribly. Lloyd's loneliness after being ignored for so long was enormous. You got the feeling that he had accepted the judgment of others that he was nothing more than a relic from the past. He asked me to pose with him in front of a giant Christmas tree. I didn't understand why he had a Christmas tree in all that California heat. It wasn't even the Christmas season. When I asked him, he just shrugged that he liked it.

The other happy experience was in meeting Jack Lemmon.

I didn't really want to go to the studios. I hate studios, and when it's possible, I avoid them. But we went on the set of *Irma la Douce*, and I was glad because I met Lemmon and Shirley MacLaine. With Jack, it was the beginning of a friendship that took some years to get going but that has lasted a very long time.

According to Lemmon, their relationship got off awkwardly.

Billy Wilder, who was directing *Irma la Douce*, invited Marcello and his interpreter to his office. For some reason, both Wilder and the interpreter got up to go down the hall. Marcello and I just sat there staring and smiling at one another because my Italian was as good as his English. Suddenly, after this long silence, he starts wiggling his fingers in a pantomime of pouring a drink and says the single word "scotch." That much even I understood, so I go looking through Wilder's drawers, and sure enough there's an old bottle of scotch. There wasn't any ice, but that broke it, anyway.

Twenty years later, the story had a sequel.

Radio City was doing this big gala called the Night of a Hundred Stars. Practically everybody in show business was crammed backstage. Suddenly, there's Marcello, who had just flown in from

Morocco, where he was doing a movie, and he looked dog-tired. I was talking to somebody else, while he was asking a waiter if there was something besides mineral water and soda. The guy says no, Marcello looks away disappointed, then spots me over the sea of heads. "Jack," he yells out, "scotch!" I ran out to a bar next door and got one for him. Twenty years and the three words between us were scotch, Jack, and scotch.

Lloyd and Lemmon aside, the Hollywood atmosphere finally snapped Mastroianni's patience.

After days of cocktail parties, I told the people with me that I wanted to return to New York, that I could have all the cocktail parties I wanted back there. Impossible, they said. I was Levine's guest, and it was important for me to meet the people he had arranged for me to see. I didn't know who they were, and I didn't wait around to find out. I just took a piece of paper and left Levine a note saying, "Mr. Levine, I'm going back to New York. Fuck you and fuck Hollywood."

For the rest of that first stay and for almost three decades afterward, Mastroianni continued to deflect the offers that he received to work in California. One project in the 1960s would have had him playing Christopher Columbus under the direction of Edward Dmytryk. Another attempted to team him with Frank Sinatra in something called *El Toro*, about the exploits of *two* Latin Lovers. Repeatedly over the years there were scripts sent to Rome with the idea of having Mastroianni and Loren pair off in a Hollywood production, with or without Ponti as producer. At times, the actor's response was the "condition" that he be the deaf-and-dumb sheriff; still other times, he snapped that there was "no heart" to American films and that he had nothing to gain by leaving European directors; always available as well was his insistence that he did not speak English well enough to avoid looking like a clown on the screen. And against the particularly persistent, he fell back on Fellini, declaring that he would work in California only with his favorite director, knowing full well that no American studio was about to underwrite Fellini's approximate approaches to budgets and linear storytelling and that the Italian filmmaker was even more averse than he was to leaving Rome.

Perhaps Mastroianni's most creative act of sidestepping, however, was his Giulio Demand.

One man wouldn't take no for an answer, so I said, "Okay, but Giulio has to fly over on Tuesdays." "Who's Giulio?" he wants to know. I tell him that Giulio is my barber, that every week I go to his place

near Rome for a haircut, and he breaks out the prosciutto and wine
while working on me. I told the producer I could no longer sit still
for a haircut without Giulio's prosciutto and wine. He decided I was
fooling around, but he got the message. And anyway, why the hell
not? If I'm such a big star like they're always saying in Hollywood,
shouldn't I have the right to have Giulio with me?

But if he declined all Hollywood offers until British director
Beeban Kidron got him to agree to do *Used People* in 1991, Mastroianni never stopped exploring projects that would have allowed
him to work in the United States—in both films and the theater—
under some Italian auspices. Despite the abrupt finish of his first Hollywood sojourn, for instance, he maintained cordial enough relations
with Levine for the two of them to announce a production project a
few months later. The film, a lampoon of the Mafia entitled *Cosa Nostra*, was to have been written by Age and Scarpelli and shot by Monicelli in New York. Mastroianni would have played a Sicilian tailor
who gets entangled with a homosexual Mafia chieftain and gets
saved by a police informant played by MacLaine. To this day, he has
expressed bafflement that the picture was never made.

In 1964, there was a tentative agreement with concert manager
Jay Hoffman for him to head a company of Italian actors, including
former Visconti troupe players Stoppa and Morelli, in New York productions of two Goldoni plays; he had to bow out because of scheduling conflicts and was replaced by Gassman. Again in 1966, Mastroianni and impresario David Merrick discussed staging a Broadway
musical about Rudolph Valentino that the actor had been doing in
Rome, but that project also came a cropper. Two other films that
would have been directed by Marco Ferreri, one in New York and the
second in San Francisco, were thwarted by a lack of capital. Another
idea to have an Italian produce a thriller directed by Alfred Hitchcock in both the United States and Italy ended with a less than scintillating encounter with the filmmaker.

> I was very disappointed because when I mentioned to Hitchcock
> how much I had liked *Psycho*, all he could say was that it had made
> a lot of money and enabled him to buy twelve-thousand head of
> cattle. I thought the reaction just a little crude and wasn't all that
> crushed when nothing happened with the film.

With most of his projects shot down for one reason or another,
Mastroianni's lengthiest stays in America until 1991 were for Ettore
Scola's *Permette? Rocco Papaleo* (Rocco Papaleo), shot in Chicago in
1971; and Ferreri's *Ciao Maschio* (Bye Bye Monkey), filmed largely in
New York in 1978. Otherwise, his visits have usually been in con-
nection with a special event or the promotion of a picture. The spe-

cial occasions included an April 1978 flight to Los Angeles for the Academy Award presentations. Nominated in the category of Best Actor for *Una Giornata Particolare* (A Special Day), the actor helped bail out producers of the ceremonies when a self-important Farrah Fawcett announced that she would not act as a presenter unless she were partnered on the stage with an international cinema icon; after Cary Grant and Laurence Olivier declined the honor, Mastroianni agreed to share the stage with the actress.

The actor took away more than the memory of Lemmon fetching him a drink when he flew into New York in 1982 for the Night of a Hundred Stars spectacle at Radio City Music Hall. His appearance was as part of the finale paying tribute to Michael Bennett's musical *A Chorus Line*, and he did his strutting with the likes of Al Pacino and Dustin Hoffman. But more important to him was "seeing some of the myths of my childhood," notably James Cagney. "It was a little sad, really. Cagney was completely paralyzed, and they brought him on in this throne." He also admitted to "a tremendous gaffe" while waiting to go on.

> Myrna Loy came up to me and said hello like somebody who had known me all her life. I was taken a little off guard and answered with a very stiff "How do you do?" I didn't recognize her. She was so frail and old.

Relatively brief as they have been, Mastroianni's visits have usually generated the kind of publicity that the backers of his latest film counted on, and then some; in Lemmon's words: "I can't name another actor anywhere who has had more stills of his work show up in the papers." In one especially publicized—and overdramatized— incident, during an October 1977 interview with Sophia Loren on the "Dick Cavett Show," he blithely tested the censorship limits of the Public Broadcasting System (PBS). In an attempt to get away from the main purpose of the interview, which was tub-thumping for *Una Giornata Particolare*, Cavett broached the inevitable theme of Mastroianni as the Latin Lover.

> CAVETT: What is a Latin Lover?
> LOREN: It's Marcello Mastroianni.
> CAVETT: So you're a Latin Lover.
> MASTROIANNI: To be a Latin Lover, you must be first of all a great fucker.
> CAVETT: A what?
> MASTROIANNI: Fucker.
> LOREN: A machine for making love.
> MASTROIANNI: Yes. To be a Latin Lover, you have to be infallible. I'm not infallible. I often fall into *fallo*.

The actor's cross-lingual pun on the Italian word *fallo* (which can mean both "failure" and "phallus") got lost in the miniuproar over his use of the undesirable six-letter word on television. Not only did the *New York Post* leap to a predictable tabloid coverage of the exchange; the *New York Times* deemed it worthy of an editorial reassurance that the republic, shaken as it might have been, still stood. Most ludicrous of all was the reaction of PBS and its WNET outlet in the New York metropolitan area. While WNET program head Robert Kotlowitz ducked reporters behind the excuse that he needed to "review the tape thoroughly," Chloe Aaron, vice-president for PBS programming, stooped to claim that Mastroianni had "meant to say 'worker' and mispronounced it."

Any doubt that the actor had known perfectly well what he was saying was dissipated a short time later when, after conceding that he had been annoyed by the attention his remarks had received in the United States, he told *Il Corriere della Sera*: "I'm half-impotent, and they're always asking me about the Latin Lover. So when they insist, I figure I have the right to come back at them with some punches of my own."

For the most part, however, the counterpunching hasn't been all that effective. Even at the beginning of 1993, during a promotional tour for *Used People,* the sixty-eight-year-old actor found himself answering the same questions about the Latin Lover.

> In Los Angeles alone, I had to do more than forty interviews in three days, and not a single one of those people skipped the Latin Lover nonsense. On the "Tonight" show with Jay Leno, he even started making a ridiculous point about whether I had ever kissed Fellini. Is that all that's in the heads of these people?

Saying *fuck* on television hasn't been his only defense.

> When I'm really weary of having to answer the same thing about the Latin Lover, I start thinking to myself that the person asking me that question is really insane. He *has* to be insane because just looking at me should tell him it's an idiotic thing to ask. So I go along with the questions and answers, all the time thinking to myself that as soon as this person walks out of my hotel room, he's going to be grabbed by two people in white coats, and while I'm off eating dinner with my friends, he'll be in a padded cell.

Such experiences as his promotional tour for *Used People* represented only the latest confirmation for the actor that Los Angeles was not his kind of city.

> My first impressions thirty years ago are still more or less intact. I'm a night person, I like to go to a restaurant with friends in the eve-

ning. In Los Angeles, though, you either have everybody boarded up in their houses with signs warning that the owners are armed and will shoot trespassers, or you have restaurants overflowing with actors. The last thing in the world I want to run into in the evening is an actor who's going to start talking about films or acting. As far as I'm concerned, that's my job in the daytime. At night, I want to talk about politics or women or sports, *anything* but movies and acting. That's why I've always preferred New York. It's a European city, not an industry town where you always run into coworkers.

Another subject that has made Mastroianni somewhat edgy during his trips to America—one that he has been asked about constantly—is the indebtedness of such Italian-American filmmakers as Martin Scorsese and Francis Coppola to the European backgrounds of their families. As he told *Attenzione,* a monthly with a large Italian-American readership, in 1981:

> I've always thought that too much was made of the Italian origins of these Americans. The idea has been abused, you know? An individual is shaped by the environment in which he grows up, by the education he receives, by the place where he lives. I'm just a little uncomfortable with people who look at a film by Scorsese and start snorting about how "all these so-called American films are really Italian films." That kind of exaggeration sounds too nationalistic to me.

Not coincidentally, the actor has been an elusive quarry for such influential lobbying groups as the National Italian-American Foundation, which has used an annual dinner in Washington to honor such Italian personalities as Loren, Fiat boss Giovanni Agnelli, and various prime ministers and foreign dignitaries. According to one foundation official,

> He's usually begged off for scheduling reasons, but I'm beginning to think that it is more than that. I think he prefers attention being paid to his work more than to himself.

Mastroianni's answer has been simpler.

> It seems odd to me that a person should get an award for the accident of where he happened to be born. If that's all it takes, everybody should get a night out and some nice parchment to hang on his wall. Maybe that kind of thing is important in the United States. It isn't to me.

15

Close-up:
The Italian Export

In the United States, Olivetti business machines, Chianti, and Marcello Mastroianni have been among the most visible symbols of Italy over the past few decades. The major difference among them is that whereas a conspicuous number of Americans have fingered Olivetti keyboards and drunk red wine, an appreciably smaller group has ever seen Mastroianni actually at work. In fact, leaving aside the dubbed and nationally distributed comedies that he made with Loren in the 1960s, most of the actor's films have been confined to art theaters in a handful of big cities and to film clubs on university campuses. Moreover, it is an exceptional evening when any television station—whether network, local, or cable—programs his pictures. Among European performers over the last half of the century, probably only Brigitte Bardot has attained comparable public recognition from people who have seldom munched popcorn while seeing what all the fuss was about.

Much of Mastroianni's notoriety in the United States has stemmed, of course, from such secondary sources as magazine and newspaper articles, appearances on television talk shows, and—attesting to the influence of the first two forums—comedians' monologues. It hasn't hurt, either, that once pronounced for the uninitiated, the actor's name glides from the tongue with the sibilant bravado of a skier proud of how he is negotiating the rises and falls of smooth slopes. As he would be the first one to appreciate, there is often an ironic hurdle to his name when it issues from an American mouth—a hurdle that owes as much to the very sound as to the persona behind it. As he has never appreciated, on the other hand, the ironic intonation has fed off the media image of the Latin Lover, sugfjgesting that maybe there is something a little *too* perfect about his name.

The greater impact of Mastroianni's public image over that of his actual work in the United States cannot be put entirely at the door of the actor's refusal until 1991 to work for Hollywood, thereby presumably forsaking vaster American audiences. By his own testimony, seconded by the recorded experiences of forerunners from Carminati to Gassman, the parts offered to him prior to *Used People* had the same Latin Lover slant and would have only consolidated on the screen what has been conveyed by the print and television media. Nor is there enough of an explanation in the infamous timidity of American distributors to circulate any foreign film, with or without Mastroianni, to audiences in the hinterlands. That might explain the lack of familiarity with his work, but it does little to illuminate the reasons behind the perduring celebrity that has separated the actor from dozens of other European performers whose most important film efforts have been weighed down by too many festival awards and have sunk in New York harbor.

In his more philosophical moments, Mastroianni has attributed the thriving of his Latin Lover image not only to the public relations machinery of the film business and to his own open squiring of some of the world's most prominent actresses but also to a fundamental American romanticism about the amatory preoccupations of Italians and Spaniards, especially. A standard synonym for this kind of romanticism is stereotyping, with the Latin Lover often only a euphemism for gigolo. That Mastroianni has rarely played such a role—and when he did, that it was in films that did not even get as far as the art houses of Manhattan or San Francisco—is neither here nor there; in the final analysis, even the stereotype of the gigolo has been secondary to a much more inclusive one concerning the actor as a Latin—the image of the Italian (or Spaniard) as not a particularly serious person.

Needless to say, Mastroianni's own characteristically bemused observations about love and life have suited this predisposition perfectly. Within such a context his small ironies about himself and others have gained rather than lost something in translation, reinforcing the stereotype. Every time that he has opened his mouth to flout his failures or inadequacies, to disclaim a gravity about his profession, or to ridicule the metaphysical significance of his latest romance, he has left himself vulnerable to the judgment that he lacks the sobriety that an adult is supposed to exhibit—left himself vulnerable not only personally but also as a representative Italian. His declarations have all been fodder for a preconception that, among other things, has little room (and even fewer movie screens) for such other Italian images as might be gleaned from the volcanic steamings of Volonté's characters, the acid misanthropies of Tognazzi's, or the stymied rectitudes of Manfredi's—not to mention for Mastroianni's own artistic forays into emotional zones of the kind in one part or another. In this connection, De Laurentiis wasn't completely wrong when, following the success of *La Dolce Vita* in the United States in the early 1960s, he tried to launch Sordi as an international star, reasoning that the actor's persona as a braying mama's boy who was too maladroit to have his haughtiness or cynicism taken seriously might enjoy regular success with a predisposed American public if promoted ambitiously enough. As it turned out, the producer could never find the appropriate script for Sordi to give America what he assumed it was accustomed to; worse for De Laurentiis, he had no part in forming the Latin Lover image of Mastroianni that ended up proving even more accommodating to stereotypical expectations on a media image level than specific roles for Sordi on the motion-picture screen might have.

The accommodation factor in Mastroianni's American popularity hardly obtrudes from the general picture of a disorganized but genial Italy that has been presented to the United States for some time, most markedly since the conclusion of World War II. In fact, if there has been a constant in official American views of Italy over the past four and a half decades, it has been that the country is a caldron of political, economic, and social crises that have prevented it from being the equal of "serious" European nations such as France and Germany. Seldom noted is the interests of various American circles to propagate such an image.

Politically, for instance, there is the so-called joke of the Rome governments that have been assembled and disassembled with almost annual regularity since the late 1940s. What the laughter has disguised here has been the practical perpetuation in power of the corruption-ridden but pro-Washington Christian Democrats, for whom cabinet shake-ups have largely meant moving from one lucrative administrative fiefdom to another, then back again. The most classic case in point has been that of frequent prime minister and frequent foreign minister Giulio Andreotti, a Christian Democrat who was wielding considerable authority in Italy even before American voters had gotten around to elect Harry Truman president. If this amounts to government instability, as sighing commentators in the *New York Times* and *Washington Post* are wont to describe it, then ruling stagnation must have switched its public identity.

Economically, Italy has come in for ritual U.S. snickering because of production inefficiencies that have proven ruinous to some of its largest companies and budget deficits that have periodically threatened to reduce the value of the lira to that of Monopoly money. What has made these problems more endearingly pathetic than identical difficulties on the North American continent, it appears, is the inability of Italy to throttle its trade unions, which have not yet gone the way of American air controllers. Indeed, if there is one folkloristic rite at which Italy excels, it is the labor strike—an anachronism that seems to stop being amusing only when too many tourists complain that they can't get their continental breakfasts, mail their postcards, and visit their museums on time.

Socially, there are any number of Italian customs that attest to a pleasant but basically frivolous, feckless people; these run the gamut from the midday siesta to the lengthy evening meal, from the myriad national holidays to the rival regional contentions that there is no such thing as a nation to be celebrated. While some pressure groups in the United States fret about all Italian Americans being written off as soldiers of the Cosa Nostra and others still deny that there is even such a thing as a Mafia, the Italians are routinely depicted as being powerless before a provision of the natural law assigning Sicily to mafiosi hoods. Also in the realm of "they were too weak to be serious," some dabblers in Italian history would even promote the notion that coming from the land that they did, the Brown-shirted goons who tortured opponents under Mussolini weren't quite as nasty as the Blackshirted goons doing the same thing at the time in Nazi Germany, presumably because they sang the more ariose lyrics of Verdi rather than the Götterdämmerung notes of Wagner while turning the thumbscrews.

The Latin Lover's place in such a tableau has been fixed for some time, going back long before the notorious U.S. senator who fumed that the Italians weren't dedicated enough to reconstruction to use some of their Marshall Plan funds to restore the Colosseum. Being both appealing (suave, virile) and weak (faithless, hypocritical), his has always been a reassuring presence for those loath to admit their own delight in transient adventure. If Mastroianni has brought anything new to the table, it has been the timing of his projected image—the launching of his stardom in the very years that Italy as a whole was being marketed, politically and economically as much as touristically, as a distraction that one would rather visit than live in. More than that, the image itself acquired an unprecedented abstract power for a generation that, if not exactly sedentary, came to surrender an increasing share of its sense of community to image makers. In this sense, not having the opportunity to see Mastroianni actually at work consolidated the Latin Lover image in two different ways: not only by excluding the possibility of different perceptions of the actor but also by deepening dependence on the figure represented by the secondary media and accepting the truth of it for its own sake.

How important have American cultural perceptions about Italy been in this process? One suggestive answer might be found in the case of another Italian Latin Lover whose professional and private life seemed to satisfy all the prerequisites—and then some—for vast popularity in the United States. He was a well-known continental actor. He was photographed constantly in the company of noted motion-picture actresses. He worked in Hollywood. He had a headline-making affair with the most famous of all American actresses and then dropped her. When he wasn't making films, he was recording love ballads. For all that, however, he never became an orchestra and balcony favorite. Some said that it was because he looked too serious and was far too articulate about his left-wing political ideas. For sure, it was true that the Tuscan-born Yves Montand was always identified as French, not Italian.

16

Organizers and Victims

If Mastroianni's first trip to America gave him a glimpse of the way stars could be treated, Fellini's *8½* was a reminder of his own conception of the actor's function vis-à-vis the film director. More radically than ever with *8½*, in fact, he became enwrapped in a filmmaker's idiosyncratic vision, with himself as its physical contours. It was an experience that he would always describe as "the truest thing that I ever did."

8½ was actually nothing more than an opus title referring to the fact that Fellini had previously directed seven features and a segment of another. The project arose from the director's long creative block in coming up with another screen subject; when all else failed, he decided to make a film about the block itself. For all that, he has never been too patient with questions about how autobiographical *8½* was intended to be or about suggestions that Mastroianni's character of Guido Anselmi was his fictional twin. Speaking with one interviewer, he declared:

> It's next to impossible for me to come out and say where the line was drawn in *8½*, where some personal facts stop and where you begin to get a portrait of an objective type. That kind of distinction doesn't interest me in the least, and I don't see the usefulness of trying to make it. When people say the film was autobiographical, I really don't know what to reply. I know only that my purpose was to deal with the life of a filmmaker who is going through spiritual anguish and confusion. If that's the character, what director would I have most logically been inspired by?

In the view of screenwriter Tonino Cervi, the trigger for *8½* was Carl Jung's *Memories, Dreams, and Reflections*. Cervi:

> One time, Fellini gave me a copy [of the Jung book]. . . . He had just discovered it a little bit before I did because, basically, he's as igno-

rant as I am. Afterward, I said to him: "[Ingmar] Bergman read this before you did, and he made *Wild Strawberries*. You've read it and you're doing *8½*." He got furious at me for saying that. He'd always felt that he was in some kind of competition with Bergman. But I think what I said is true.

For those accustomed to his expansiveness (detractors called it megalomania), it did not come as too much of a surprise that Fellini initially thought of two of the cinema's most accomplished actor-directors, Charlie Chaplin and Laurence Olivier, for the role of Guido. Although the Chaplin notion foundered soon enough on second thoughts about his advanced age, the pursuit of Olivier continued for some months. With Fellini himself customarily evasive on the subject, varying motives were attributed to the British actor for finally saying no: Some reports said that he was reluctant to absent himself from his recently gained post as creative director of Britain's National Theater Company; others, that he had lost whatever enthusiasm he might have had for the film when Fellini refused to give him a script. But not everyone believed that Fellini was determined to land Olivier in the first place. John Francis Lane, an American journalist based in Rome, recalled a trip that he made to London with Fellini to see Olivier.

> Afterward, Fellini said to me, "It must be very difficult to work with him." My own impression was that he knew all along that it was going to be Marcello and that his hunt for another actor was an elaborate deception. I think what was really going on was that he didn't have a clear idea of what *8½* was going to be, so he was trying to keep his backers at bay with all his talk of needing an actor like Olivier while he worked out the film in his head.

Mastroianni has also had his doubts that he was only the director's second or third choice.

> Federico didn't give up on Olivier just because he asked for the script, the way some people said. The reason was that he realized that Olivier was too "grand" an actor to give him what he wanted; he was simply too different from Federico himself. I resembled him much more—Catholic, weak, antihero.

The plot of *8½*, such as it is, revolves around the memories, fantasies, and practical torments of the director Guido as he goes through the motions of mounting a film in which he does not believe. His principal antagonists at his various levels of consciousness are women—his wife (Anouk Aimée), his mistress (Sandra Milo), and an ambitious actress (Madeleine Lebeau), among others. But equally pervasive are the "positive" characters all portrayed by Claudia Cardinale—the Ideal Woman, the actress named Claudia Cardinale, and the Ideal Woman that the actress Claudia Cardinale plays in Guido's film. Out of all his overlapping dreams, hallucinations, and objective struggles, the protagonist eventually sees his way to a concluding circus parade of every person he has ever known or imagined, the scene signaling resignation to his own fabulous perceptions of the human comedy as an energetic spectacle that is never staged too far away from a cemetery.

Although Mastroianni was the only member of the cast to go into 8½ with a full script, neither he nor Fellini attributed too much importance to it. For the actor, the key to interpreting the part of the director was his intimacy with Fellini and his own sense of well-being that once again, and perhaps even more so than he had in *La Dolce Vita*, he was able to play at an adult game. Betraying his own feeling that he was embarked on a role more biographical than Fellini cared to admit, he also gave greater emphasis than usual to the physical aspects of his character.

> Thanks to my familiarity with Federico, I was able to transfer to the screen all those elements that some people call autobiographical. It didn't take very much to get down some of his tics and faces. The main thing I had to do was to raise the timbre of my voice to make it more like his. My own voice is somewhat grave, and this annoyed him at the beginning. Overall, it was like playing one of those childhood games with a friend, where one of you says, "Okay, you're the cop, and I'm the robber. Let's go."

Fellini's view of Mastroianni's role also laid stress on some physical refinements.

> Not even Marcello knew exactly what the film was, even after we had discussed it at great length. What he gave me most of all, and what I will always be grateful for, was his complete trust and friendship. With that, and his ability to go right to the heart of whoever he plays, his character grew from hour to hour. If he complained about anything at the start, it was that I insisted he lose some weight and look a little older than he was through a few makeup touches. The role was of a man being eaten alive by his neuroses, so I thought that called for somebody who didn't look like he had just gotten up from the table after a sumptuous lunch. The aging effect wasn't to make him resemble me more (after all, I'm only a couple of years older than he is), but to dull that perennial look of his of the endearing, sweet boy from Frosinone. I didn't want him coming off that *simpatico*.

Despite Fellini's reputation as an actor's director, other members of the cast didn't get off so easily. Milo, for one, confessed to being both lost as to what she was supposed to be doing and exhausted by the director's endless takes of her scenes. She said it was Mastroianni who got her through the first difficulty.

> There has never been a greater co-worker than Marcello. I was so intimidated by Fellini, did not have the slightest idea of what I was doing half the time, but Marcello kept saying, "Stop worrying about it. You were great. Wait and see if you don't win a Nastro d'Argento for this." I thought that it was just something that he was saying out of kindness to relax me, but I *did* win it!

Because Fellini wanted her to look as different as possible from the wife character played by the thin Aimée, Milo had to put on ten to twelve pounds for the part of the mistress.

> He practically spelled out a diet for me. It bothered me, but I didn't say anything. I knew going in that Fellini was one of those people who devours everyone around him. They say he's an actor's director, and maybe he is, but except for Marcello, who has a far more personal relationship with him, every actor who has ever worked for him has become something of a Federico Fellini creature. So I fell, too, and put on the weight because he made it sound so essential. Then, the first day that I had to go before the cameras, I showed up already pretty nourished, and it's a scene of Marcello and me eating. All Fellini said to me was, "Okay, Sandrina, you eat, drink, talk, eat some more, drink some more, talk some more." We did that damn scene sixteen times, and after the last seven or eight takes I had to throw up from all the food and drink. Finally, with my sixteenth chicken leg, I told him I couldn't do it anymore, and we stopped. The next morning, we go to see the rushes, and at the end of all those sixteen takes, Federico goes, "Let's do it again!" I almost had a heart attack then and there. But by an act of God or something, we ended up doing it only twice more before he was satisfied.

As Mastroianni had been in *La Dolce Vita*, Cardinale remained most impressed by the difference between working for Fellini and for Visconti, for whom she was then also shooting *Il Gattopardo* (The Leopard).

> 8½ was the first time that I used my own voice on the screen, that I wasn't dubbed by somebody else afterward. Long before we began shooting, Fellini would call me up and get me talking about my character at great length. It was only when we began shooting that I realized that the things I had said on the phone had become my dialogue. . . . He made everything seem to come out as though by accident. It was absolutely the opposite of working with Visconti, where everything was planned down to the last detail.

But for the American journalist Lane, Fellini's treatment of Milo was far more typical than the director's relationship with the admiring Mastroianni or Cardinale.

Maybe Marcello doesn't notice it because he's got a special relationship or because he thinks he can smooth over Fellini's excesses by offering his own encouragement to the people he's acting with. But if you talk to the people who've worked with Fellini over the years, you'll discover that a lot more of them were destroyed by his chaotic way of working than were helped along in their careers. The only actors he doesn't bother are stars like Mastroianni, who love him and who, at bottom, could get along without him, anyway.

For all the personal support she received from Mastroianni while doing 8½, even Milo has admitted that she was exasperated by the actor's relationship with the director.

They really got along like an older and a younger brother. Marcello was always listening to whatever Federico said like the young brother who has nothing but admiration for his older brother. As far as Marcello was concerned, Federico was God, the gospel. I love Federico, too, but I never really liked Marcello's attitude toward him. You can love somebody as a friend and a fellow artist, but that shouldn't prevent you from judging him, too, from saying what you don't like about him if that becomes a problem.

For his part, Mastroianni has denied that there ever was a problem with Fellini on 8½ that might have called for a sterner attitude on occasion. Other comments he has made on the filming make it clear that his approach to the character of Guido the director left him very vulnerable to Fellini's guidance, authoritarian or not, as the case might have been.

8½ was a sort of psychoanalytic session, almost a self-psychoanalysis, because Guido was the portrait of a man of my generation, of a sensible, intelligent man, a kind of illustrative antihero. He was a prototype of the forty-year-olds of the time, with all their fragility and confusion, a symbol of a generation that had nothing more to give. That kind of person is no longer of use to anyone. Now we need people with much clearer ideas than Guido had. But as far as the film itself was concerned, as something produced in the period in which it was, I think it was a beautiful X ray.

Italian critical reaction to 8½ was divided among those who viewed it as Fellini's masterpiece and those who viewed it as a masterpiece of decadence to be lamented rather than praised. But even those who rejected the film as "a complete surrender to narcissism," as one reviewer put it, conceded that in terms of visual language it marked an advance on *La Dolce Vita* and the director's other works. With regard to Mastroianni, his performance was rated as being among the best of his career, with most of the quibbling coming over whether or not he had "done Fellini" as rapaciously as the director's own character might have warranted. Fellini's own cryptic remarks about the role of Guido notwithstanding, the uniform assumption was that the film was highly autobiographical. Criticism abroad was even more favorable, with many reviewers flattering Fellini more than they knew by deciding that 8½ was as much of a cinematic personal statement as any of the Swedish films of Ingmar Bergman. A minority of nays was led by *New Yorker* magazine critic Pauline Kael, who found the character of Guido not so much a film director as an idle dreamer who would have liked to have made movies. Among the numerous awards won by 8½ were the 1963 Oscars for Best Foreign Film and Best Costume Design for a black-and-white feature (Piero Gherardi); the picture had also been considered a favorite for Best Screenplay written directly for the medium but ended up losing out to the insipid but expensive *How the West Was Won*.

If Mastroianni has always cited 8½ among the handful of films that he is most proud of having made, his very next project, *I Compagni* (The Organizer), is also on the list. Based on a screenplay by director Mario Monicelli, Age, and Furio Scarpelli, the same trio that had been behind *I Soliti Ignoti*, *I Compagni* was set against the background of one of Italy's first industrial strikes, among textile workers in Turin toward the close of the nineteenth century. Shot in nearby Cuneo, the film cast Mastroianni as a radical professor who helps to organize the workers, then has to flee when a combination of imported scabs and the Italian militia doom the uprising. Although the professor shares some fugitive moments with a prostitute (Annie Girardot) who shelters him from the authorities, he goes off at the end dedicated to pursuing his mission as a revolutionary intellectual.

I Compagni had been written initially for Alberto Sordi, but he backed out when Monicelli refused to soften the professor's ideological character. Sordi had also objected to the shabby appearance of the protagonist; Mastroianni, in fact, goes through the film under a heavy coat, scarf, and hat, his face all but hidden under a beard and glasses. In the view of cowriter Age, the casting switch probably cost at the box office.

As well-known as he was, Mastroianni didn't have the automatic audience in Italy that Sordi did—people who always went to "a Sordi film" just because he was in it. On the other hand, Mastroianni made everything a lot more coherent from a dramatic standpoint. He fit the character beautifully, and he tackled the part with great enthusiasm.

Monicelli:

What Mastroianni did in that film was absolutely beautiful and, for somebody of his stature, very risky. He never tried to make the professor some kind of little saint. His professor was an intellectual who understands a great deal but who's a bit of a lost soul himself, somebody distracted and prone to error as much as anybody else. It is despite these human frailties, and here's where the drama is, that the professor comes to realize that what is really important is not the defeat of the moment but the long-range sense of union and solidarity. I don't think that there's any doubt that Marcello conveyed this.

Although most Italian critics joined Monicelli in applauding Mastroianni's performance, they were split on the film as a whole. In a period in which Fiat workers were on the verge of staging the most significant work stoppages in Italy since the end of World War II, left-wing journals shrugged off the picture as popularized history, owing its inspiration more to the need for the *commedia all'italiana* to find stronger subject matter than to a desire to throw an artistic light on the labor struggle. Less austere comment backed Monicelli's view that the film succeeded in its avowed purpose of portraying the professor and the Turin workers as having been defeated only temporarily. Given the union situation in Italy at the time, *I Compagni* stirred a great deal of political and editorial debate for months afterward. Age, for one, lamented the fact that more people ended up discussing the film than actually saw it.

If just the members of the left-wing parties in the country had bothered to see it, we would have had millions of spectators. As it was, not even the grandsons and relatives of the workers depicted in the picture went near it.

The film fared better abroad. In the United States alone, it won Italy another Oscar nomination in the category of Best Screenplay, was cited among the five best foreign pictures of the year by the National Board of Review, and helped to win Mastroianni a 1965 Golden Globe Award as World Film Favorite (Male). *I Compagni* also won over audiences in Britain, though only after nervous British distributors publicized it by ignoring Mastroianni's actual physical appearance in the film and plastering a stock shot of his unbearded face on posters. The distributors admitted that whatever the actor himself wanted to do, they were not ready to play around with his Latin Lover image.

Mastroianni's own estimate of the film was that it was "stupendous." He told one interviewer many years later:

> When it came out, nobody went to see it because the title, which was meant to be ironic, was taken seriously. A lot of people thought that anything called *The Comrades*, as it was in Italy and France, had to be something about the reds or about a Communist-Socialist way of seeing things. That immediately divided prospective viewers into two camps—the people who didn't want to see anything that they thought would glorify the Left, and the people of the Left who didn't trust Monicelli and us to be telling *their* story, supposedly, in a comedic vein. In the end, nobody at all went to see it when it first came out. Then, however, when it came out on television many years later, everybody went crazy for it. In other countries, I've never had that problem. People in America and Britain and France have always liked it. When they mention what they call *The Organizer* or *Les Camarades!*, it's always to praise it. It's really one of the postwar classics of Italian cinema.

The actor's next two projects—*Ieri Oggi Domani* (Yesterday, Today, and Tomorrow) and *Matrimonio all'Italiana* (Marriage Italian Style)—reunited him with Loren in familiar comedy territory; the third member of the 1950s triangle—De Sica—was also on hand as the director of both pictures. The films were an attempt by producer Carlo Ponti to rev up his wife Loren's stalled career and succeeded in that aim; in the United States, they were considered commercially viable enough to be dubbed into English and released on neighborhood circuits around the country rather than in the usual art houses catering to European productions.

If there was anybody skeptical about the aspirations of *Ieri Oggi Domani*, it was De Sica, who made no attempt to conceal the fact that he had taken on the project only after failing to find backing for a film of his own. Although Mastroianni also acknowledged the purely commercial calculations behind the productions, he was much more sanguine about the results, terming *Ieri Oggi Domani*, especially, "a pleasure from beginning to end." As it turned out, the film brought him a British Oscar, though some London opinion regarded the prize as equal recognition for his work in *I Compagni*.

Ieri Oggi Domani consisted of three tales that pitted Mastroianni and Loren in different roles as sex partners. The opening story, "Adelina," was written by Eduardo De Filippo, casting Loren as a contraband cigarette dealer in Naples who, though arrested regularly, stays out of jail by exploiting a law that prohibits pregnant women from being put behind bars for such minor offenses; Mastroianni was the sexually weary husband who has to keep up his end of the ploy. In "Anna," based on a short story by Alberto Moravia, Loren plays a rich Milanese wife who dallies with the far more humble Mastroianni before returning to her husband. The third tale, "Mara," was written by De Sica's longtime collaborator Cesare Zavattini and revolved around a seminarian's (Mastroianni) sexual awakening with a prostitute (Loren). While the Moravia episode was quickly forgotten, both the De Filippo and Zavattini tales became part of Loren-Mastroianni screen lore—the former because of the zaniness of the premise, the latter because of a well-publicized striptease by Loren and the reaction of the Mastroianni character to it. Loren, who had earlier suffered a miscarriage during the filming, admitted that the striptease scene was one of the most nerve-racking of her career and that she had been sick to her stomach for several days leading up to the shooting. As indelible as the actual striptease, however, was the reaction of the Mastroianni character when she abruptly ended her seduction with the announcement that she had decided that he was better off going back to the seminary; the actor's look of incredulity and the single line *"Cosa?"* (What?) at realizing that Loren wasn't going to shed the remains of her underwear was marked by many critics as one of the most exquisitely droll moments in Italian film comedy and had a great deal to do with the prizes he would win. Otherwise, *Ieri Oggi Domani* was generally seen as a successful commercial venture that, at the same time, confirmed De Sica's fall from his more ambitious days as the maker of such classics as *Ladri di Biciclette*.

In part because he knew that he was embarked on a similar box-office entertainment with *Matrimonio all'Italiana*, De Sica approached it moodily—a fact reflected in the letters that he wrote during production and that were subsequently collected in book form. Making matters worse, the film was plagued by illnesses to key cast members, necessitating a great deal of rescheduling to accommodate the absent; Mastroianni also had to take leave because of the death of his father-in-law, the composer Carabella. One of De Sica's letters sniped at the actor for being distracted, asserting: "Mastroianni would like to get away from it all. Where he is concerned, working is martyrdom." Another missive mocked the actor's habitually polite form of addressing his "uncle" in the third person and as *"Commendatore."* Near the end of production, the director admitted to another correspondent that the film had "aged me five years."

Matrimonio all'Italiana was based on *Filumena Marturano*, a 1947 comedy by the Neapolitan playwright De Filippo. In the title role, Loren played a prostitute who is hired by a businessman (Mastroianni) to double as his lover and his aged mother's maid. Many years pass, with Filumena holding on to the hope that the business-man will marry her. Instead, he announces his intention to marry someone else, whereupon she fakes a fatal illness and persuades him to marry her on her ostensible deathbed out of charity. When he real-izes that she has deceived him, he tries to get the marriage annulled, but she trumps that move by revealing the existence of three sons whom she has been supporting secretly for years, one of whom is sup-posedly the businessman's. After some futile attempts at identifying which of the boys is his, the Mastroianni character resigns himself to his wife and three children.

Most Italian critics wrote off *Matrimonio all'Italiana* as com-mercial fluff, not even bothering to lament De Sica's supposed decline, as they had with *Ieri Oggi Domani*. Most of the praise was reserved for Loren in her dominating role as Filumena—a fact that neither displeased nor surprised Mastroianni.

> Vittorio was really a tired man during the shooting. But he could still find the energy to protect Sophia. She had a very difficult role, and he did everything possible to make it easier for her. There was a great sense of mutual trust in the way they got along with one another. They understood each other's sense of humor; they had their deep bond of being Neapolitans.

Shortly after completing *Matrimonio all'Italiana*, Mastroianni expressed some interest in starring in Arthur Miller's *After the Fall* on the Italian stage. The more he explored the project, however, the more he realized that he was drawn to the subject matter (the main character is a thinly disguised Marilyn Monroe) rather than to the somewhat monotonous male protagonist. Around the same time, the French magazine *Paris Jour* published the results of a poll of fourteen internationally known actresses in which they were asked to name the actor with whom they most wanted to work. When Mastroianni emerged with the most votes (from onetime costars Loren, Cardinale, Aimée, and Girardot, as well as from Joanne Woodward), the Latin Lover publicity gained another wind, making the disgruntled actor more than ripe for Monicelli's *Casanova '70*.

In *Casanova '70*, Mastroianni played an Italian army officer attached to NATO who can perform sexually only when he feels that he is in danger. This complex leads him through a series of misad-ventures with the lovers and wives of military superiors, diabolical noblemen, and others dedicated to doing him harm. In the end, he narrowly escapes a murder conviction and is last seen going off with a woman (Virna Lisi) he can supposedly love without recourse to his sense of peril.

Although *Casanova '70* stirred only mild interest among Italian critics, with several of them suggesting that Mastroianni was slightly less than driven in the title role, the actor has always claimed a personal and cultural importance for the film.

> I've always liked the opportunity to demolish the image of the Italian Latin Lover. It really isn't a very pleasant label. In my traveling here and there, I've always come up against this image of the Italian as some kind of sexual bull or ram. Fine if it's true, but let's take a closer look to see if it is true. And even if there is something to it, wouldn't it be interesting to add to that quality a sensibility in Italians that foreigners rarely acknowledge? That's why I've always liked doing Italian characters who are vulnerable and fragile in love, who may love for its own sake more than some other people but who are nevertheless controlled by the psychological as much as the physical aspects of romance. Maybe not all Italians need the danger fantasies of a character like that in *Casanova '70*, but the film was made with the delicious intent of undermining that conventional image of the Italian as a ram or bull with nothing in his head.

The actor's next undertaking, Elio Petri's *La Decima Vittima* (The Tenth Victim), found him in the most unexplored of all Italian cinema territories—science fiction. The project also prompted some clashes between the actor and producer Ponti and a series of hard feelings and misunderstandings among the actor, the director, and several teams of screenwriters. The only thing that Mastroianni, Petri, and the writers agreed on at the end was that Ponti had been ultimately responsible for most of the conflicts and that *La Decima Vittima* emerged as a perfect example of what can happen to a good film when a producer decides he knows everything better than his cast and crew.

According to Petri, the idea of adapting Robert Sheckley's novel *The Seventh Victim* for the screen occurred to him in 1962, but without any supporting enthusiasm from a producer. Finally, in 1964, Mastroianni read the book, liked it, and brought the project to Ponti. That was the beginning of the trouble. Petri:

> Ponti didn't want to make a film with me, and he certainly didn't want to make a science-fiction picture. He never stopped sneering at the whole idea. But what he did want to do was make a picture with Marcello, so that seemed to carry the day. But he never stopped interfering. For months I worked with Tonino Guerra and Ennio Flaiano on the script, and in the meantime Ponti was paying other people to write adaptations. His methods would have broken

the spine of an elephant, and we were exhausted before we ever got to actually shooting.

At one point, Petri even accused Mastroianni of encouraging the rival scripts—an allegation denied by the actor.

We all had great problems with Ponti. This was a hallucinating story about a world in which, wars having been outlawed, these powerful people decide that a game of "hunter and victim" will satisfy the human need to kill. Ponti decided that was too grim and wanted everything done with more humor. This made everybody extremely uncomfortable, and at one point Elio had the idea that we were all ganging up on him to lighten the story the way Ponti wanted. That simply wasn't true. Where the real problem was, was that Ponti had promised the American distributors, without consulting any of us, that the story would have a happy ending. It was either that or no picture at all. What we had gotten into, in other words, was a typical case of the film *industry* overtaking everything else. So instead of the tragic story that Sheckley had written, we ended up making a bastard that pleased nobody. It was the classic case of a producer screwing up because he thought he knew better than an intelligent director like Petri.

The critics generally agreed that *La Decima Vittima* was neither fish nor fowl, though most of them blamed Petri for not being faithful to the book and took Mastroianni to task for appearing satisfied to play the protagonist with short blond hair rather than contributing a true performance.

Onscreen in *La Decima Vittima*, the actor's chief antagonist— but ultimate love—was played by Ursula Andress; offscreen, there was more love than antagonism between the two. The affair took place amid Mastroianni's resignation that he was not about to commit himself to anybody or anything. "Just once in my life, I would like to make a definitive decision," he could still say to a Swiss magazine many years later. "The few times I tried to do it, I stopped halfway. Especially when I was doing *La Dolce Vita*, I tried to find the courage to say to my wife, 'I'm leaving,' but I couldn't do it." People close to Andress said that the Swiss-born actress had few reservations about breaking off because she was primarily interested at the time in having a settled home and family.

Mastroianni's problems with Ponti on *La Decima Vittima* amounted to only a foretaste of his difficulties with the producer over his next commitment with director Marco Ferreri. A man who liked to parade his eccentricities and who would always appeal to the actor's instinct for risk as much as Fellini could tap the "boys' night out" side of his personality, Ferreri cast Mastroianni as a businessman who becomes obsessed with the question of how much pressure a balloon can take before it explodes. Under the working title of *L'Uomo dei Cinque Palloni* (The Man with the Five Balloons), the director had gotten about 80 percent through his allegory when Ponti stepped in to protest the film's denouement. (After finally exploding his balloon, the businessman goes to the window of his apartment and simply jumps out.) Upon further reflection, the producer decided that the entire film was an aberration and ordered a halt to production. This set into motion a totally new film and years of confusion about what had been made by whom when.

Mastroianni:

Ponti came to me one day after seeing what we had filmed and said he wasn't going to let it be released. "I can't allow something like this to circulate," he said. "It would cost me a fortune, and it would hurt you, too." But then, despite hating what he had seen, he tried to save what he thought could be saved by ordering the footage cut down to a sketch. Then he asked me to do two other sketches—one directed by De Filippo and the other by Luciano Salce—so he could package the whole thing as an anthology film. He told me he wanted to call it *Oggi, Domani, Dopodomani* (Today, Tomorrow, the Day After Tomorrow). That had nothing at all to do with the content, but it sounded like *Ieri Oggi Domani*, which had made him a lot of money.

The actor's response?

I thought to myself that it was crazy, but I was also counting on the fact that even in a mutilated version, Ferreri's piece would be much better than the other two, so I should stick with it. But I also said to him, "Okay, but *L'Uomo dei Cinque Palloni* is still the story of a suicide, so why don't we make the other two sketches also about suicide so we can have a coherent theme?" He looked at me like I was a lunatic. But I didn't drop the idea. I figured I had some maneuvering room with him because he wanted me so badly to fulfill obligations to distributors, so I asked Ferreri if he would mind if I approached Pasolini with the idea of three suicide sketches. Ferreri said fine, and Pasolini loved the idea. He wanted to do a sketch about the Roman Petronius Arbiter. He saw that as "a festive suicide." So I go running back to Ponti overwhelmed with my own genius and tell him that now that we have two brilliant directors, Ferreri and Pasolini, we only need to find another one of their stature to do something really original. He looked at me as though my brains had fallen out of my head. "Are you absolutely insane?" he screams at me. "If we did what you're suggesting, this film would have everybody in the country scratching his balls to ward off the evil eye! You can't release a picture about three suicides and expect people to come see it!"

Instead of by Pasolini and by two other suicide tales, *Oggi, Domani, Dopodomani* was filled out by two totally unrelated stories—"L'Ora di Punta (Rush Hour)," directed by De Filippo, and "La Moglie Bionda (The Blonde Wife)," directed by Salce. In "L'Ora di Punta," Mastroianni played a young scientist on the verge of a nervous breakdown who visits some married friends (Salce and Lisi) and ends up sitting around in terror as they go through a nightly brawl that always ends with the husband pulling a gun on the wife; the next morning, the scientist realizes that he has witnessed next to nothing, since the sound of machine-gun fire nearby indicates that every couple in the neighborhood engages in similar fights, and often more lethally. In "La Moglie Bionda," the actor was cast as a bank teller who attempts to sell his free-spending wife (Pamela Tiffin) to an Arab sultan but ends up in a harem himself.

Critical opinion was divided over whether the De Filippo or the Salce episode was the more stupid. On the other hand, as Mastroianni had foreseen, the Ferreri episode was treated far more benevolently, and there were several calls for Ponti to release the originally planned *L'Uomo dei Cinque Palloni*. At least immediately, this was small consolation for the actor, who was roasted for having lent his presence to the Ponti-inspired episodes. Moreover, the very image that he thought that he had been walking away from in doing the Ferreri film descended again, thanks to one of his costars. In a widely reprinted article that originally appeared in *Newsweek* in November 1965, Tiffin declared:

> I want you to put it in capitals that I am the first American actress to play opposite him, and I'm very proud of it. . . . He's really a hunk of a man. He's romantic, he's elegant, he's sensual, he's a Latin Lover, and yet he's a teddy bear, too. There's something cuddly about him. And that voice of his! It makes your bones vibrate!

Three years later, Ponti did indeed have a change of heart about the original project, advancing the money for Ferreri and Mastroianni to complete their film. Although there were a few minor script changes (the generic businessman became a candy manufacturer initially drawn to the balloons as a publicity gimmick), *L'Uomo dei Palloni* (The Man with the Balloons) maintained its nihilistic edge, with the protagonist's lover (Catherine Spaak) leaving him because of his obsession, the man bursting his balloon and jumping out a window, and everything ending on the cynical note of a passing motorist (Tognazzi) complaining that the suicide had chosen *his* car to land on. Despite his seeming conversion to finishing what Ferreri and Mastroianni had started, however, Ponti had still another change of mind and in 1969 was reluctant to release the film anywhere outside of France, where it was shown under the title of *Break-up*. It took another decade for it to be shown publicly in Italy, by which time it had become largely a cinematic curiosity. Its most ardent supporter was Moravia, who declared in his weekly *L'Espresso* column that *L'Uomo dei Palloni* was "a vivid portrait of the solitude of modern man," ranking it among the best work done by Mastroianni and Ferreri up to that juncture.

Mastroianni himself has never needed much encouragement to extol Ferreri.

> He's a man of few words, in fact, none. He gets tired explaining things, so he doesn't bother. It's up to the actor to grasp what is going on. Like Fellini, he assumes that the actor will understand the director's world immediately. I believe that he is one of the most interesting directors there is, and not just in Italy. He's always surprising you with his details, and he leaves an actor a lot of room to work. Not everything we've done together has been a success, but it's always been a creative experience.

With the distance of some years, the actor also became a little more philosophical about his differences with Ponti, as regards both the Ferreri project and *La Decima Vittima*.

> It's not that I've ever really disliked him in any way. After all, he gave me a lot of work, and I don't think anyone will deny that the things we filmed with Sophia worked out for everyone concerned. I suppose what I regard as his main defect is that he's one of those producers who believes he's the only one who knows anything. Mind you, this doesn't make him different from a lot of others; back in the 1960s, especially, there were a lot of little Mussolinis going around. Ironically, ever since television began to dictate everything in the 1970s, I've missed working with people like Ponti. At least with them, an actor or a director knew who the "enemy," if I can use that word, was. And don't forget that along with all the vulgar things they were responsible for, producers like Ponti were also behind many quality films.

In 1965, Alessandro Blasetti announced with no little fanfare that he had the creative energy to make only one more film. As his swan song, the never modest director said that he wanted to "teach a conclusive lesson about the damage caused by egoism . . . which is at the root of all hatred and violence in the world." With his valedictory tone, Blasetti had little trouble in rounding up a who's who of

Italian performers whom he had helped along the way: Mastroianni, De Sica, Lollobrigida, Mangano, Manfredi, and Walter Chiari. *Io, Io, Io . . . e gli Altri* (Me, Me, Me . . . and the Others), as the film was called, followed a journalist (Chiari) from one tale to another as he sought to confirm his presupposition that people looked out only for themselves. The biggest counterargument in the picture was offered by the character played by Mastroianni, a friend of the journalist's who still has the capacity to value the love between others and who, ignoring the danger to himself, tries to save a worker falling off a scaffolding, only to get killed for his efforts.

Given its commemorative feel, *Io, Io, Io . . . e gli Altri* found few Italian critics ready to bash it for its simplistic plot line, most of the commentary devoted to Blasetti's long career. Mastroianni adopted an equally polite stance, noting that he could have hardly said no to a director who had taken such a paternal interest in him at the start of his career. Even though Blasetti's retirement announcement turned out to be premature and he directed other films, *Io, Io, Io . . . e gli Altri* ended his working relationship with the actor.

17

Close-up: One of the Boys

M astroianni's feeling of security with his choice handful of Italian directors has not always been shared by fellow players,
least of all by the actresses with whom he has costarred. Especially
during the 1960s and 1970s, where he found psychological suste-
nance and creative incentive, many of them complained of finding
men too self-absorbed to realize that they were being abrupt, callous,
and even cruel. For Catherine Spaak, who costarred with Mastroianni in Marco Ferreri's *L'Uomo dei Palloni*, the working atmosphere was decidedly misogynist.

Spaak:

> I am sure that Ferreri does not like women. He behaves so
> strangely. One second his head is in the clouds; the next second he
> demands that you do the most absurd kind of thing. One time we
> were shooting on the thirtieth floor of a skyscraper, and he sud-
> denly ordered me to throw the script out the window. When I asked
> him why, he just yelled at me, "Do it! Do it!" He also had this rou-
> tine in the morning when you showed up for work. You were sup-
> posed to walk right up to him, and with this vague air of his, he
> would always say, "Angel, angel, come here to me," and everybody
> in the crew would immediately respond in chorus, "I can't because
> the devil is tempting me!" Only after we had gone through this little
> ritual could we start work.

Spaak's admitted feeling of humiliation resembled the reaction
of 8½'s Sandra Milo, who claimed that Fellini's often cavalier treatment of cast members other than Mastroianni, particularly of the
women, spoiled her satisfaction at winning awards for her performance in the motion picture. Longtime Rome-based newsman John
Francis Lane has been among those disputing Fellini's reputation as
an actor's director, asserting that the filmmaker took delight in ridiculing some of his players. According to Lane, Fellini was also insen-

sitive to the untenable situation that his working methods created for actress Barbara Steele during *8½*.

> At first, Barbara was very happy to be in *8½*. But then she realized that her contract not only said that she had to be available for a certain number of scenes but that she had to remain on call indefinitely and without pay for as long as the production took, just in case Fellini needed her again. She ended up having to stay in Rome for almost six months, during which time she couldn't accept other offers. When the film came out, her best scenes were on the cutting-room floor, and she practically disappeared from the industry. I'm not saying this was unique to Fellini, it's part of the Italian industry, but he's never lost a moment of sleep over people like Steele or ever had a reason to think about how his approach to work might affect other people.

To be sure, Ferreri and Fellini have never held a patent on directorial excesses, self-indulgence, or insensitivity. John Huston, to name only one of scores of directors, became notorious for macho games that left his stars stranded in perilous situations and for such brutal ploys as secretly replacing water with gin so that he could get a more convincing performance from an actor doing a drunk—even though the player in question was a recovering alcoholic. What is striking about the complaints of Milo and others, however, was Mastroianni's reputed habit of turning a blind eye to on-set tensions if his favorite directors were involved, sometimes even when he was the one who ended up paying the biggest price. For instance, while he said plenty—and none of it positive—about the largely inanimate character that he portrayed in *La Notte* for Antonioni, merely a professional acquaintance, he was all but mum about the idiotic roles that he did in *Oggi, Domani, Dopodomani* for Salce and De Filippo—the former an old friend whom he had known since the days of Visconti's stage company, the latter the master of the Neapolitan theater whom he revered. After *Adua e le Compagne* and *Fantasmi a Roma*, he swore never again to work with the fanatically meticulous Pietrangeli because of the director's mania for endless retakes, but he carried on stoically when close friend Fellini insisted on a comparable number of reshootings for many scenes in *8½*. In *La Notte*, he found it natural to strike an alliance of mutual grievances with Jeanne Moreau, but in *8½* he kept a diplomatic distance from Milo, giving her moral encouragement without confronting Fellini about some arduous situations in which he was as involved as the actress. To a significant extent, in other words, the actor's on-set behavior during the period was determined less by what he was asked to do than by who asked him to do it. When the request came from his immediate circle or from the older generation of filmmakers (Visconti, De Sica, Blasetti, De Filippo), with whom he acted like the *bravo ragazzo* of his earliest film roles, an open conflict was out of the question.

In his relations with producers, he has also generally avoided trouble, leaving money and contractual matters up to others. ("Who wants to get into all that back-stabbing business? You sit back, watch them go at one another, get a few laughs, and then go back to work.") One striking note over his lengthy career is the fact that he has been involved in only three films with the usually ubiquitous De Laurentiis. He has denied, however, that this anomaly has had anything to do with the distrust by other Italian actors over the years of some of the producer's financial associates. ("What—they never wondered about where the money of some other producers came from? If De Laurentiis had a good project, I don't see why I'd say no.") With Ponti, he has had brother-in-law–type squabbles that Loren's presence has prevented from degenerating too far; excluding the ambiguous results of the fight over *La Decima Vittima*, he was for a long time grateful enough for his success in the comedies with the actress to give the producer the last word, even on aberrations such as *Oggi, Domani, Dopodomani*. If there has been any other quid pro quo for his minimal professional resistance, it has been in occasional public twitting of Ponti, both as producer and as husband of his "sister" Loren. For his part, Ponti has seldom risen to the bait, generally exuding the same air of an older brother-in-law resigned to the antics of his wife's family.

At the crossroads of his career in the latter part of the 1950s, Mastroianni's most confident relationship among producers was with Franco Cristaldi, the youngest producer in the history of the Italian film industry when he did his first feature in 1953 at the age of nineteen; it was Cristaldi who oversaw *Le Notti Bianche, I Soliti Ignoti, Divorzio all'Italiana*, and *I Compagni*. With him, Mastroianni felt free enough to tempt friction on artistic and production matters, such as when nerves were being frayed over the unexpected costs of *Le Notti Bianche* and on the question of Petri's being allowed to direct *L'Assassino*. Although they later went their separate ways, Cristaldi once characterized his working relationship with Mastroianni as only the most publicized part of a deeper mutual trust. He told Italian television in 1984:

> After being in the film business for more than thirty years, I think that I can say with some experience that it is easy to find bad actors who are wonderful human beings and easy to find accomplished actors who are terrible human beings. That is where Marcello is the

exception, because he is both a great actor and a wonderful human being.

This testimonial notwithstanding, Cristaldi was still a producer whose priorities were not quite the same as those of the writers, directors, and actors with whom Mastroianni had begun spending his time as far back as the 1950s (although they would have been the first to deny any superior artistic airs). With the principal exception of the locally born Petri and actor Paolo Panelli, their common denominator was that they were bourgeois Romans only by adoption. This abetted their feeling of detachment toward the capital, making them more Roman than the Romans in their sense of irony about the life around them; at the same time, however, it helped to inure them to the enervating cynicism and most debilitating aspects of the *menefreghismo* (who-gives-a-damn attitude) evident in wide swaths of Roman society. If they were all attracted to motion pictures through individual ambitions, abilities, and opportunities, it was equally true that the milieu of the industry was ideal for satisfying the outsider's instinct to create something of a manageable Rome of his own—the one employed constantly as a film location amid the normal comings and goings of residents, merchants, politicians, and tourists. In this, Mastroianni's lament about sometimes having to work in the artificial atmosphere of a studio such as Cinecittà was not just a job complaint but a protest against not being allowed to appreciate the city as he (and his intimates) had become accustomed to appreciating it. Conversely, Fellini's impulses toward abstracting Rome in *La Dolce Vita* could not be satisfied by simply shooting real streets in a conjectural fashion (since he already assumed that this was the only way to see the concrete Rome) but required major construction work at Cinecittà.

Like Mastroianni, the contemporaries who were closest to him had been tried by Fascism and World War II without having been traumatized by it. All of them preferred the 20th Century–Fox and Paramount Americans who had fueled their dreams during Mussolini's reign to the Marshall Plan Americans who arrived in Italy after the war to manipulate the corruption-ridden and repressive Christian Democratic governments and would seldom be able to refer to America for the rest of their lives without using a tone that was an uncomfortable mix of exhilaration, dejection, and scorn. If they were not all registered members of the Italian Communist party (the country's largest and most organized opposition force), they were still far more apt to vote as independents for the Communists than as sympathizers for the watered-down Socialist and Social Democratic parties, both of which were implicated in almost as many scandals and

CIA-inspired operations as the Christian Democrats. Intellectually resistant to the censorship laws that were clamped down on the film industry, they were inevitably involved as actors, directors, writers, or producers in the films that were most responsible for eroding the power of the restrictive statutes.

If there were lean stretches here and there, they generally worked a lot. Not only were they talented in their given fields; they seemed to pose none of the commercial problems to money people that the neorealist directors (Rossellini, for example) did by making films that rarely circulated beyond art theaters. The payoff was that when they weren't shooting something, they were making plans to film or talking to media interviewers about work that had just been released. They also worked a lot *together*. Many times, work amounted to the practical development of ideas initially swapped over a restaurant table; just as frequently, the creative package put together for a production included not merely above-the-line acting, directing, and writing talent but also the behind-the-scenes people (Mastroianni's brother, Ruggero, for example, had become one of the most sought after editors in the industry) close to the circle or its individual members.

But perhaps most important of all, Mastroianni and his friends fed off similar fantasies—the fantasies of mid-century Italian males (and they were almost exclusively that) who had broken through the bankruptcies of Fascism's sexual pomposities, of the Madonna-or-whore alternatives of the church and its secular publicists, and of the predicated genderlessness of political class action but who had not found a substitute ideological repository for them. Their quest for that substitute—mirrored in all their major films of the 1960s and early 1970s—led them in many directions. For Fellini, the road was that of the psychocentric mythology suggested by Jung; Madonnas were still Madonnas, and whores were still whores, but as grotesque nightmare and hallucinatory anguish in which nobody was more awake than anybody else. For Ferreri, the path was primal allegory in which women were reduced initially to apes (as in *La Donna Scimmia*, or The Ape Woman) and then the apes themselves became love objects (as with *Ciao Maschio*, or Bye Bye Monkey), while men were viewed as becoming one with either their solipsistic obsessions (the balloons in *L'Uomo dei Palloni*) or the commodities provided toward such an end (eating themselves to death in *La Grande Bouffe*). Petri, the most logically explicative of the group, took the more direct tack of political commentary, correlating sexual complexes and ideological choices in such films as *Indagine su un Cittadino al di Sopra di Ogni Sospetto* (Investigation of a Citizen Above Suspicion), leaving himself vulnerable to attacks from both the Italian Left establish-

ment and Movement radicals in the United States and other countries, the latter of whom ridiculed his seemingly simplistic discovery.
Subsequently, Scola stressed the same fusion of sexuality and ideology, although usually more as a historian than as a driven social
critic.

As a performer, Mastroianni's articulation of fantasies was, on
one level, much more circumscribed than that of his director friends,
who exercised ultimate visionary control over their work. In fact, the
most popular fantasies associated with his screen endeavors were
those brought to movie theaters by audiences and reinforced by tabloid segments of the media—the actor as the Latin Lover. But if Mastroianni regularly dismissed that perspective as a stereotype having
nothing to do with him, he also willy-nilly established a discernible
pattern in his choice of roles, in his professional behavior in the
course of rendering them, and in his public analyses of them that
indicated an emotional and intellectual challenge similar to that
faced by the Fellinis, Ferreris, and Petris. As he told the *Herald Tribune* in 1962:

> Our generation is stuck at a crossroads and going two ways—or at
> least looking two ways. We have our roots in the past and we walk
> in modern streets. From the past we carry many questions about
> values given us as truths which are not workable truths. They are
> part of the useless baggage of life.

The actor's biggest step in trying to articulate the state of his fantasy world was the most obvious one: making himself available for
the projects of his friends, no matter how dissimilar they were in
their approaches to illuminating a crisis that, while undoubtedly also
spiritual, political, social, and moral (even zoological, according to
Ferreri), was especially one of imagination. If the directors betrayed
differing psychological, allegorical, and social-political propensities,
he showed himself more than willing to adapt to any one of them in
the given character of the moment. That he was seldom out of place
in such disparate visions—but was, on the contrary, usually lauded
as their total incarnation—attested not only to his histrionic gifts and
to the artistic rapport that he had with the filmmakers but also to the
commonality of their quest under various guises for solid imaginative ground. By Mastroianni's own evaluation of his most significant
characters during the first decade or so of his stardom, his chief contribution was personifying the antihero—the man essentially stymied by his fantasy landscape and whose strivings, whatever the
specific emotional color or resolution of a role, were motored by a
profound exasperation. Even when that exasperation was not explicitly equated to a particular character's relations with women,

women—in everything from the murder victim in Petri's *L'Assassino* to the gallery of female archetypes in Fellini's *8½* to Casanova's accumulated paramours of the past in Scola's *La Nuit de Varennes* (That Night at Varennes)—were at least an emblematic occasion for crisis. What was constant, as the actor tried so frequently and so futilely to explain to whoever would listen, was not the Latin Lover but the Latin who didn't feel free enough to love, the Latin damned even at his most energetic to being only a Latin Rover over a daunting human terrain.

Fortunately for Mastroianni, there was much more to his fantasy world than this; if there had not been, his versatility and resilience as an actor might have dried up as soon as he had shot his last scene for Antonioni in *La Notte*. As fundamental as they were in his films, even the women characters of *L'Assassino*, *8½*, *La Nuit de Varennes*, and so many others belonged to only one of his imaginative spheres. Coexisting with it was the second fantasy world *of* the films, of the adult playgrounds of the movie sets that he has never been reluctant to call the best part of working in motion pictures. If the landscape within his films was all existential exasperation, comic or dramatic frustration, the tableau around the films was, in the best of instances, just the opposite—precise guidance and clear direction. At times, the actor has contended that, as with *La Notte*, an insufferable set and an insufferable film were the two sides of the same coin; on other occasions, most notably on Fellini and Ferreri productions, he has credited the atmosphere of the set with being primarily responsible for a well-rounded performance.

In entering *both* fantasy worlds with his commitment to a project, the actor effectively precluded his involvement in any third world of artistic tensions and abuse. He could not afford the further perspective. As much as he had steeped himself in an antihero character of a film story before the start of actual film shooting, he had also immersed himself in the role of the actor who was going to enjoy what he was doing because he was able to count on a director able to play one fantasy world off against the other. Even his widely reported (and self-confessed) habit of coming out of character the instant a director yelled "Cut!" after a take amounted to coming out of only one of his characters; in his ability to go immediately from a wrenching dramatic scene to a catnap or a snack while the next setup was being prepared, he in fact remained within his second character as the totally secure performer for whom the set was a fantasy world unto itself. As the chief designer of both of these worlds, the director, once given trust in undertaking a project, was not only not to be challenged over some external consideration but wasn't even seen externally.

For their part, the directors, at least the slyest of them, did everything possible to strengthen their image in Mastroianni's eyes, making even their deepest probings into his emotional reserves seem like a mutual conspiracy against both the *business* of filmmaking and the transitory importance of the character that he happened to be doing for them. If the actor could describe his experiences with Fellini on 8½ as a psychoanalytic process, it became clear in other stories about all-night toots and abrupt outings to look up people they hadn't seen in years that it was one in which the role of the couch was analyzed as much as the character of Guido. If he could note with admiration Ferreri's aversion ever to saying anything, it was because the director's eccentricities never seemed more explicable than within the pliable dimensions of his adult playground.

The impact of such trust on Mastroianni's screen work was double-edged. On the one hand, it generated swells of internal freedom, translated through his rich and varied recitative abilities, for characters that, on the surface, were anything but free, especially with women characters. On the other hand, it consolidated his place as one of the boys, one of the adopted Romans who would always need another creative venture to continue across the ruins of the fantasy world of mid-century Italian males.

18

Lovers and Strangers

If there were two running motifs in Mastroianni's public remarks in the first half of the 1960s, they were his ridiculing of the Latin Lover image solidified by *La Dolce Vita* and his proclaimed disinterest in the theater. Thus, there were a few snickers in March 1965 when he announced his intention of returning to the stage in a musical centered around the life of Rudolph Valentino.

For Mastroianni, however, there wasn't that much of a contradiction.

> If anything, Valentino was made into a parody as the Latin Lover. The subject could hardly be approached solemnly. But why he mainly interested me was because he was an actor, and that was a role that I hadn't really done before. That was really the only thing that we had in common.

But there was in fact more than that involved for the actor. To begin with, he had been anything but happy with his film roles since *Ieri Oggi Domani*, and the scripts sent to him would have had him repeating either the handsome, apathetic intellectuals of *La Notte* or the crazed barons of *Divorzio all'Italiana*. For another, he had overcome a years-long dread of appearing in public as a song-and-dance man by doing an Italian television variety show.

> There were these twins, the Kessler sisters, and we did a little soft-shoe thing, and I loved it. Since I had been a kid, I'd always admired Fred Astaire, and there I was doing something exactly like him!

In fact, the self-confidence carried over to his viewing of Valentino films and his first rehearsals for *Ciao, Rudy* in the fall of 1965.

> The interesting thing was that as far as being a great dancer was concerned, Valentino was no big deal. All you ever see in those old films is a whoosh here and a whoosh there, and it's all over. I really think he was a worse dancer than I am.

171

As a final expression of his interest, Mastroianni put up about half of the estimated $240,000 needed to mount the production. It had the promise of a shrewd investment at the time.

> Staging Broadway-type musicals in Italy was a very rare thing, and it was hard to attract investors. We thought that with me in there financially as well as in the play, it would be easier to get things going. There was also talk of taking the play abroad if it worked out, and that would have made us a profit fairly quickly.

It didn't quite work out that way. When *Ciao, Rudy* opened at Teatro Sistina in Rome on January 7, 1966, the book by Sandro Garinei, Pietro Giovannini, and director Luigi Magni was generally rapped for being too indecisive between comedy and drama, while Armando Trovaioli's score elicited only a tepid response. A number of critics praised Mastroianni's Rex Harrison–like presence as an actor who sang-recited his way through the show, giving him even higher marks for his footwork, but even they concluded that he had devoted more energy to his role than the part or the play warranted. A smaller segment of reviewers thought the entire venture was ill conceived and the actor too wooden by half. Potential agreements for moving the production to New York and London died in the early negotiation stages, as did another plan to adapt it to film. After a three-month run in houses usually filled to capacity by Mastroianni's popularity, he bought his way out of a longer contractual commitment and hung up his tango heels.

For all that, the actor has always insisted that *Ciao, Rudy* was important to him in terms of expanding his horizons. "I enjoyed myself madly," he said. Costar Raffaella Carrà also took away positive memories of the actor's commitment to the project. Carrà said, laughing, some years later:

> When we began rehearsals, there was a little bit of apprehension because he was Marcello Mastroianni, the star. But once he arrived, there were no problems at all. He was so incredibly disciplined, going through all the routines over and over again like somebody in the chorus. You could tell that he had had a great deal of theatrical training. And he was really enthusiastic about doing what to him was new—the singing and the dancing, the big production numbers.

The films that Mastroianni made around the time of *Ciao, Rudy* were very much a mixed bag artistically but involved him with some of the most important people in his life.

His oddest venture in the period was *The Poppy Is Also a Flower*, an American-financed production with vague sponsorship ties to the

United Nations and to that body's efforts to stamp out international drug cartels. Supposedly inspired by an "idea" by Ian Fleming and directed by Britain's Terence Young, *The Poppy Is Also a Flower* starred normally subordinate players Trevor Howard and E. G. Marshall as two UN agents who track a heroin shipment from the Near East to various European cities before they finally unmask the ringleaders of the traffic (Gilbert Roland and Anthony Quayle). Mastroianni was in a couple of scenes in the role of a Naples-based Italian representative for Interpol; like several other cameo performers (Yul Brynner, Omar Sharif, Rita Hayworth, Stephen Boyd, Eli Wallach), he contributed his services gratis on behalf of the avowed propaganda purposes of the film. That purpose was not especially clear to critics on either side of the Atlantic. They wrote off *The Poppy Is Also a Flower* as nothing more than a high-minded cops-and-robbers show and as a dim reflection of the postwar American production of *To the Ends of the Earth*, which told a similar story.

For Mastroianni, the highs and lows of *Poppy* were in performers Howard and Hayworth.

> Howard was one of those actors I used to think about back in the days of Eagle-Lion. I'd also considered *Brief Encounter* one of the most beautiful films I'd ever seen. Then when we finally get to work together, what is it? It's a scene in a ship's cabin where I'm supposed to be listening to Howard and Marshall interrogating Quayle in English. I had a single line in the scene—"Not yet." Howard and Marshall start talking, but suddenly both of them start coughing and wheezing like old men. There was dust or something in the cabin, and it took us forever to shoot the talking part of the scene. Then we're all supposed to walk through the narrow door of the cabin to leave, but we can't get that right to save ourselves. I think it took us nine hours to shoot the damn thing and for me to say "Not yet."

A sadder memory was Hayworth. "She looked terrible. This was one of the great beauties, and it tore my heart out to see how she was no longer the woman I'd known from Hollywood movies, but someone who, it turned out later, was just very sick."

Howard also once recalled a less than scintillating shoot on *Poppy*.

> Marcello was an extremely charming, deferential man. But I had the feeling that he didn't know what the hell he'd gotten himself into with all these Englishmen and Americans running around, and only wanted to get everything over with as quickly as possible. The truth is, he wasn't the only one in that film who felt that way.

Mastroianni couldn't afford as much impatience for his subsequent project, *Spara Forte, Più Forte . . . Non Capisco* (Shoot Loud, Louder . . . I Don't Understand), for the simple reason that it was his third venture at producing. Despite his less than exhilarating experiences on the production side of *Contro la Legge* in 1950 and *Le Notti Bianche* in 1957, he was talked into once again putting on a second hat by Joe Levine.

> Levine liked me a lot. He thought that I was some kind of good-luck charm for him because of the money he had made off the films of mine that he had distributed. So he came to Rome and said to me: "You do so many pictures for others, why not do one for yourself? I'll be your partner."

The result was Master Film, the first project was *Spara Forte, Più Forte . . . Non Capisco,* and Mastroianni had found a new reason to spend most of his waking hours on the telephone.

> It was a disaster. Levine never bothered even to read the scripts that were sent to us. He had an absolutely blind trust in me. He could never get it into his head that I've never been able to organize anything, starting with myself.

According to Richard Levine, the son of the late producer, a partnership with the disorganized Mastroianni was not atypical of his father. "He didn't always do things just because they made sense," in Levine's view.

> I'm not knocking either one of them, but they were both strange men, and you can't expect to find so-called mainstream explanations for the things they did. I suppose the main thing was that to my father it made sense at the time. Who knows why?

At the beginning, there seemed to be at least one solid benefit for Mastroianni in being a producer. "I wanted to do De Filippo's play *Le Voci di Dentro* (The Voices Inside) as a film and I wanted Eduardo himself to direct it. I'd always had an enormous admiration for him. But despite his reputation in the theater, he had done few films, and they hadn't exactly been up to his gifts. I don't know why: Maybe because producers didn't trust him and preferred him only as an actor, or because he himself had been aloof about the film industry. But because of Master Film, I had the opportunity to choose him as my director, and so we did *Le Voci di Dentro* with the title of *Spara Forte, Più Forte . . . Non Capisco.*"

The rather dense plot of the Neapolitan farce cast Mastroianni as a dreamy sculptor who lives with an aging uncle (De Filippo)—a fireworks expert who communicates with his nephew only through the code of firecrackers and cherry bombs. The sculptor's overly vivid imagination leads him to accuse a neighboring family of fortune-tellers of plotting to kill a wealthy customer, the fortune-tellers turn out to be indeed would-be murderers and try to kill the sculptor, and the ostensibly imperiled client is revealed as a gangster bent on fleeing the country. Also flitting around is a prostitute (Raquel Welch) with whom the Mastroianni character is in love. Everything ends in an explosion provoked by one of the uncle's experiments, killing him and the gangster and sending the sculptor and the prostitute off together in search of happiness.

Most Italian critics trashed *Spara Forte, Più Forte . . . Non Capisco* as an adulterated version of *Le Voci di Dentro*, taking particular aim at De Filippo for lending himself to the warping of his own play. A typical comment was that of the daily *L'Unità*, which observed that "the original work itself might not have been a masterpiece, but it was certainly sewn together better than this. . . . *Spara Forte, Più Forte . . . Non Capisco* just doesn't convince. . . . Jumping here and there, without clarity, it is hard to understand where and at what it is shooting." Mastroianni came off much better, especially in a *Vita* magazine review by Gian Luigi Rondi, who declared in part:

> That he is one of Italy's best actors has been known for some time. That he has always tested this reputation in some particularly hard parts is also on the record. But with this otherwise forgettable adaptation of *Le Voci di Dentro*, it seems to us that he has delivered the best that can be gotten from Italian comedy.

The actor agreed with most of the critical reservations, blaming the film's shortcomings on the pressures from American distributors that forced the character of the prostitute to have more screen time so that it could accommodate a recognizable actress like Welch.

> The distributors insisted on Welch, and even though her part remained relatively small, it was enlarged enough to imbalance a lot of things. The film really wasn't convincing. Anyway, I have never regretted making it because it allowed me the honor and privilege of being directed by Eduardo.

Master Film's second (and last) project was an adaptation of *L'Étranger*, the Albert Camus story set in colonial Algeria. Titled *Lo Straniero* (The Stranger) as a film, it initially attracted Mastroianni because "I wanted to restore my artistic virginity." In the event, it left even more people unhappy than had the De Filippo movie; before it had become history, several people had accused each other of not having grasped the essence of the Camus tale.

For some years, several Italian directors—among them Mauro

Bolognini and Francesco Rosi—had made attempts to transfer the French fiction to the screen; Bolognini had even signed a contract to make it. In the end, however, the final choice fell to Camus' widow, Francine, and she selected Visconti. Originally enthusiastic about the project, the director went to his favorite leading man—Alain Delon—to play the central role of Meursault, but the actor, in part because he was still smarting over personal and professional tensions with Visconti during the shooting of *Il Gattopardo* (The Leopard), demanded more money than producer De Laurentiis was willing to pay. After a couple of casting forays elsewhere, including a stab at acquiring the services of Marlon Brando, a deal was struck with Master Film for Mastroianni to take over the starring role and to act as coproducer.

From the beginning, Visconti made it clear that his former theatrical pupil had not been his idea. Worse, he accused Francine Camus of objecting to the screenplay that he and Georges Conchon had put together and that had been the key to his interest in the film in the first place. As the director told an interviewer a couple of years following the picture's release:

> *Lo Straniero* contained a great theme, or so it did in the script that Conchon and I did. What ended up on the screen was another thing altogether, little more than a literal version of what Camus had written. What we were trying to do was to make something that had the echoes of *L'Étranger* but that was updated with references to the OAS campaign in Algeria and the Algerian war of independence. In our view, that was what Camus' book had been about, even though it had been written so many years before those events took place historically. But the widow didn't want to hear anything about that. She just wanted a faithful film version of her husband's novel, with no modern interpretation. Then all the other problems began to weigh in. Delon seemed to me far more suited to the role of Meursault than Mastroianni, but Mastroianni was who there was. What could I do? De Laurentiis was intent on making the film at all costs, and I had a contract with him that I couldn't get out of. I resigned myself to shooting it, telling myself that the Camus novel was still the Camus novel and was hardly something just to be thrown away. But, overall, it still came out as little more than an illustration of the book, and I never felt part of it, as I did with other films.

To placate Francine Camus, De Laurentiis brought in veteran Italian screenwriter Suso Cecchi d'Amico to rework the Visconti-Conchon script. To calm his own apprehensions about Visconti's truculence and the director's insistence that the film would be even more of a fiasco if it wasn't shot on location in Algeria, raising the specter of production costs spiraling completely out of hand, he quickly assembled a low-budget spaghetti western for filming in North Africa so he could ascertain the organizational skills of Algerian crews. When De Laurentiis announced himself as satisfied with the results of these two moves, however, he was still very much in the minority. Even the script doctor, Cecchi d'Amico, came to share Visconti's reservations, including that over the casting choice for the character of Meursault. "Maybe Marcello wasn't exactly the actor needed," the screenwriter allowed later. "Maybe he didn't give the film enough dimension."

For his part, Mastroianni was hardly oblivious to the hornet's nest stirred by his involvement in the project. In the actor's view, much of it was caused by a misunderstanding of the character of Meursault.

> "Why Mastroianni?" people kept asking. But the character of Meursault was no intellectual, not one of these mysterious archangels that Gérard Philipe had always played and that some saw in an actor like Delon. Meursault is a Mediterranean type—an optimist, a thoroughly normal man who likes girls and food and being with friends. This is what makes the character so extraordinary— the fact that he was so healthy, very normal and very Mediterranean.

To put it mildly, such a reading was not Visconti's, and only the director's preannounced detachment from the project worked to prevent serious creative tensions during filming. Even at that, however, Visconti could not resist taking a couple of potshots at the actor even years later. After directing *Death in Venice* with Dirk Bogarde in 1971, for instance, he told an interviewer:

> Bogarde had a professional side, British, and much deeper, much more disciplined in every way. Bogarde never stopped being in his character in *Death in Venice*. Even when he went home, he was still Aschenbach. He was Aschenbach for two and a half months. Mastroianni, on the other hand, is a fellow who sees a plate of tagliatelle or spaghetti and completely forgets he is doing Meursault. He eats, and then he picks up his character again. That's very different. It's the Italian side—a bit frivolous.

In outline, *Lo Straniero* follows the *pied noir* Meursault along an apparent road of emotional indifference as he attends his mother's funeral, picks up a woman (Anna Karina) only a couple of hours later, helps a somewhat disreputable friend (Georges Geret) out of complications with an Arab lover, keeps his own lover at bay whenever she proposes getting married, and finally kills the brother of the Arab woman for no ostensible reason. At an ensuing trial, he is condemned to death as much for all the testimony brought to bear about his callousness as for the concrete fact of having killed the brother. For Meursault, the outsider, all of this adds up to a final conclusion that the world is absurd and that death is his only reality.

Only too familiar with the preproduction troubles surrounding the film, most Italian critics agreed with Visconti that the director's heart was not in it, taking him to task for either not pulling out of the project altogether or not making the best of a bad situation. The compliments that there were came mainly for the first half of the film, with Moravia in *L'Espresso* going so far as to claim that Meursault's actions before the trial were sometimes far more comprehensible in the picture than they had been in the book. On the other hand, Moravia was among the louder voices condemning the lengthy trial sequence and "the carting out of an ideology . . . that depended on caricatures to function and . . . that still rendered the character of Meursault as more of an intellectual idea than as a real character." In circumstances of the kind, according to Moravia, it was inevitable that Mastroianni would begin to look lost. Other reviewers did not show as much mercy toward the actor. Pietro Bianche of *Il Giorno* found that "the psychological density and metaphysical emptiness of Meursault . . . has eluded him." Leo Pestelli of *La Stampa* was only one of several who found Mastroianni's "sympathetic looks . . . exactly wrong for the theme of absurdity that emerges in the second half of the film." Filippo Sacchi of the weekly *L'Epoca* put it more bluntly:

> It should have been evident to a blind man that it was not possible to marry Mastroianni to the character of Meursault. This has nothing to do with the actor's unquestionably formidable talents. It is a problem of physical and moral compatibility. It is either there or it is not there, and no miracle of direction, no acting bravura, can create it if it isn't there already. . . . It is to Mastroianni's credit that he seemed to be getting away with the improbable for the first quarter or so of the film. But the fact remains that he is absolutely the opposite of what Meursault should be.

Perhaps taking a cue from their subject, two of Visconti's biographers also called *Lo Straniero* a low point in the director's professional career, with one of them, Geoffrey Nowell-Smith, even scoring him for making a "travesty" of the Camus work. Other foreign opinion was more lenient, and although the picture hardly precipitated a rush from either award givers or audiences, it was accorded a generally respectful reception. Mastroianni found himself in much more agreement with this reaction than with that of the Italian critics.

> The reviewers attacked Visconti for having adapted the book too literally and for not having given the film a more personal interpretation, but many of these same people knew that Camus' widow had been adamant that the original text be followed to the letter and that Luchino couldn't do anything else. In any case, I've always thought it a very beautiful piece of work, and the more that it has been shown on television, the more that seems to have become the prevailing opinion. The last word isn't always pronounced the first time that a film is released.

What had become pronounced by the middle of 1967, on the other hand, was the actor's financial straits. Although he had been far and away the highest-paid male actor in Italy for a number of years (and equaled only by Loren overall), he had begun to attract creditors through his personal spending habits, his unsuccessful venture with *Ciao, Rudy,* the indemnity that he had to pay for getting out of his contract with the musical, and the failure of Master Film's two productions. (Because of his commitments to the play and *Spara Forte, Più Forte . . . Non Capisco* and *Lo Straniero,* he also had to turn down several roles that would have more than satisfied his debts.) It was this financial situation that, following the flop of *Lo Straniero,* prompted him to accept offers for two films that, by his own admission, he would have normally turned down, if for entirely different reasons.

Diamonds for Breakfast, a British-Italian coproduction, was the first film shot in English in which the actor agreed to star. In addition, it was directed by Christopher Morahan, making his debut behind motion-picture cameras after several years in the theater and television. That Mastroianni waived his usual strictures against both shooting in English and working for a novice owed to both the hefty salary he was offered and the presence of Ponti as producer. "I told Ponti that the only three things I knew how to say in English were *fuck,* which was the first word I learned, *hello,* and *good night.* He said 'Stop worrying, I'm the boss, and you'll be okay.'"

Although he would later call *Diamonds for Breakfast* "terrible," the actor also had mellower moods when he insisted that he liked the film and that this plus the opportunity to go to England had been as important in his decision as the money.

> It was a very entertaining comedy. Going to London appealed to me because it was a period when I wanted to get out of Italy, to travel some. I had begun having second thoughts about all the offers I had

received from abroad. While I wasn't ready to go to Hollywood, London seemed like a good compromise. I suppose the fact that I didn't speak English also made me feel a little adventurous. Ponti got me a teacher, and I learned my lines phonetically, like a parrot. London was a wonderful place to be in those days—all the hippies and Mod types on King's Road, the Beatles. It was one of the best times I ever had.

Diamonds for Breakfast cast Mastroianni as an exiled Russian aristocrat who makes ends meet by operating a boutique in Hampstead. One day, while visiting a castle that is hosting an exhibition of Russian crown jewels, he slips on a banana peel thrown away carelessly by a sculptress (Rita Tushingham) and cracks his head, setting off visions that he has been entrusted by his ancestors with recovering the gems. He rounds up a gang of eight women, including the sculptress and his aged aunt Anastasia (Nora Nicholson), and through one piece of chicanery and another, gets the lord of the castle to organize a charity exhibition of Russian costumes studded with the jewels. The gang outfoxes the heavy security laid on for the benefit, whisks away the stones with the help of carrier pigeons, and makes good its own escape. But when the thieves return to Aunt Anastasia to help her with the birds, they discover that the old woman has already taken off for Monte Carlo and, in line with family tradition, will lose all the loot at the baccarat table. The aristocrat has to be satisfied with his love for the sculptress.

The film was generally received for what it was: a light caper comedy that told all the obvious jokes about the Romanovs and the Soviet Union and that relied heavily on Mastroianni's charm. Critics who bothered chided the actor for agreeing to a prefabricated role in the eyes of British and American audiences—the Latin Lover who surrounds himself with women even to pull off a heist; in this sense, according to some reviewers, the aristocratic exile was a lot closer to Rome than he was to Moscow or Saint Petersburg.

Ultimately far more controversial than *Diamonds for Breakfast* was De Sica's *Amanti* (A Place for Lovers), a tearjerker that appealed to the director as much as to the star for purely financial reasons. Produced (once again) by Ponti and scripted by a small army of writers, *Amanti* told the sodden tale of an American divorcée (Faye Dunaway) who rents a sumptuous villa near Cortina, apparently to get away from America and her broken marriage. Out of little more than whim, she begins an affair with an Italian engineer (Mastroianni) that soon enough has him wondering why she refuses to think about anything except the present. In predictable soap-opera style, he eventually discovers that she is suffering from a fatal disease. The film ends with the lovers determined to get as much out of their time together as they can, though there is also a fleeting (and wholly contradictory) suggestion that the divorcée's X rays might not have been as bad as feared.

For reasons that escaped even Mastroianni, Italian critics reacted to *Amanti* more benevolently than they had to some of his other work in the period, notably *Lo Straniero*. Although De Sica came in for his share of jabs ("he seems to have directed the proceedings with only one hand"; "he is working more tiredly than ever"), the film overall was treated as a competent attempt to emulate Hollywood's "women dramas" of the 1930s, with Mastroianni and Dunaway congratulated for having acquitted themselves professionally within that framework. All of this mystified the picture's leading man, who had little but derision for *Amanti*, at least after the fact. In a number of interviews, he rejected it as "a commercial operation—nothing more." More striking was his fallback on a stereotype of the Italian male attributed to him by Rex Reed in a *New York Times* interview published in June 1970: "Ridiculous! Why would an Italian accept an invitation from a dying woman? Why? If I knew she was sick, I would not make her have sex. It was a stupid movie."

It did not require particular insight to connect some of Mastroianni's more heated responses to *Amanti* to the love affair that he initiated with Dunaway during the making of the picture—a stormy relationship that, for more than two years, had her jetting from the United States to Europe for weekends, and had him pursuing her to California. Associates of the actress attributed her with wanting to wed Mastroianni and have a family, then finally with losing patience before his refusal to divorce Carabella. In a biography of Dunaway put together by Allan Hunter, she was quoted as declaring: "There's no good way to end a romance. You can either sit and talk out all the things that went wrong, or you can just say good-bye. In this case, the word was *ciao*."

Almost a quarter century after the fact, Mastroianni acknowledged that the affair "almost destroyed me. I loved her very much, and I know she loved me. It ended up being a very painful relationship. I have never talked to her since. I have loved three or four women in my life, and except for Faye we parted as friends or still are friends. I really don't want to see her again."

With rare exceptions, however, the actor has also flatly denied the authenticity of the numerous quotes attributed to him by reporters on both sides of the Atlantic about his time with Dunaway.

While we were together, we were very discreet, and now lately, after all these years, magazines are popping up with so-called details about us. They are absolute lies. One magazine in America even had a quote where I supposedly described her as having a smashed nose and an old woman's hands. I suppose science fiction has always been popular in America.

One of the few quotes that he has not disowned was blaming himself for the breakup.

I could not decide to say the one thing there was to say, so she left. Women get tired of the falsities you bring them. For a time you succeed in subtly dictating your game. Then one day you hear—"You seem to be sweet and polite. Instead, you're a monstrous egotist. You play according to your rules, nobody else's." And it's mostly true.

As for Carabella, she assumed, at least in public, the stiff upper lip that had been her trademark for some time whenever another woman came into the picture, insisting that "Marcello and I will grow old together." Even in public, however, the veneer occasionally cracked under indications that Mastroianni was more serious about Dunaway than he had been about his other flings, Carabella referring to the American actress only as "that one."

19

Close-up: The Ideal Woman

Much of what Mastroianni has had to say about women over the years has had the profundity of a stand-up comic looking for sympathy as much as laughs. On more than one occasion, he has sounded like a Latin Woody Allen, with his ironic plaints playing to the nods of the gods rather than to those of the nearest psychotherapist. That he has felt compelled to issue quotable pronouncements for media representatives intent on consolidating his image as a bedroom expert has been only half the problem; the other half has been his own often-stated self-perception that since he is doomed to fester within the complexes of the average Italian male of his generation, he might as well make the best of everything. In contrast to characters that he has played on the screen, this cosmic fate has, equally by his own admission, absolved him of any special urgency in seeking some definitive clarity. In the words of Catherine Deneuve, he has, in his private life, responded by behaving like somebody who "arrives through the door and leaves through the window."

An integral part of this attitude has been the actor's recurringly expressed concern with an "ideal woman"—that nonexistent creature whose approximate incarnations invariably assume greatest importance as a flawed approximation; that is, in the end, discardable. In this, Mastroianni has hardly been alone, as shown by his friend Fellini's characterization of such an entity in 8½ and by the numerous purely symbolic women in the work—with or without him—of Petri, Ferreri, and Scola. It was also Fellini who, in *La Dolce Vita*, had the Mastroianni character address the topic by declaring to the woman played by Ekberg:

Who are you, Sylvia? You are everything, you are everything. Do you know that you are everything? Everything. Everything. You are the first woman on the first day of creation. You are the mother, sister, lover, friend, angel, devil, earth, home. Ah, yes, that's what you are—home.

In general, Mastroianni's fancies about what makes up the ideal woman have been drenched in the terms of reference of his middle-class Italian Catholic upbringing: Mothers, Madonnas, and whores course through his imagery. At times, he has taken to psychiatric and political vocabularies, although with the kind of mechanical tone suggesting that, for him, the mothers, Madonnas, and whores still covered the concept best. In speaking of Jeanne Moreau, for instance, he once pronounced her "a total woman—a lover one moment, a mother the next." His own footloose ways he has ascribed to "the Madonna putting her finger on me when I was born and saying that this would be the way I would always be, looking for a woman who may only exist in my mind." He told another interviewer:

> The absolutely ideal woman is somebody that you meet once, then never again. She must be a worry for you. She must make you feel uncertain of her. Who is she? *What* is she? Maybe she is a whore. Then you waste no time. You just throw yourself at her.

By the test of such a single fleeting encounter, Deneuve, with whom he lived for several years in Paris and Rome and fathered a daughter, failed.

> The ideal woman is amusing. She makes you feel happy and contented. When I first met Deneuve, I was convinced that she was such an ideal. But when I got to know her better, I realized that she was not at all like that. Who she was was Catherine Deneuve, the mother of my daughter Chiara.

On the other hand, Marilyn Monroe, whom he never met, passed the test.

> Maybe I liked her more than any woman. I never knew her, but it was obvious that she couldn't make it alone. This made me want to protect her, to possess this small blond cloud. . . . She was the last of a species.

As regularly as he has shared his notions of the ideal woman, the actor has described her opposite.

> I would say that the worst kind of woman is the one who, whatever you do, says you're acting like a fool. When you are desperate, she tells you not to make a scene, that you're not in some theater. She has a talent for keeping you tense when you take her out with your friends, and your friends end up saying: "Poor Marcello. He's so nice when he's by himself, but he's so dull when he's with her."

La Decima Vittima (The Tenth Victim) represented one of Italy's few forays into science fiction on the screen. Among those appearing with a blond-haired Mastroianni was Ursula Andress.

In the first of the three tales making up *Ieri Oggi Domani* (Yesterday, Today, and Tomorrow), Mastroianni played an overwhelmed husband who must keep his wife, Sophia Loren, constantly pregnant so she won't be sent to jail for selling contraband cigarettes.

None of the troubles besetting the set of *Matrimonio all'Italiana* (Marriage—Italian Style) were evident in this shot of Mastroianni with Pia Lindstrom and director Vittorio De Sica. Lindstrom, the eldest daughter of Ingrid Bergman, had a small role in the picture.

Mastroianni and Loren were teamed again in De Sica's *I Girasoli* (Sunflower), a torpid soap opera that gained a great deal of attention because it was a coproduction with the Soviet Union.

Amanti (A Place for Lovers) brought Mastroianni together with Faye Dunaway—the beginning of an offscreen relationship that kept gossip columnists busy for a couple of years.

Dramma della Gelosia: Tutti i Particolari in Cronaca (The Pizza Triangle) marked the first teaming of Mastroianni with director Ettore Scola. Also starring were Monica Vitti and Giancarlo Giannini.

La Moglie del Prete (The Priest's Wife) was one of the lesser Mastroianni-Loren efforts.

Although hailed abroad, Fellini's *Intervista* came in for some hard knocks from Italian critics for supposedly exploiting Anita Ekberg's physical appearance. Here the actress is flanked by Mastroianni and Fellini.

Ça N'Arrive Qu'Aux Autres (It Only Happens to Others) was the first of the actor's four films with Catherine Deneuve, with whom he took up residence in Paris and had a daughter.

A grave Mastroianni actually did his lines in Greek for Theo Angelopoulos's *O Melissokomos* (The Beekeeper).

As far back as 1972, Mastroianni had voiced interest in doing a film version of François Billetdoux's play *Tchin-Tchin*. It finally got to the screen in 1990, costarring Julie Andrews and distributed in America under the title of *A Fine Romance*.

After decades of saying no, Mastroianni finally agreed to do an American picture in 1991—Beeban Kidron's *Used People*. His costars were (clockwise from left) Marcia Gay Harden and past Oscar winners Shirley MacLaine, Kathy Bates, and Jessica Tandy.

Mastroianni and MacLaine in a scene from *Used People*.

Anybody would be dull when she takes that attitude of critic and judge, making sure, like she was some kind of press agent, that you always cut a respectable figure, that you don't make a fool of yourself. Women often have a conformist idea of decorum, dignity, and authority. The worst kind of woman doesn't realize that it's fun to show off, to parody your shortcomings.

Or, again:

The worst kind of a woman has an embarrassingly totalitarian idea of love. No matter how modest, how intelligent they may appear at first, they invariably want to possess and change you. Why? Didn't she like me the way I was when we first met? If she did, why does she now want to make so many changes? Why does she always invade everything? Why must she know everything—what I did, where I was, whom I met, what I think? Why does she always give orders? Why does she always say things like "You must decide *now*. Clear your head. Tell him directly to his face. Call him up right now and tell him what you really think. Don't put it off like you always do. Don't lie, because I'll know, anyway. Smoke less. Drink less. Eat less." The worst kind of woman will say things like that even to some wretch who has been stranded in a desert for a month and hasn't had anything in his mouth all that time except his mirages. Whatever you may be to other people, to her you will always be a retarded minor in need of her as a protective, terrifying mother.

And still again:

They all want to change me. It never fails. They scream at me. They have presumed that I can give them clarity and solidity and go crazy when it becomes obvious that I can't give them any such thing. I would rather be a lot less loved and more respected, taken for what I am.

Even the most casual sifting of such remarks makes it evident that where Mastroianni is concerned, the principal difference between the ideal woman and the worst woman has often been only a couple of hours. He has never denied it. Quite the reverse; it has always been part of the Mastroianni package that he has been the first one to endorse those who have found him the perfect product of, in the words of one writer, "the matriarchal Catholic conception of male sexuality." While she was alive, he grimaced and moaned and sighed at some of his mother's blurtings about him in much the same way that some of his eccentric screen characters bewailed their fate at the hands of an ogre of a mother; at the same time, he could laugh off in absolute security some of her more patently spiteful digs at him, such as when she told an Italian television interviewer that, as a child, she had sometimes thought of him as a girl more than a boy. (His sardonic reply: "Mind you, she didn't say I wore dresses.") Nor has he hesitated to go along with those who have accused him of being (among other things) "an overaged baby," "a perennial teen-ager," "an infuriating narcissist," and "a study in boorish egotism." If he has bothered to refute anything, it has been the number of his reputed conquests, not the lack of substance to the majority of them.

> Every time I go to a restaurant with ten people, photographers take pictures. As soon as they develop them back in their darkrooms, they crop out eight of the people and sell the pictures showing "proof" of my new affair with the woman sitting on my right.

Rounding off the picture has been his standard answer to the question, posed many times over the years, of what his reaction would be if his wife had a lover. "If it ever did happen," has been the customary response, "I wouldn't want to know about it." (The blithe-ness of this hypocrisy is especially impressive in the face of the fact that Carabella had already been linked for some time to actor Luis Suarez while Mastroianni went on giving such a reply.)

Impeccably consistent in his inconsistency, completely faith-less in his perseverance, and immaculately indecisive about priori-ties outside those involved in doing his stage and screen roles, he has admitted to only a modicum of guilt about the possible consequences of his behavior for others. He told Curtis Bill Pepper in the *New York Times Magazine* in 1987:

> Of course, there's some. But then you justify it. You say, "Okay, but what else could I have done? I'm immature. I was born that way. The Madonna put her finger on me. I pay my taxes, I'm a good actor, I win prizes. What more do you want?"

In the opinion of Sophia Loren, it is useless to expect that Mas-troianni will ever change. For Loren, however, the most striking fea-ture of the actor's private life has not been his insensitivity toward others but the emotional monotony that he has surrendered to. As she has been quoted by her biographer A. E. Hotchner:

> Marcello is a man beset with problems, continually buffeted by problems he cannot solve but which torment him, and for years they have been the same. People in his life have changed, but the problems remain the same, and Marcello has refused to change his life in order to ease those problems. I figure that he must like the problems, and the torment.

Mastroianni's living style has hardly been discouraged by his surroundings. For one thing, the Italy that he knew until the early

1970s practically assumed philandering and double housekeeping as a working alternative to (nonexistent) divorce rights. For another, many friends and associates have led lives similar to his own, though without the publicity attending his entanglements. This has been true not only of his contemporaries but also of his "uncle" De Sica, who remained officially married for twenty-five years to his first wife while living all the time with Spanish actress Maria Mercader and finally had to obtain French citizenship to dissolve the marriage. Most of all, however, the actor's gallivanting has been reinforced by his profession.

According to Mastroianni, it has been more than coincidence that his longest relationships, aside from the one begun in the late 1970s with Italian television director Anna Maria Tatò, have been with actresses.

> They understand my immaturity the fastest. They know exactly where it comes from. Why shouldn't they, since it is in them, too? They sense immediately what is reality for this imbecile—at least in the beginning they do—and that makes it possible to cut through the false presuppositions that men and women sometimes have about one another when first meeting.

But more than merely with actresses, the longest affairs have been with women whom the actor knew initially as costars; he even met his wife as a fellow performer with the Visconti company. Although innumerable costars have ended up spending more time together offscreen than on during a film shoot, in Mastroianni's case the recurrence of the phenomenon has lent still another dimension to his view of the movie set as an adult playground; that is, by design or not, the romances have prolonged for him the reality of a given production beyond a final wrap. Only in the cases of Carabella and Deneuve, the mothers of his daughters, did he consent to extend yet further his avowed fantasy world into another joint professional project.

But the fantasies carried over from the film set have had more limitations than those imposed by some final take. Whether puncturing his screen image as a Latin Lover or bemoaning his advancing age, Mastroianni has put obsessively confessional American actors to shame by candidly charting his physical vulnerabilities and deficiencies. On one occasion, for example, he told an interviewer of a London adventure that ended ignominiously when the woman with him made a crack about his skinny legs: "I could not make love to her again." Continually over the years, he has referred to his "impotence," "half-impotence," and "temporary impotence"—if normally from the safe shore of a problem said to have been since overcome.

In 1988, regarding his relationship with Tatò, he acknowledged the growing factor of age, telling one reporter that "things *down there* [his emphasis] aren't as good as they used to be." To a Swiss magazine, he has declared:

> It is hard if a woman wants you but you don't want her. You are not some kind of vending machine—put in one thousand lire and the gasoline begins flowing. But that's when you start to hear all the complaints. "You don't love me anymore. I can't excite you because you don't really want to be with me." Then come the quarrels and sulkings and silences and cruel remarks, all of it ending up as contempt. But it simply isn't true that when things like that happen, it means that the man isn't in love with the woman. Sometimes a man just doesn't feel like it, the way a woman sometimes doesn't feel like it. A man is very fragile sexually. The least little thing is liable to make him impotent.

A similar motif has been the actor's advice to those smitten with his Latin Lover image to look closer to home for their phallic icon. He told an American magazine writer in 1981:

> If it's the great seducer you're looking for, you'd be better off talking to Mr. Smith down the street. He has had a lot more love affairs than I have had, and I would guess that he has probably been much better at them than I would have been.

Ruminations of the sort have left the suggestion that in many of his escapades Mastroianni has been the classic hound chasing after the bus, catching up to it, then wondering what to do next. The pursuit had been expected of him, including by himself, so that was what he did, but after that mechanics were sometimes less than their own reward. At least with regard to the actresses that he has pursued, however, there seems to have been one long-range, self-protective calculation from the beginning. Of the women whom he has singled out for understanding him the fastest, he has also said: "My wife is very intelligent. She knows that actresses are the least threatening women in the world and that their professional exhibitionism is superior to their danger to her."

However questionable that might have been in Dunaway's case, in particular, Carabella's predominantly stoic public posture over forty-odd years of marriage has been an indispensable premise for Mastroianni's rovings after the ideal woman and immediately subsequent discoveries of the worst woman. If anything has changed in her attitude toward his open philandering, it has been in the exhaustion of her own weariness, progressing from her barely concealed bitterness over Dunaway to a distant respect for Deneuve to a philosophical indifference toward Tatò. In 1978, she could remain piqued enough by the personal complexes of her husband to tell the Italian weekly *Oggi:*

> I feel privileged because I stand on the balcony and watch. From above I see him in the middle of all his emotions, looking for air to breathe. Marcello has always wanted to be in a prison, and he has often imprisoned himself with his own hands.

Ten years later, she was back to generic ethnic sociology, telling Curtis Bill Pepper:

> You have to understand the nature of the Latin male. He likes to wander, to feel free and potent. So you let him go, absolutely, without strings—and sooner or later, he'll come back home.

A few months after that, her own most important sense of purchase was reflected in another comment that

> jealousy has long been banned from my life. I respect the freedom of others, and I expect them to respect mine. If my husband has needed a period of wandering, should I be hindering him? I have always cultivated my own interests and own friends.

For his part, Mastroianni has seldom voiced anything but gratitude for the room Carabella has left him, claiming more than once that "I consider my marriage a great success. My wife is my great friend, and I am hers." In the wake of such assertions, some of the actor's longest associates have contended that he found his ideal-worst woman decades ago in Carabella and that everything else since then has been sound and fury signifying very little. The most extreme expression of this opinion has come from Carlo Ponti, with the contention that

> Mastroianni doesn't have any psychological problems, but he likes to think he has. He has created a real confusion because he has gotten it into his head that he's the person that Fellini created on film.

However self-contradictory that assessment, it is not alone in citing the actor as a character in a shadow play of his own inspiration, being performed primarily for himself and his wife. The freedom that he has had to run around, in the view of one friend, has merely been an adult reenactment of his boyhood excursions into the mysterious streets of Turin and Rome when he saw himself as a fearless adventurer.

> At the end of the day, he knew that he still had a home to go back to, that no matter how contrary he had acted with his mother, she would be there for him. Just like his mother effectively under-

wrote all his petty thieveries and ramblings around with his gang, Flora has been his insurance with Dunaway and the others. He has never been able to lie to her any more credibly than with his mother.

As seductive as such analyses might be from a psychological perspective, they are hardly equal to the welter of human travail that has engulfed Mastroianni and everyone connected to him through the way that he has conducted his life. As Fellini once put it, "He didn't fall in love with Dunaway in the streets of Turin, and a lot more than a penknife was gained and lost." If there has been any single explanation at all, according to the director, it is to be found in the one priority that has consumed Mastroianni for a half century of his life. "Forget about the Madonna making him the permanent *bambino*," Fellini told Pepper in the *New York Times Magazine* in 1987.

> He would follow Dante into the circles of hell, seeing the lost and the doomed, yet also talking to taxicab drivers and ballroom dancers, looking always for another acting role—and, like Dante, hoping to find the beauty of a lost love, the first love. . . . Everything about his life, his art, his loves, his going from place to place, always saying that he is somewhere else . . . it's to go on acting.

Only Mastroianni himself has been more explicit. Carabella and his mother might have filled archetypical roles in a matriarchal Catholic society. Dunaway might have been the woman who "almost destroyed" him. Deneuve might have been "a real person who is the mother of my daughter." Tatò might have been "a woman made of flesh, unlike dolls . . . a real woman." Loren might have been "the ideal sister." Others might have been situated somewhere along the scale extending from the ideal to the worst. But nowhere has the process of ideal-worst been more constant than in the flow of Mastroianni's commitment to work. In his initial enthusiasm for a project. In his rendering of it under varying circumstances of satisfaction and dissatisfaction. In his ability to forget about one project to go on immediately to the next—the more different the better. In knowing that the success of given roles is neither here nor there, that he has the ultimate security of being constantly in demand. In being able to talk retrospectively about what enchanted him and what disappointed him. In liking himself for always being available for some new adventure, and in agreeing with critics when his efforts have been deemed as half-hearted. How else to say it than in his repeated descriptions of an actor as "a little whore," "a liar," or "a chosen child of the Madonna"—or, as in another declaration, that "the actor is fundamentally like a beautiful woman"?

Somewhat like the character in Ray Bradbury's *Martian Chronicles*, in other words, Mastroianni has given every indication of having come closest to finding his ideal woman and his worst woman when he has looked at his own reflection.

Part Three

Mastroianni

20

Going Abroad

Two clouds hung over Mastroianni's work in the late 1960s and early 1970s. The first was his volatile relationship with Dunaway, which in the best of times drove him to her California home or her to his latest location, but which in the worst of times distracted him from wherever he happened to be and whatever he happened to be doing. The second was another crisis in the Italian film industry, brought on this time not only by the gargantuan production-distribution appetites of Hollywood but also by the crash landing of Italy's postwar economic takeoff and by the consolidation of free television as a major entertainment rival. By the turn of the decade, De Laurentiis had bowed to the failure of his grandiose Dinocittà studio complex on the outskirts of Rome and transferred his operations to the United States (amid parliamentary accusations of some financial skullduggery), Ponti had acknowledged bankruptcy, and numerous other producers had fallen by the wayside. Those who made money did so largely on the strength of soft-core sex comedies and minor features that starred popular Italian singers of the period (most prominently, Gianni Morandi and Adriano Celentano).

In his efforts to find alternative financial sources, Ponti stepped up his foreign coproduction deals, at one point concluding a multi-million-dollar pact with the shah of Iran to shoot several pictures in the Near East country. One of his other ventures was *I Girasoli* (Sunflower), a joint Italian-French-Soviet production that was shot extensively in Moscow and the Ukraine and that reunited Mastroianni and Loren under De Sica's direction. From the start, the actor made it clear that his main interest in the project was the chance that it gave him to get away from Rome and visit the Soviet Union. Even years later, his fondest recollection of the film was having to speak Russian in several scenes with actress Ludmila Savelyeva and Moscow extras. "De Sica said I spoke it like it was Arabic."

To judge from the letters that he sent friends in Italy during the shooting, that was about as close as the director got to humor. In the same testy tone that had marked his chronicling of *Matrimonio all'Italiana* some years before, De Sica had little but complaints about the production—about Mastroianni showing up for work appreciably overweight, about the insistence of absolute strangers in restaurants to wine and dine (or vodka and caviar) him and the actor until the early hours of the morning, and about his constant need for an interpreter. This time, even Loren came in for criticism, the director declaring at one point that the actress's greatest failing was that she was "always jealous of other actors," in the case of *I Girasoli*, particularly of Savelyeva. Among his other headaches, De Sica disclosed, was having to put up with the constant criticisms of the Soviet actress by Loren's coterie; this, in turn, he wrote one associate in Rome, made him like Savelyeva even more.

The story of *I Girasoli* was a somewhat converse variation on some of the melodramas that Mastroianni had done in the 1950s, when he was the prisoner of war returning home to find that everyone had thought him dead and had arranged their lives accordingly. This time, Loren played the Neapolitan wife who, after the war, journeys to Moscow to trace the husband (Mastroianni) that she is convinced has survived a Soviet prisoner-of-war camp. When she finds him, however, it turns out that he has lost his memory from a wartime blow, is unaware of his Italian marriage, and has since settled down with a local woman (Savelyeva) and started a family. After several melodramatic tos and fros, Loren persuades the man she still loves to remain with his new wife and children.

The most benevolent critical reaction to *I Girasoli* was that, as both a story and a coproduction, it espoused antiwar sentiments and thereby contributed to a thawing of Cold War tensions between East and West. The more prevalent view was that it was a mediocre soap opera that pulled out all the Hollywood-type stops (the musical soundtrack was provided by Henry Mancini) to disguise the further decline of De Sica and the standard performances of the costars.

Although he would later declare himself proud of the Russian lines that he had in the film, Mastroianni has also admitted that he spoke them only after pleading with De Sica to be able to speak in Italian and dub everything subsequently. (The director said no because of the disparity in lip movements between the two languages.) He couldn't even consider such a net for his next project— the British production of *Leo the Last*, shot entirely in English by John Boorman in London. Moreover, unlike *Diamonds for Breakfast*, he didn't even have Ponti around this time to provide psychological support from the producer's office.

I liked Boorman, and I liked the script. Plus, it seemed like the time for me to do risky things, to stretch myself beyond what even some of my friends thought I should stick to doing.

Like *Diamonds for Breakfast, Leo the Last* cast Mastroianni as a foreign aristocrat living in exile in London. When he isn't using his binoculars to indulge a birding passion, he is training them on black neighbors in the ghetto surrounding his mansion. Overwhelmed by their daily misery, he invites a family into his home, precipitating a conflict with his own relatives and retainers and winning only the most detached kind of gratitude from his temporary wards. Only when his relatives get him declared insane and he retaliates by launching an attack on the mansion, in the process destroying the house and most of the contiguous area, is Prince Leo released from all his demons.

For Boorman, Mastroianni was the ideal actor to play Leo from the beginning.

> I thought of Marcello for the role because I'd seen him in *I Compagni*. In that film, he had played an essentially passive character who still managed to attract all kinds of trouble to himself. That was the way I saw Leo, too.

According to costar Billie Whitelaw, Mastroianni was as ideal a working companion between takes as he was before the camera.

> Even twenty-five years later, the first thing that comes to mind when I think of Marcello is what a superior professional he was doing that film. I think I learned a great deal from him. There was never a problem, never any condescending airs. We met in the morning with Boorman, we went through the scene, then we just did it. My only doubt was that even if he did have problems, he probably was too courteous to say that he did. For my own part, I knew that unless I was absolutely horrendous, he would just go on.

What particularly impressed Whitelaw was that the actor maintained his imperturbability through some physically dangerous scenes.

> The film ends with a sequence where everything blows up, and the shot called for Marcello to be standing in front of all this havoc. Well, there were a couple of other actors in the cast who created an enormous fuss with Boorman. But not Marcello. At one point, he just kind of ambled over to them and said, "C'mon now, I want to go to bed. It'll be all right. Let's just do it." For the life of me, I never understood how the insurance people let him do some of those

scenes, with fireworks and explosions all over the place. As far as he was concerned, it was a drawing-room scene.

The reverse side of the coin was that Mastroianni showed absolutely no sentimentality about what he was doing. According to the actress:

> Shortly before the final scene was supposed to be shot, we had an incredibly devastating fire. Everything went up in smoke, and prop boys were diving through windows to save what could be saved. I actually started crying—it seemed like such a terrible waste. But Marcello just looked at me and smiled and said, "Oh, don't worry about it. They'll put it out and start rebuilding tomorrow morning." And then he just walked off to his trailer, absolutely confident that nothing tragic had happened. It was just part of the business, and he wanted me to remember that.

Most Italian critics were unimpressed with *Leo the Last*, with the consensus being that any credibility built up by the film over the first half was destroyed as soon as the Mastroianni character began to act like a revolutionary spokesman for England's poor minorities. In the words of one critic, "There is supposed to be a political message here, but it defies finding." English and French reaction was more sympathetic, and Boorman ended up taking a Cannes prize for his direction. Both Whitelaw and Mastroianni have always seconded the acknowledgment.

Whitelaw:

> Generally speaking, my reactions to films is that I am either happy I did something or sorry that I did. In the case of *Leo*, I'm very glad that I did. I think John is always a little ahead of other people in some of the subjects he tackles, and I think this was a perfect example.

Mastroianni:

> I think it is a very good film, but nobody went near it. Whenever somebody comes up to me and starts telling me how much he liked it, I say, "Okay, that makes fourteen of you. All fourteen of you who saw it liked it."

The actor had much more luck with his next project, *Dramma della Gelosia: Tutti i Particolari in Cronaca* (The Pizza Triangle), the first of his numerous films under the direction of Ettore Scola. The tragicomedy cast Mastroianni as a Roman bricklayer who falls in love with a flower vendor (Monica Vitti) and leaves his somewhat gross family for her. In short order, however, she is drawn to a pizza maker (Giancarlo Giannini), prompting a whirl of misunderstandings, breast beatings, attempted compromises, and suicide attempts. The bricklayer emerges the worst for the chaos, eventually walking the streets without a home or job and thinking only about his lost love and the rival who has taken her away. He gets his vengeance by killing the vendor and beating the pizza man to within an inch of his life on their wedding day. His mental instability allows him to get off with a relatively light sentence of five years.

Italian critics found a lot to distrust in *Drama della Gelosia*: the film's constantly shifting tone from comedy to drama and back again; the vaguely condescending view of the proletarian backgrounds of the main characters; even some physical touches that seemed aimed more at evoking past Italian films than at developing the characters at hand. (The Mastroianni character, for example, wore his hair in a couple of scenes somewhat the way that he had as the ridiculously scheming Baron Cefalù in *Divorzio all'Italiana*.) Even those who liked the picture generally found it "astute," as one critic put it, rather than particularly moving. Although he, too, came in for only mild praise, Mastroianni ended up riding his performance to a Cannes Festival prize for Best Actor—an outcome that he has sometimes confessed to being puzzled by. In contradiction to other assertions that *Dramma della Gelosia* was "a very beautiful film" and "a small classic that was probably ahead of its time," he has also told interviewers, "I haven't any idea why they gave me that Cannes award. I don't think I did anything particularly different, and I'm not sure the film did."

Mainly because it afforded him another opportunity to be out of Italy, the actor returned to England for Franco Indovina's *Giochi Particolari* (The Voyeur), a morose tale of an Italian couple (Mastroianni and Virna Lisi) who have little to keep them warm except money and an 8-mm camera that provokes him into increasingly dangerous games. The predictable outcome has the Mastroianni character being killed on his own film by a lover (Timothy Dalton) that he has deliberately thrown together with his wife. *Il Corriere della Sera* spoke for most Italian dailies in branding the endeavor an attempt to give "class" to the soft-core films then making money in the country, noting in passing that Lisi's modest stripteases were bound to disappoint those drawn to theaters by a lurid advertising campaign. Mastroianni has referred to *Giochi Particolari* as "one of the things done in the haze" of his tempestuous times with Dunaway.

The haze did not lift perceptibly for *La Moglie del Prete* (The Priest's Wife), another Ponti production with Loren. Directed and cowritten by Dino Risi, *La Moglie del Prete* saw Loren as a would-be suicide who is dissuaded from her act by a sympathetic voice (Mastroianni) on a suicide emergency hotline. She tracks down her rescuer, and not even the discovery that he is a priest sways her from declaring her love. He reciprocates her feeling initially and announces his intention of leaving the priesthood but then changes his mind when he is offered a promotion to monsignor. When he takes the advice of wilier clerics to suggest to the woman that instead of marrying they live as clandestine lovers, she leaves him to his rather tenuous vocation, not telling him that she is pregnant.

"Inane" was one of the more charitable words used to describe *La Moglie del Prete*. More than one Italian critic also confessed to being bored by still another variation on an aggressive Loren character passing herself off as Common Woman in her husband's glossy commercial productions, and for once the Loren-Mastroianni pairing on a marquee failed to attract audiences to any appreciable degree. As though he needed other handicaps, Mastroianni's performance was further undermined by the decision to hire a Scots dialogue coach (the film was shot in English), making him sound worse than he had in his earlier projects in England. This added up to a hat trick, since his attempts at doing a northern accent in the Italian version of the film were also scored. The actor has seconded such criticisms.

> I've never been able to do dialects the way, say, Giannini and Volonté can do them. What I've always tried to do is to catch the musicality of the different regional speeches in Italy. Sometimes I get it right; sometimes I don't. In that film I didn't.

Dialect was also a major consideration in *Scipione Detto Anche l'Africano* (Scipio the African), directed by Luigi Magni, who had staged *Ciao, Rudy*. An ironic look at the Roman Empire, *Scipione* had the title character (Mastroianni) speak the modern dialect of the Italian capital in an effort to underline his social antagonism to Cato the Censor (Vittorio Gassman), his main foe. In the end, in fact, such popular touches and a parallel emphasis on Scipio's domestic problems with his wife (Silvana Mangano) practically overwhelmed the costume aspects of the study of the former Roman hero's declining years. The result, according to most critics, was "a bizarre but ultimately mediocre" reworking of a story that had provided the Italian cinema with one of its biggest spectaculars during the Fascist years.

For Mastroianni, however, *Scipione* proved far more memorable for what occurred offscreen during its production than for what a modest number of spectators got to see. To begin with, there was one of his costars—his brother, Ruggero.

> Rossetto—that is what we have always called him in the family— had been one of the biggest editors in the industry for years, but he

had always wanted to be an actor. In fact, he had become a little frustrated that nobody had ever offered him a part. Well, when I suggested he play the part of Scipio the Asian, the brother of my character, Magni didn't hesitate. Nobody was more elated than my mother. When she saw the film, she said to me, "You're pretty good, Marcello, but this time Rossetto beat you to the punch."

The critical consensus was otherwise, with most reviewers suggesting that Ruggero stick to editing.

However enthusiastic he might have been to have his brother at his side at the start of production, Mastroianni soon fell into what he described as "total despair" over his breakup with Dunaway.

> The worst time was when we went down to Pompeii for some night scenes. I thought of everything around me as a cemetery. I was so depressed about Faye that I didn't know what the hell I was doing and didn't especially care. One night, I jumped up on a horse for a scene where I was supposed to go galloping off. Gassman, who wasn't exactly bubbling, either, because of some liver problem that he had, looks up at me and goes, "Jesus, I didn't know you could ride!" When I told him it was the first time in my life I'd ever been on a horse, he got all white and said, "But aren't you afraid up there?" "What the hell do I care?" I said to him. "I want to die, anyway. Besides, you've made films where you've ridden a horse." "Like hell I have," he says to me. "You think I'm crazy? I hate horses. Any horse that I've been on for a film has been fake."

Hoping that Dunaway would change her mind, the actor couldn't wait for dawn to come so he could finish work in Pompeii and make the three-hour drive back to Rome to see if she had left any messages. With no word, he then got back into the car and returned south for the next evening's work.

> I just wasn't sleeping, and that made me even more impossible for everybody. When I'd walk into the hotel where the troupe was staying and hear them making plans to play cards or something, I would feel this great hatred for them. I was so wrapped up in myself that I didn't see anybody or anything. One time, walking down a hall at Cinecittà, I went right past my brother without noticing him. The set was like a morgue. I was in my state. Gassman had his liver worries. Mangano was distracted by something having to do with her husband [De Laurentiis] being in America. Magni was never effusive on the best of days. . . . One day, I was in the middle of a scene with Silvana, when the cameraman said we had to stop because there was a fly buzzing around. I said to him, "Why stop? The fly is the only damn thing around here that's alive."

If Mastroianni got over his Dunaway blues, it was mainly because of Catherine Deneuve, whom he had met only fleetingly a few years before but who had made an indelible impression on him.

> I had gone to the George V to meet Roger Vadim. He was accompanied by a young woman who struck me as the last word in beauty and elegance. Vadim said to her, "Please wait here, I must talk to Mastroianni for a few minutes." Without a word, she sat down at some distance from where we were. The few minutes turned into more than an hour. Vadim was talking about some project that he had in mind, but I kept looking over to where this delicate woman was sitting. She didn't move the whole time. She wasn't smoking or reading or looking at her watch or getting up to make a phone call or having a drink—absolutely nothing. She just *was* there. Calm, beautiful, content as a plant, as though her whole life consisted of waiting patiently for Vadim. Well, animal that I was, I was incredibly touched. I thought to myself, "This is the ideal woman."

Deneuve was with Mastroianni when, following *Scipione*, the actor had another opportunity to travel abroad—this time to Chicago for Scola's *Permette? Rocco Papaleo* (Rocco Papaleo). There was a catch to the assignment, however.

> Scola was enthusiastic about the film, and I trusted him. But even though there seemed to be more producers than actors involved, nobody was willing to pay us what we earned normally. So we said to hell with it and agreed to work for a percentage of the profits. Naturally, there wasn't a lira of profit.

Permette? Rocco Papaleo gave Mastroianni the part of a Sicilian immigrant originally drawn to the United States by the prospect of entering the Golden Gloves but long since reduced to a series of humble jobs, most recently that of an elevator operator in an Alaskan mine. When he goes along with some of the miners to a boxing match in Chicago, he gets caught up in a whirl of misadventures that pit his deep optimism against the brutalities of the Windy City. Only when an attractive woman (Lauren Hutton), whom he thought had returned his affections, dumps him contemptuously does he arm himself with a bomb and go off intent on wreaking havoc on his next abuser.

The film was panned just about everywhere that it was shown as more grotesque than satirical. Even Mastroianni has acknowledged it as something considerably less than a masterpiece, shrugging to one interviewer that "for the people connected with it, it was like a baby born badly—you have to love it in any case." Lauren Hutton, for one, has not disguised that feeling, going so far as to say that her experiences on *Permette? Rocco Papaleo* "changed my life." According to the actress, that was the last impression she had expected when she first showed up for her two-month stint.

> It was only my second film, and I had no idea what I was doing. I was the Green Child personified. To make it worse, the producers had found me an interpreter who loathed me. She was a thirteen-year-old girl who was the daughter of a Turin industrialist who had decided that the best way to keep her away from her left-wing radical friends was to send her abroad and work on the film. She showed up expecting to see this big capitalist actress in furs or something. Not even the fact that I was always in jeans broke the ice. I was nothing more than the exploiter class. I assume she interpreted everything accurately, but I was never sure.

Equally intimidating was that Hutton's first shot was a complicated track that called for her to hit Mastroianni with her car.

> I idolized this man ever since I saw him in *La Dolce Vita*, and here I am in this car supposed to run him over as soon as I meet him, jump out, and then go through a page and a half of dialogue. That's when I told Scola my little secret—I didn't know how to drive. We got that message through, and whatever the man was thinking, he just said to me, "No problem. We'll pad the car so you don't hurt Marcello." I was mortified. But they just went about attaching half an inch of foam rubber to the front of the car. I didn't dare look at Marcello while all this was going on, even though he was as natural as could be, talking to everybody, not giving away for a second that he was on the verge of being killed by this woman in the streets of Chicago in the interests of making a movie.

The first take of the scene didn't do much for the actress's confidence.

> Scola kept saying it was an automatic, so there wasn't much I had to remember. Well, I started off like I was supposed to, but he shouldn't have told me where the brake was because I kept hitting it. Finally, Deneuve, who was standing there and watching, came to my rescue. She jumped into the back of the car and got down on the floor so she couldn't be seen. And then, as the camera started rolling, she kept yelling two things to me—"Cheat," which meant that I should get my profile into the shot, and "Hit him!" We did that damn thing eight times, with Catherine in the back yelling those things to me. And the astonishing thing was that each and every time, Marcello hit the ground and started writhing in a completely different way. I may not have known what acting was, but I knew *that* was it.

For Hutton, the experience wasn't confined to the professionalism that Mastroianni showed on the set.

Marcello and Catherine were always cooking. He had this fagioli
soup that he especially liked, and both of them were shocked that
I never ate. Well, before the two of them got through with me, they
had taught me how to eat, how really to love food. Between that and
what I watched him do before the cameras, I'm really not exaggerating when I say I felt that my life changed with that picture.

During his stay in Chicago, the revived actor went out of his
way to meet with as many local residents as possible. On one occasion, he held a seminar for college students at the Goodman Theater,
where he discussed film and theater for several hours. There was little doubt among those on the scene at the time that Mastroianni's
improved mood was due to the company of Deneuve.

Back in Rome after *Permette? Rocco Papaleo*, the actor appeared
as himself in a cameo role for Fellini's *Roma*, then realized one of his
oldest ambitions by costarring with Anna Magnani in *Correva l'Anno
di Grazia 1870*. Shot for Italian television but shown in other parts of
Europe theatrically (and titled simply *1870*), *Correva l'Anno di Grazia 1870*, written and directed by Alfredo Giannetti, cast Mastroianni
as a veteran nationalist who is dying in prison when Rome is finally
liberated from the papacy and united to Italy. The last scene—cited
by many as the dramatic raison d'être for the whole exercise—has
the patriot's wife (Magnani) describe the liberation to him in meticulous detail so that he can feel that he is a part of the victory before
dying.

The mild critical response to *Correva l'Anno di Grazia 1870* did
not dim Mastroianni's enthusiasm for having had the opportunity to
work with Magnani. "I couldn't remember when I had been so
excited," he told one interviewer.

With due respect to all the others I have worked with, she was a
unique actress, a woman of incomparable greatness and intelligence. And generosity! There was one scene, for instance, when she
was supposed to have this long monologue about a lot of political
things in the script. At one point she turns to Giannetti and says,
"What the hell is this? I'm going on forever here. Mastroianni is
supposed to just sit there and listen? No, I have a better idea. I'll say
something, then he'll say something, and so on." Maybe it was
because she had some respect for me, I don't know. But I certainly
never saw any basis for that reputation of hers as some kind of terrible ogre on the set. Believe me, compared to a lot of other stupid

actresses who thought they were big stars and had directors running all over the place to satisfy some whim, Magnani was a giant.

The actor was so taken with the experience that he made plans
with Magnani to make a film version of the French play *Tchin-
Tchin*,which had caused some controversy at the 1971 Spoleto Festival, with Daniel Gélin and Betsy Blair in the leads. As it turned out,
Mastroianni did the piece both on the stage and on film, but without
Magnani, who died about a year after the release of *Correva l'Anno
di Grazia 1870.*

The next move abroad was to Paris for Nadine Trintignant's *Ça
N'Arrive Qu'Aux Autres* (It Only Happens to Others), costarring
Deneuve. It was during the making of this film that the actor and
actress moved into an apartment on the swank Avenue Georges Man-
del, maintaining a residence there for about three years. On May 28,
1972, the couple's daughter Chiara was born.

Ça N'Arrive Qu'Aux Autres was a semiautobiographical treatment of the tragedy that had struck Nadine Trintignant and her
actor-husband Jean-Louis Trintignant a few years before, when they
had awakened one morning to find their nine-month-old daughter
dead in her crib. In the film story, the couple played by Mastroianni
and Deneuve also lose a daughter (who had the same name as the
Trintignants' real child), then shut themselves up in their apartment,
severing all ties to the outside world and contemplating suicide. After
the initial shock wears off, however, the pair makes a try at rediscov-
ering life, ending up in the country at a wedding for strangers and
giving every impression of having overcome the worst. But it is not
that easy: Returning home and coming across a photo of their daughter, the husband and wife once again descend into gloom, the film
concluding on an ambiguous note about whether the revival they felt
in the country will get them through.

The autobiographical nature of the film prompted reviewers to
move gingerly in their appraisals, with many reluctant to come right
out and say that aside from Deneuve's performance, in particular, it
barely moved beyond its tragic premise. A typically careful evaluation was that of the Milan daily *Il Giorno,* which observed that "some
people might find such an undertaking of dubious taste, while others
believe that it could be useful therapy for the people personally
involved in such a misfortune." For his part, Mastroianni took every
opportunity to praise Trintignant's "professionalism," denying that
the set had the air of a funeral parlor and stressing his satisfaction at
being directed by a woman for the first time in his career.

Although established in Paris, the actor reached back to some of his oldest friends in Rome for his next project, *La Cagna* (Liza), an allegory directed by Marco Ferreri and based on Ennio Flaiano's novella *Melampus*. Ferreri:

> Mastroianni and Deneuve wanted to work together again, so I thought of Flaiano's story. That was the easy part. The fact is that we ended up changing the original story a lot, and it's a good thing Marcello was involved because I could not have seen eye to eye only with Flaiano, who thinks that cinema and literature are sacred.

What Mastroianni brokered was a very Ferreri-like story about a Parisian cartoonist who leaves his wife and grown children to live on a deserted island in the Mediterranean. With only his dog, Melampus, as company, the cartoonist makes do by living in an old German bunker, fiddling around with a crash-landed Luftwaffe plane, and periodically taking a raft over to the mainland for supplies. His routine is brusquely interrupted by the arrival of Liza (Deneuve), a spoiled blonde who has gotten bored with companions aboard a yacht that has put into the island. Despite the cartoonist's efforts to get rid of her, Liza remains behind after the yacht has sailed and, to get the Mastroianni character's attention, kills his dog. From that point on, she herself takes on the aspects of a canine (*cagna* in Italian meaning bitch), submissive to the cartoonist's every desire. After an interlude in Paris, where the cartoonist only confirms his hatred for civilization, the pair return to the island. The end of the film finds them reduced to even greater isolation by the destruction of the raft during a violent storm and by the failure of the refitted plane to get any further than the runway.

Italian and French critics had a ball deciding whether the male or female character was ultimately the more degraded figure, but otherwise agreed that *La Cagna* was fully in line with Ferreri's misanthropic view of life. Both the director and Mastroianni conceded, however, that the film wavered too uncertainly between satire and tragedy, creating the impression of shock for its own sake.

If wanting to work with Deneuve had been the springboard for *La Cagna*, the need for money for supporting his new household had a lot to do with the actor's appearance in Roman Polanski's *Che?* (What?). Filmed largely in a villa on the Amalfi coast, *Che?* represented Polanski's attempt to modernize the adventures of Alice in Wonderland. In the picture, a young girl (Sydne Rome) wanders from room to room in the villa, encountering a series of bizarre characters whose common denominator is that they are impervious to her attempts at getting through to them. One of the inhabitants is a middle-aged seducer (Mastroianni) who attacks the heroine twice before she makes good an escape.

One school of opinion found *Che?* respectable but too abstract for its own good. The majority view dismissed it as claptrap, observing that its most noticeable dramatic progression over two hours was in the increasing nudity of the Rome character as she wandered from room to room. For the *New York Times*, among others, the only relationship between the film and Lewis Carroll was at the level of heavyhanded porno parody. The distributors agreed: After the picture's initial release and death at the box office and following the arrest of Polanski on a morals charge, *Che?* was reedited and reissued as a soft-core porn feature under the title of *Diary of Forbidden Dreams*. Mastroianni has shrugged off the film as

> one of those promising ideas that turns out to be a disaster and that the actor has to rebound from. . . . It was not very convincing. Polanski was not a director suited for southern climates. In the script there was a real sense of cruelty and threat, you really feared for the character of the girl. But none of that came out.

Mordi e Fuggi (Sting and Run) found the actor back under the direction of Risi in an uncertain drama about a couple (Mastroianni and Carol André) who get kidnapped by terrorists fleeing the scene of a murder and who get to despise each other while in the hands of their captors. Critics who paid any attention to it at all chided Mastroianni for seeming to be satisfied with doing a Sordi turn as a cowardly hostage. The project's only defender was Risi, who insisted even a decade later that *Mordi e Fuggi* had been ahead of its time in depicting terrorism in Italy.

Mastroianni didn't fare much better in a subsequent portrayal of Nazi terrorism during World War II. *Rappresaglia* (Massacre in Rome), directed by George Pan Cosmatos and based on Robert Katz's study of the 1944 massacre of several hundred Rome prisoners in retaliation for an underground ambush of a German patrol, cast him as an emblematic priest who seeks to obtain the intervention of the Vatican to put a halt to the executions. When the priest elicits nothing more than a generic disapproval of the looming reprisal from a Holy See bent on not alienating the occupation Nazi forces, he joins the victims at the Ardeatine caves. Although Katz himself collaborated on the screenplay, the fictional account of the reprisal was much softer on the stance of Pope Pius XII than the book had been. In addition, the casting of Richard Burton as German commandant Herbert Kappler often had the Nazi character come off sympathetically.

The legal and political fallout from *Rappresaglia* proved far more durable than its artistic impact, which was next to none. Despite the diluted condemnation of the Vatican vis-à-vis the book, the film prompted an elderly niece of Pius XII to sue Katz, Pan Cosmatos, and producer Ponti for insinuating that the pontiff had effectively collaborated with the Nazis. A lower court ruled in her favor, delivering sentences of up to eighteen months for the defendants; only a lengthy appeal process kept them out of jail. The suit was, in fact, only the centerpiece of numerous political machinations around the film. Aside from those with Vatican interests, some Italian politicians were nervous about the continued presence in the country, in solitary confinement, of the real Kappler. They only breathed more easily when, on August 15, 1977, the ex-commandant managed to "escape" from the fortress where he was being held to West Germany.

Mastroianni's next project—*L'Événement le Plus Important Depuis Que l'Homme A Marché sur la Lune* (A Slightly Pregnant Man)—was one that he would brand "the absolute worst" of his career. Once again, the picture arose from his desire to work with Deneuve, and ideally in a comedy. Their willing partner was director Jacques Demy, who not only quickly banged out a screenplay but also used his own house and its environs for most of the location work.

L'Événement centers around a Parisian driving instructor (Mastroianni) who is diagnosed as pregnant. Before long, he is a cause célèbre, embarked on a lot of predictable gender-switching jokes with his hairdresser-lover (Deneuve). The film ends with the delivery of the child and signs that other men around the world will also soon be in need of maternity clothes.

As savage as many critics were with the film, the most significant testimony to it probably came from director Demy. He didn't make another picture for five years and even then needed a Japanese production company to finance him. As for Mastroianni, he tried to write it off as another case of "the actor having to get up off the floor to feel alive again with his next project."

In the event, he still had some staggering to do—not all of it metaphorical.

21

Close-up: The Romantic Socialist

Mastroianni's association with the political Left in Italy has never been as systematic as that of some other noted figures in the country's film industry (e.g., Volonté), but it hasn't been a cursory indulgence, either. Like Fellini, Scola, and others, he has usually supported social and cultural initiatives that in an American context would be defined as liberal. As a voter, this has left him across the street from the political power structure epitomized by the Christian Democrats and their on-and-off governing partners from the Social Democratic and Socialist parties. Just as often, it has made him a free-lance backer of the Communists as the only viable alternative to the entrenchment of the Christian Democrats in Italian political, business, and cultural life. But over and above immediate balloting preferences, the actor has personified the somewhat paradoxical position that many prominent artists and intellectuals of his generation have adopted within a society in which the concept of an Establishment has always meant decidedly different things to different people and sometimes rival things to the same people.

Asked once how he characterized himself politically, Mastroianni replied:

> I don't like fervid position taking. I suppose I'm a romantic socialist in the old sense, with a small s. I hate labels and imposed ideals. I can't get too enthusiastic, either, about all those values that are supposed to be typical of the average Italian—God, Nation, Family. But what remains with me is the realization that the world could find a solution (to its problems) with the kind of justice that would also allow the poor to survive and affirm themselves.

In the same vein, he had this exchange with the monthly *Attenzione* in 1981:

209

MASTROIANNI: Gian Maria Volonté has justly used his profession for political ideals. I've made films that you would call politically committed, too. But the commitment was, let's say, very Latin.
ATTENZIONE: In what sense?
MASTROIANNI: Well, in the sense that I don't belong to any political party. I have great sympathy for the non-Communist Left because I believe it is logical, normal, that a nation like ours go that way. What I would really like, I suppose, is for Italy to be a socialist country, but in a serious way. A healthy, democratic socialism.
ATTENZIONE: But you don't see that happening?
MASTROIANNI: How can it happen when nobody there is serious? If we were serious, we would have had a democratic socialist republic since 1946. But the fact is that Italy is led by clowns and charlatans, and that's why we're in the situation we're in today. And you certainly don't see any of these buffoons examining their consciences when something like the Red Brigades comes along. Who was it who helped create the Red Brigades? All these charlatans with their scandals and corruption, that's who.

With the exception of a suspicious drop-off in film offers for a few months after his appearance in 1976 in Petri's *Todo Modo,* a film that went after some noted Christian Democratic leaders with little subtlety, Mastroianni has seldom sensed professional repurcussions from his criticisms of Italian ruling circles; certainly nothing along the lines of the threats leveled against De Sica in the early 1950s following the release of *Umberto D.* One reason has been his international standing and personal traveling itch to go wherever a promising part was to be found. Another has been his emphasis on roles and films that convey social and political injustices through what he has termed "the laughter of Pulcinella."

You can't expect to tell the truth, and get people to appreciate the truth, by lecturing them. The truth is damn unpleasant. So you get people to *enjoy* the truth. When Italian cinema has been most successful, it's been successful in this way. And it's no wonder it's never been especially popular with these people we have been saddled with in our governments.

Or, again:

People are tired of having to live so politically intensely. Everything they do from the moment that they get up in the morning is political, so why should they be eager to run into a movie house for more of the same?

Along with his cachet as an international star and his aversion to screen militancy, Mastroianni has avoided trouble with the petulances of power through his identification, loose as it might be, with the leftist establishment of Italy. For some four decades following the founding of the republic in 1947, in fact, three distinct politico-cultural nuclei of significance prevailed in the country. One was that of the "Christian" values of the Christian Democrats and Vatican-influenced loyalists. A second was represented by the Italian Communists, who were inspired far more by the solidarity principles of the Resistance and by the stated goal of a "national road to socialism" than by any profound regard for the policies of the Soviet Union. The third nucleus was that of the self-identified "laics"—centrist forces that dismissed the Christian Democrats and Communists as complementary religions and that vaunted their appreciation for the pragmatic ways of the Anglo-Saxon countries in everything from business organization to mass-media manipulation. (Less important, although not always less visible, was a fourth bastion of neo-Fascist cultural values.) On a level of political parties, accommodations of the moment could obscure the distinctions; on a broader cultural plane, however, the differences were not dispensed with so easily, so that everything from national regions to city neighborhoods to publishing houses to street fairs maintained a fundamental ideological association. In the context of these competitive circles, there was hardly any hesitation on the part of the Christian Democrats to herald Sordi as one of their own, just as there was little timidity on the part of the laics to boast of having a Gassman or a Manfredi in their ranks or on the part of the Communists to publicize support from the likes of Mastroianni, Volonté, Fellini, and Petri. In the 1980s, much of this demarcation began to fade in the face of such new factors as regional self-assertion, the dying out of the old guards, the replacement of East-West pressures by those from multinational corporations and financial markets, the reorganization of the Communist party, and the incursions of the European Community, but prior to then, well-known figures linked to any of the circles could count on as many defenders as attackers, not just in the media but, if need be, also on the floors of Parliament and in ministerial corridors.

Like Fellini and many others, Mastroianni's principal reason for providing independent support to the Communists at appointed elections was that they posed the most serious opposition to the cretinization of public life attributed to the Christian Democratic power structure. It was, in the actor's words, "a question of honor" to resist in particular the censorship policies of the Christian Democrats that, far from being confined to motion pictures, were even more oppressive on the state-run television network, where government speeches usually held sway over images of the real Italy. In his later years, he broadened his attack against television as a medium per se, not merely as a fiefdom of individual political parties but as a phenomenon that had been imported only too successfully from the idealized Anglo-Saxon countries of the laics. As he told *Il Corriere della Sera* in November 1983: "It is shameful how our society has been taken over by TV quiz shows, lotteries, and the like. It's pathetic seeing the public encouraged to do these things."

But for all his strongly held views, Mastroianni has never been regarded as a prominent presence in the periodic waves of overtly political films that have washed over Italy, most conspicuously in the late 1960s and early 1970s. With a handful of exceptions in the scores of pictures that he has made, the most frequent explicitly political context to his roles has been that of Mussolini's Fascism (*Cronache di Poveri Amanti, Per le Antiche Scale, Una Giornata Particolare*, etc.)—works that, whatever their other merits, could have ideologically excited only the most obscurantist interests. In some other films where revolution was synoynmous with Italian nationalism, such as in *Correva l'Anno di Grazia 1870* and *Allonsanfan*, the actor portrayed characters doused by as much pathos or cowardice as by heroism, ultimately affecting a presence that overwhelmed any literally political significance. In fact, by the standard of treatise pictures, the only truly political films in which Mastroianni has figured have been Monicelli's *I Compagni* and Petri's *Todo Modo*—the first role representing the closest he has come to rendering a romantic socialist on the screen and the second one drawing considerably on the explosiveness that the director always saw as the actor's most untapped gift.

By Mastroianni's own criteria, however, *I Compagni* and *Todo Modo* were far from being his only political films. In his view, every time that he took on a role that dealt with some contemporary social aberration, he was making a political comment. As he once declared,

> The Italian cinema is the only artistic medium that has cried out against all the misgoverning and constantly criticized our decrepit institutions. *Divorzio all'Italiana*, for instance, was a denunciation of a very real problem.

On other occasions, he has included *Il Bell'Antonio* and *Signore e Signori, Buonanotte* in the same category. On the other hand, he has usually omitted from the list fatuous melodramas laid against a background of some political topic; for example, the urban terrorism of *Mordi e Fuggi*.

In the final analysis, if there has been a consistent political assumption to Mastroianni's screen roles, it has been that most generic of all saws that man is a political animal. Taking together the numerous characters he has portrayed and the unrealized goals of his romantic socialism, his additional contribution has been to underline how the political animal has rarely been allowed to prowl beyond its cage.

22

Dark Days

Mastroianni's first three screen ventures with Deneuve amounted to two near disasters and a catastrophe. *La Cagna* threatened particular ruin to director Ferreri, who suddenly found himself a dirty word in the Italian and French boardrooms where film financing was approved. But Ferreri had two aces. The first was his friendship with four of the most bankable actors working in Europe in the early 1970s—Mastroianni, Tognazzi, Michel Piccoli, and Philippe Noiret. The other was the diabetes that he almost died of early in 1973.

As Tognazzi was to recount it, *La Grande Bouffe* (Blowout) arose from the elaborate meals that he and Ferreri had once devoured in the actor's Rome apartment. "When everything was out on the table, all of it seasoned to a turn, we would survey it very carefully, then say to each other almost ritualistically, 'This is going to kill us.' Then we would dig in." When the director had dug in once too often and had to be admitted to a Swiss clinic, he has acknowledged, "I began thinking about death." No sooner had he gotten back on his feet than he wrote the script for *La Grande Bouffe* and, with the indispensable backing of his four players, overcame resistance to financing the picture.

La Grande Bouffe was as intimate a film ever made by Ferreri— a fact indicated by having the four stars use their own first names as a quartet of middle-aged professionals (Tognazzi a restaurant owner and chef, Mastroianni an airline pilot, Piccoli a television producer, Noiret a magistrate) who gather at a villa with the intention of eating themselves to death. Although the four indeed end up as corpses, the Mastroianni character reaches his objective only after announcing that sex and automobiles, not food, are the path through life (and to disgruntled death); after an impotent tussle with a prostitute brought to the villa for the occasion, he ends up freezing to death in an automobile that he has devoted his final hours to repairing.

Some critics voiced suprise that Mastroianni, the biggest box-office name of the quartet, was killed off first, while Noiret, probably the least known, ended up with the largest role. The reason had nothing at all to do with dramatic considerations, reflecting instead Ferreri's loose relationship with his players. Mastroianni:

> Deneuve and I had been planning for some time to take a vacation in Jamaica, so I asked Marco to kill me off first so the trip wouldn't be ruined. Then Piccoli had another picture to make, so he was killed off. Ugo had to do something else, so he didn't want to stick around till the end, either. Noiret was like the cat that swallowed the canary.

Reaction to *La Grande Bouffe* covered all the bases. Its savagely grotesque premise made it one of the most discussed films of the year, this aiding its commercial fortunes and restoring Ferreri to the good graces of his backers. Wherever it was shown, it sparked solemn debate about the consumer society and, somewhat as with Fellini and *La Dolce Vita*, about whether its director was a sentinel against modern immorality or a parasite opening the gates to it. Among the prizes it took was the International Critics Award at the 1973 Cannes Festival. But on the other hand, the film was also scored by numerous reviewers for not venturing far beyond its premise and for ultimately playing witness to the suicides rather than explicating them sufficiently. In Italy and France especially, Mastroianni and Piccoli also came in for a share of critical bruises. The usually sympathetic Moravia, for instance, told his *L'Espresso* readers that "Piccoli is only convincing, and Mastroianni not even that." French periodicals were particularly upset that Piccoli's character farted almost as much as he ate, and took the actor to task for lending himself to a role of the kind. As for Mastroianni, he has generally confined himself to insisting on the "high morality" of the film as a whole.

With Yves Robert's *Salut l'Artiste* (Salute the Artist), Mastroianni returned to the slighter, more melancholy ironies of a scuffling second-rate actor in Paris who keeps reality at bay by running to one minor job after another. His brittle world begins to fragment only after a partner (Jean Rochefort), with whom he has been a staple for dubbing studios, advertising agencies, and casting directors, decides to leave show business for the security of a regular job; in short order, his wife (Carla Gravina) and lover (Françoise Fabian) also puncture his balloons. While showcasing what was probably Mastroianni's best performance since *Dramma della Gelosia*, *Salut l'Artiste* was undone by a distribution company (Paris/Euro International) that went bankrupt shortly before it was due to release the picture. Those who saw it, and there weren't many, saw it only a couple of years after completion, and usually as a movie-theater fill-in.

At one point in *Salut l'Artiste*, the character of the actor is told by his mistress: "On the screen you may be a presence, but with me you are mainly an absence." Similar words might have been heard from Deneuve offscreen around the same time as the French actress's household relationship with Mastroianni neared an end. The couple's last hours were played out during the filming of *Touche Pas à la Femme Blanche!* (The True Story of General Custer), a wild satire directed by Ferreri that transplanted Custer's "last stand" to the backdrop of the Parisian quarter of Les Halles, the vast market area then being knocked down and serving as an unofficial home to the French capital's roofless poor.

Although Ferreri has always claimed that *Touche Pas à la Femme Blanche!* was addressed to "all the children of the world," it is doubtful that anybody under fifteen grasped its ambitious—and often explicit—surrealistic attempt to meld the story of Custer (Mastroianni) with that of the contemporary exploitation of Third World peoples. Conversely, adult critics generally sounded like children who had just seen a modern variation on a Gary Cooper western, giving the film a high score for its entertainment value and bizarre casting (Tognazzi played an indian named Mitch; Piccoli, Buffalo Bill) and waving off the profundity of its satirical intent. If Mastroianni had been dismissed as inadequate in *La Grande Bouffe*, in *Touche Pas à la Femme Blanche!* he was equally hailed for centering the story's absurd style. For the actor, as much as for the director, this added up to a half victory:

> What some people seemed to expect from Ferreri after *La Grande Bouffe* was another scandalistic treatise of some sort on modern society. It *was* a denunciation, but done in such a surrealistic key that it wasn't considered as important as the previous film.

Touche Pas à la Femme Blanche marked the end of Mastroianni's first lengthy sojourn in France. To some Italian reporters he claimed that his return to Italy was motivated entirely by professional reasons. Typical was his declaration to the Rome daily *Il Tempo* that "I have worn out my interest in France. Their films have remained very behind, rooted in old concepts and classic concerns." For some time, however, the breakup with Deneuve led to some heavy drinking. Adding to his gloom were the death of De Sica and his inability to finalize a couple of projects that he wanted to do with Visconti, who was ailing and who would also pass away within a short time. At one juncture, he fell into such a depression that he had

to turn down the role of the Fascist district leader in Bernardo Bertolucci's *1900* that eventually went to Donald Sutherland.

The actor's first film upon returning to Italy was *Allonsanfan*,
directed by brothers Paolo and Vittorio Taviani. His role was that of
a weary aristocrat in the early nineteenth century who has spent long
years in prison for his support of republican causes and who little by
little betrays all his ideals, in the process causing the deaths of innumerable comrades. He himself gets killed during one last feverish
stab at believing that he has retained some of his principles. Although
he was praised by some critics for his performance, Mastroianni was
mentioned by many others as the film's chief problem because of his
rather resigned reading of the protagonist. This became even more of
a point of discussion following disclosures that the part had been
intended originally for Volonté, who had turned it down because of
his own political principles of not wanting to portray a negative revolutionary character. While Volonté was bashed in some left-wing
circles for not knowing how to separate the ego of an actor doing an
unsympathetic part from the general tableau of a film with ideological aims, Mastroianni was by extension attacked for lacking the ability to provide the kind of psychological friction in the role of the
traitor that his fellow actor might have displayed; that is, he wasn't
political enough. It was one of the few times that questions were
raised not only about his performance in a given film but also about
his emotional range.

As bleak as the character in *Allonsanfan* was, its self-delusional
rationalizations did not quite total up to the classic screen villain.
The same thing could not be said for Mastroianni's next three undertakings, when, for about the only time in his career, his dark mood
made him receptive to decidedly black-hat parts. The first of the trio
was *La Pupa del Gangster* (The Gangster's Doll), which again found
him with Loren under the direction of Giorgio Capitani. Based on a
short story by Cornell Woolrich, *La Pupa del Gangster* was equally
inspired by the MGM crime film *Party Girl*, with the hood portrayed
by Mastroianni as obsessed by Rita Hayworth as the character played
by Lee J. Cobb in the American feature had been by Jean Harlow.
Otherwise, the Ponti production added few nuances to the melodrama of a hooker (Loren) who helps the police get their hands on her
protector for a murder charge. The picture died a quick death.

In Giuseppe Patroni Griffi's *La Divina Creatura* (The Divine
Nymph), Mastroianni was back to operating a stable of prostitutes,
this time for an aristocratic clientele on the eve of Mussolini's ascen-
dancy to power. Instead of being arrested at the end, the actor's bad
guy dons the black shirt of the Fascists and is represented as a symbolic figure of the Italy to come. Such high-toned significance with a

capital S and some enthusiastic reaction to Mastroianni's performance as the nasty pimp could not save *La Divina Creatura*, even
with an advertising campaign that emphasized the charms of costar
Laura Antonelli.

The actor's third straight heavy was for Bolognini's *Per le
Antiche Scale* (Down the Ancient Stairs), in the part of the chief of
staff of a psychiatric clinic in the 1930s who casts a Svengali-like
power over his female patients and colleagues while trying to bend
to his will the newest arrival, a psychiatrist (Françoise Fabian) whose
approaches to treatment would jeopardize his sense of control. It is
ultimately disclosed that the doctor is obsessed with the fear of going
mad himself—a destiny borne out to some degree by his final realization that in Fascist Italy insanity is even more pervasive outside the
clinic than in its wards. While relatively more layered than his characters in *La Pupa del Gangster* and *La Divina Creatura*, Mastroianni's
personage in *Per le Antiche Scale* borrowed heavily from the two earlier roles, with some critics contending that he seemed more interested in emphasizing the physician's evil manipulativeness than the
incipient madness that had been the key to the original book by
Mario Tobini.

After appearing as himself in Scola's *C'Eravamo Tanti Amati*
(We All Loved Each Other So Much) in a scene that re-created the
Trevi Fountain sequence from *La Dolce Vita*, the actor hit his stride
again with Luigi Comencini's *La Donna della Domenica* (The Sunday
Woman), based on a popular thriller by Carlo Fruttero and Franco
Lucentini. Mastroianni played a detective who prowls around high
society in Turin to get to the bottom of the murder of an architect.
Before he has resolved everything, he falls for a wealthy woman (Jacqueline Bisset), who, however, turns out to be more interested in a
one-night stand than in any relationship with the socially inferior
policeman.

Aside from garnering good notices for his performance, *La
Donna della Domenica* brought Mastroianni the renewed attention
of European and American gossip columnists for his off-the-set relationship with Bisset. Some associates of the actor said that they had
a six-month affair; others pegged it as a romance that ended almost
immediately after postproduction dubbing of the film. Mastroianni's
usual retort was to point to Bisset as an example of the way photographers isolated his dinner companions to create headlines; on the
other hand, he was visibly annoyed to be dragged back to Turin some
months later for a premiere of the film with the actress, especially
when an unexpectedly low turnout mainly consisted of publicists
and of reporters eager for more juicy tidbits. If nothing else, the conjecture about Bisset pushed aside other stories that had linked the

actor to two of his costars in *Per le Antiche Scale*, Marthe Keller and
Barbara Bouchet.

In the middle of all the talk, Carabella appeared for the one and
only time on the screen with her husband, in Flavio Mogherini's
Culastrisce Nobile Veneziano (Lunatics and Lovers). As small as her
part was, it marked Carabella's most conspicuous professional
appearance since leaving Visconti with Mastroianni in the 1950s to
concentrate on raising their daughter. The inevitable media spin on
the casting was that it marked a reconciliation between the pair—an
interpretation refuted not only by subsequent facts but by the insistence of both Mastroianni and Carabella that there had never been a
breakup requiring a reconciliation.

Culastrisce Nobile Veneziano combined some of the elements of
Fantasmi a Roma and *Leo the Last* to relate the story of a Venetian
marquis (Mastroianni) who wanders around his palazzo speaking to
the ghost of his wife, becomes the target of building speculators who
attempt to get him committed so they can seize the property, and
fends them off by hiring a prostitute (Claudia Mori) to pose as his
spouse. When the prostitute decides that she likes the aristocratic life
too much just to go away again, the marquis gets rid of her by sending
her aloft in a hot-air balloon, thereby freeing himself to go back to
babbling to the phantom of his real wife.

Culastrisce Nobile Veneziano netted Mastroianni little beyond
his salary. If it had any impact at all, it was as the first Italian feature
to be ripped by critics for transposing the glossy filming techniques of
television commercials to the big screen and presuming that this
would be sufficient for making a motion picture. For Mastroianni, it
was quickly forgotten in the uproar over his subsequent project, *Todo
Modo* (One Way or Another).

Directed by Petri and adapted from a novella by Leonardo Scia-
scia, *Todo Modo* was an iron-fisted allegory about a group of
extremely powerful politicians, government officials, and business
leaders who gather annually at a religious retreat for "spiritual exercises." In fact, the retreat is merely an occasion for them to work out
more of their power games under the sometimes cynical, sometimes
lacerating supervision of Father Gaetano (Mastroianni). When bodies
start piling up, suspicion passes from one survivor to another, until
all of them are also eliminated. The last survivor is a state official
known only as M (Gian Maria Volonté), who, surveying all the
destructiveness around him, concludes the lethal saraband by blowing out his brains.

Todo Modo's clear references to the power circles of the Italian
Christian Democratic party made inevitable the numerous obstacles
thrown in the path of the project's progress from script to screen.

Alberto Grimaldi, for one, had to throw in the towel as the producer when he could not find an Italian or French distributor. His successor, Daniele Senatore, resolved that impasse with an unlikely recourse to Warner Brothers, which felt emboldened by the presence in the cast not only of Mastroianni and Volonté but, in the small role of M's wife, of Mariangela Melato, then enjoying some notoriety as the star of Lina Wertmuller's films. For all that, Petri still had enormous difficulty in persuading Cinecittà to make one of its lots available. Equally predictably, a phantom organization known as the Unione Uomo-Natura (Man-Nature Union) filed suit against the film immediately upon its release for defaming the Italian chief of state; the legal maneuver netted little more than some brief publicity.

While *Todo Modo* gave rise to a nationwide guessing game about the true identities of the figures depicted on the screen, there was little need of conjecture about the inspiration for the central character of M, who right down to his initial represented Aldo Moro, the Hamlet-like government leader who was killed by terrorists a couple of years later. According to both Petri and Volonté, in fact, one of the film's initial problems was that the actor had submerged himself far too deeply in the persona of the Christian Democratic chieftain, producing a caricature that necessitated some significant reshooting. Another problem was the insistence of Warner Brothers to release the film on the eve of crucial Italian elections that amounted to a referendum on Moro's attempts to reach a governing agreement with the opposition Communists. Petri:

> We did not know when we were planning the release that there would have been elections, which were called at the last minute. Instead of being viewed as a commentary on the ruling class in Italy, therefore, the picture was seen as a direct attack on Moro and those who favored an agreement with the Communists, which had not at all been our intention. Warner Brothers couldn't have cared less about such internal ramifications. They were interested in a film that would provoke controversy, whatever direction it took. The result was that the Communists attacked *Todo Modo* publicly even more than some of the Christian Democrats who were against Moro's initiative. In private, of course, the Communists kept telling us how much they liked the film.

With one exception, the film ended up being blasted from every critical sector in Italy, with Volonté coming in for some particularly heavy notices for mimicking Moro rather than delivering a dramatic performance. The exception was Mastroianni's unusually aggressive portrait of the retreat supervisor that the actor himself has always cited as one of his most fulfilling roles and that Petri would point to as a perfect example of "the angry Mastroianni being the best Mastroianni." But the political pollution around the film was such that even when the Italian industry conferred an award on him as Best Actor of the year, it did so without specifically mentioning *Todo Modo*. As he declared during the award ceremonies:

> I don't know what else they could have given it to me for except *Todo Modo*, considering some of the other things that I've done lately. Obviously, Petri's film continues to bother a lot of people in power.

Mastroianni's next project also annoyed the Italian establishment, and this time there were no prizes. *Signore e Signori, Buonanotte* (Ladies and Gentlemen, Good Night) was a cooperative effort among some of the country's leading directors (Scola, Comencini, Monicelli, Magni, Nanni Loy), writers (Age, Scarpelli, Benvenuti, Ugo Pirro), and actors (Mastroianni, Manfredi, Gassman, Tognazzi, Paolo Villaggio) satirizing a typical day at a television studio. The film was actually an anthology of sketches parodying popular Italian programs, with Mastroianni playing the linking role of an anchor. As in all such initiatives, quality varied from skit to skit, with Manfredi gaining most of the attention for his role as a cardinal who fakes an illness so he will be elected pope. It was mainly because of this episode that the Vatican organ *Osservatore Romano* decried the entire film as "squalid," while other critics bemoaned the fact that there wasn't equal ferocity in some of the other segments.

Following *Signore e Signori, Buonanotte,* Mastroianni was more idle professionally than at any other time in his career (nine months). Most of his time was spent resolving his tax problems and getting to know his daughter by Deneuve, Chiara. According to the actor, Carabella was equally eager to host the child and at one point even suggested to Deneuve that she raise Chiara in Italy (a proposal politely refused by the French actress). There was considerable speculation at the time that as the main figures involved in *Todo Modo*, Mastroianni, Petri, and Volonté had become victims of a subtle blacklist in Italian film circles. Mastroianni has attributed his inactivity more to a combination of the tired roles offered to him and a personal weariness that made it difficult for him to recognize a fertile opportunity even when it was in front of him.

> For a long time, I was proud of the fact that I was the antihero of my generation. Then I realized that it was a dead end, that I wasn't getting beyond it. I became furious with myself and with others who didn't tell me this.

He told another interviewer of the period:

I thought to myself, I have lived a lie at one time or another about everything—in my relationship with people, with my country, with myself. I looked in the mirror and said, "How boring and oppressive you've become!" In the past, I had fit very easily into the role of victim. But suddenly I kept asking myself whether I had given more than I had taken.

As it turned out, he emerged from his funk with one of his key roles, as the homosexual in Scola's *Una Giornata Particolare* (A Special Day).

Largely a two-character play on film, *Una Giornata Particolare* is set against the background of Adolf Hitler's summit visit to Rome on January 6, 1938, for talks with Mussolini. With her Fascist husband and six children out from under foot to catch a glimpse of the Nazi leader, a housewife named Antonietta (Loren) is tending to her normal chores when the flight of her canary brings her into contact with her neighbor Gabriele (Mastroianni), a radio announcer who has just been fired for his homosexuality and anti-Fascist sentiments. The story then peels away the layers of political, domestic, and sexual repression that have suffocated both characters. Although they also eventually fall into one another's arms, it is clear that Gabriele makes love more out of pity and solidarity with Antonietta than because of any converting sexual thunderbolt. In the end, he is hauled away by the Fascist police, to be sent into internal exile, while she has only the consolation of a gift he has left for her—a copy of *The Three Musketeers*.

According to Scola, the first impediment to getting *Una Giornata Particolare* into production was the lack of enthusiasm from his eventual backers about both the script and the main players.

> Their first objection was that, in their words, "nothing happens" in the story, that all the spectacular scenes that there might have been around Hitler's arrival happened offscreen. As far as Marcello and Sophia were concerned, they kept saying that both of them were too old.

In the director's view, however, there was no better pair to play the couple.

> When I thought of the story of these two people humiliated in their sexuality, it seemed right to have them played by actors who had always been used as symbols of triumphant sex. It seemed like another way of celebrating virility and beauty as absolute values, not as commercial commodities.

For Loren, the role was the avenue out of a series of forgettable projects in Italy and abroad that had done a great deal to eclipse her star power. The death of her estranged father during shooting also gave her an emotional edge that she had not felt in a long time, she has admitted.

> There is a climactic scene in which I have to seduce Mastroianni. I prepared my fantasy for that scene for several weeks prior to shooting it. When the camera finally turned, I was really and truly that housewife making aggressive love to that passive man Marcello was playing. No fakery; in my mind, I was completely that woman having sexual intercourse at that moment.

Although he has usually listed *Una Giornata Particolare* among his most gratifying experiences, Mastroianni did not share Loren's self-absorption with his role; on the contrary, most of his comments indicate that the character of Gabriele simply restored his normal self-confident way of approaching a part as Mastroianni Doing. . . .

> So many people thought there was something extraordinary about playing a homosexual. I never could figure out why. For me, it was just one more case of saying, "Hey, I'm not who you think I am. I have an awful lot of limitations. Here, for instance, here's another one." It is the way I have always worked. And fortunately there was Scola as the director—one of those people who is always ready to listen, who creates a wonderful atmosphere on the set, who doesn't consider himself God's gift to the world.

In general, Italian critics were more impressed with the acting of Mastroianni and Loren than with the film as a whole. For many, the setup between the major characters was reminiscent of a Hollywood vehicle in which sentimentality, anger, happiness, and pain added up to a leaden parade of emotions aimed at nothing more than displaying the range of the players. Numerous foreign reviewers voiced the same reservations. In the end, it was Mastroianni who took away the major honors, including another Oscar nomination for Best Actor. While saying that he was flattered by the acknowledgment, he also had few illusions about winning the Hollywood prize.

> I can see them giving it to someone like John Travolta because that would let them finance more John Travolta films, knowing that they would make a profit from them. But if they give it to me, then what? I won't be there for them to make some money for the next couple of years.

The Oscar was given to Richard Dreyfuss for *The Goodbye Girl*.

One of the more ironic footnotes to *Una Giornata Particolare* was written in Poland, where it was pulled from theaters briefly because projectionists ran it immediately after a newsreel. Much of the newsreel was devoted to a visit by Communist party secretary Edward Gierek to Rome.

23

Close-up: Table Projects

For all the films that Mastroianni has made, he could compile a list almost as long of projects thwarted for one reason or another. Some of them have been little more than whims given extra life by the abetting fantasies of associates; others have been thought out enough to reach serious negotiation stages. One has gained legendary status as the most famous film never made in Europe.

Of the screen initiatives that went on with other actors, the most successful was probably *Un Homme et Une Femme* (A Man and a Woman), the 1966 French love story that broke international box-office records and that numbered two Oscars among its many awards. According to Mastroianni, Anouk Aimée urged him to costar in the film with her, but he was put off by the then-unknown director (Claude Lelouch), the production's unpromising financial situation, and even the necessity to play a widower. The male lead ended up going to Jean-Louis Trintignant, and Mastroianni ended up saying, "I made a mistake."

Two projected roles that the actor had looked forward to, on the other hand, were a film biography of composer Giacomo Puccini and a screen version of *Macbeth*. Both pictures would have been directed by Visconti, and both fell by the wayside with the filmmaker's death in 1976. Aside from everything else, the Puccini role would have been a gift to his mother, who had never gotten over his performance as Donizetti in *Casa Ricordi* in 1954. Doing *Macbeth* had shaped up as another event—the actor's first sally into a major Shakespearean role in any medium. His trust in Visconti for undertaking the venture was such that he did not seriously consider doing the film after the passing away of the director.

One of Mastroianni's favorite talking pieces over the years has been his deflection of Hollywood offers by holding out for the role of a deaf-dumb sheriff. Slightly more seriously, he sought to sell Petri on the idea of doing a comic western in which he and his brother,

Ruggero, would be teamed as feared gunfighters who enter a town and who, similar to the thieves in *I Soliti Ignoti,* ransack only the food shelves of the general store and the kitchen of the local steak house. Petri was also the target of a proposal in the 1960s to do a satire on Vincent Price horror films; according to Mastroianni, the film would have been entitled *Necrofilia* (Necrophilia) and feature old friends Buazzelli and Panelli, as well as his brother, in one scene of comic carnage after another. Once again, the director dismissed the idea as café talk. For his part, the actor has noted how his enthusiasm for the western spoof preceded Mel Brooks's success with the genre in *Blazing Saddles* in 1974 and how *Necrofilia,* if it had been made, would have gotten to theaters before the droll horror stories filmed by Dario Argento.

A third contemplated lampoon carried echoes from Visconti's rebuke of the actor as sounding like Tarzan shouting to his apes.

It was going to be called *Old Tarzan and Old Cheetah.* Imagine Cheetah in white fur having to push Tarzan up a tree. When he cries out, none of the animals pay attention to the demented old fool. The leopard skin? Maybe it's just a piece of hide covered with shit marks.

As late as 1989, the actor was proposing the same basic story, but with the setting Siberia and the character's name switched to Tarzanovich.

It would be a way of getting into Tarzan's real drama—the fact that he was never found but just kept wandering around like an imbecile, waiting for a beautiful white huntress to come along. What's more pathetic than seeing an old man growing old alone? The way I see Tarzan in such a film, he's a hero for people like me who are no longer in the prime of life. Africa or Siberia, it would be a great film.

A curious number of the unrealized projects and movie fantasies that Mastroianni has confessed to have involved the United States or characters with a strong Hollywood association. Aside from the sheriffs, Vincent Price monsters, and Tarzan, there have been his stymied desire to costar with Marilyn Monroe, the Joseph Levine parody of the Mafia, and another expressed ambition in the 1960s to work with Kim Novak. Even when an American setting did not appear to be called for, the actor envisioned just such a background. Thus, in the late 1960s, he went so far as to acquire filming rights to the Israeli novel *Piotrus,* with the intention of shifting the story's locale from the Middle East to New York.

I thought it was a fascinating idea. It was about a man who was at the end of his rope who sells himself to a woman. The woman is a landlady, and she locks him up in the only bathroom in her building as a way of forcing her other tenants out so she can sell the property at a great profit. I brought it to Ferreri, and he was very enthusiastic. But then everything got bogged down in the usual pre-production things, and my rights to the novel elapsed.

It was with Ferreri as well that he wanted to shoot a property called *The War Eagle* in San Francisco.

The story was simplicity itself. A man finds a young girl in a park, spends a beautiful day with her, then goes home and wrecks his apartment in despair at never again being able to see the world the way the girl does. Our idea was to make the girl Chinese so that she was not just an innocent but also a symbol of a civilization far more adult and far more advanced than ours. That suggested that we do the film in San Francisco because of the large Chinese quarter that is there. Ferreri and I even made a trip to scout some locations, but nobody with money wanted to hear anything about it.

As for why America even for subjects conceived in other settings, the actor has suggested a combination of factors.

When some of these ideas first came up, there weren't too many European filmmakers who were shooting in the United States. I think somebody like Ferreri, for instance, had another way of seeing America that would have been striking on the screen. Then, too, it seemed easier to sell some projects with an American location. That didn't prove to be so in the end, but it had been a consideration.

Mastroianni's fantasies about shooting in the United States have been matched over the years by those American filmmakers intent on having him work for them in some distinctly odd undertakings. What the actor has described as probably the most bizarre proposal he ever received came from blood-and-guts director Sam Peckinpah. According to Mastroianni, Peckinpah first approached him in London in 1969 during the shooting of *Diamonds for Breakfast*.

I still only had about three words of English, and the only thing I really knew about him was that he made all these violent westerns with people dying in slow motion. From what I understood, he wanted very badly to make a film about somebody who runs into Harrod's department store in London because he is being chased by himself. Once inside the store, the character just disappears. I suppose it was meant to be some kind of a commentary on the consumer society, but I wasn't even sure about that. In any case, I thought it was a fascinating idea, but he went off and I stopped thinking about it.

Almost ten years later, however, Peckinpah was in Rome, proposing the same idea.

It was one of the strangest afternoons I ever spent. We arranged to meet in the main restaurant of the Hilton Hotel. He comes in, not looking all that well, takes in the restaurant, and insists we move to another restaurant upstairs in the hotel. We're hardly seated up there, when he takes another look around and says that he doesn't want to be overheard, let's go somewhere else. For the next two hours, we ran from one place in that hotel to another, and every time we sat down, he'd get another attack of paranoia. Even after that experience, I think I still might have done the film if everything else worked out. But then Peckinpah died, and that was the end of it.

In the late 1980s, following his triumph in Nikita Mikhalkov's *Oci Ciornie* (Dark Eyes), it was reported that Mastroianni was going back to work with the Russian filmmaker in an international production entitled *The Siberian Barber* that would have costarred Meryl Streep. But although the picture figured prominently in a publicity campaign heralding the return of Angelo Rizzoli to producing, it never moved beyond the talking stage. Similarly, the actor was cited as one of the chief conquests of private European television operator Silvio Berlusconi near the end of the decade; according to Berlusconi's office, Mastroianni had agreed to star in a miniseries entitled *The Last Waltz in Vienna*, playing the role of a melancholy journalist who uncovers a plot to defeat East-West détente but who can't get anyone to believe him. In the event, no contracts were ever signed, and the actor spent most of the period abroad completing theatrical features in Greece and Hungary.

Much longer was the saga of *Il Viaggio di G. Mastorna* (The Voyage of G. Mastorna), the most famous film never to go before the cameras on the Continent. The travail began in 1965, when Fellini approached De Laurentiis with a mystical tale of what a famous cellist encounters following his death. The name of the title character was a play on Mastroianni's name, suggesting the way that a Rome variety-hall emcee might have introduced the actor to the audience. *("Ed ecco a voi—torna Mastroianni!")* In its original outline, as written by Fellini and novelist Dino Buzzati, the film resembled a modern retelling of Dante's journey through the afterworld; in De Laurentiis's view, however, Fellini's ambitious budget for location shootings in the United States, Germany, and other countries mainly threatened a trip into the world of after-bankruptcy, and the producer eventually pulled out. Over the next twenty-five years, the director made periodic announcements that what he called his "film of films" would be his next undertaking, but each time he was detoured by other commitments. At one point, the picture was so close to production that gigantic sets, including a replica of St. Peter's Cathedral in Cologne, were already awaiting actors at Cinecittà; on another occasion, everything was ready to go when the director suddenly fell ill. That illness, along with his on-and-off optimism about getting started, generated considerable conjecture that Fellini had become superstitious about the project and its death theme—an allegation that the filmmaker denied emphatically.

As for Mastroianni, he was so certain that the picture was going to be his follow-up endeavor to 8½ with the director that he took cello lessons for fingering dexterity. It was also partly because of *Il Viaggio di G. Mastorna* that he ended his 1966 run in *Ciao, Rudy* earlier than stipulated by his contract and had to pay a forfeiture indemnity. Still, because of scheduling conflicts or financial shorts, nothing happened for years. In the mid-1970s, Fellini and the film were back in the news, but without Mastroianni; as with 8½, the director had developed a fancy for Laurence Olivier in the role of the protagonist. This cooled the enthusiasm of prospective American backers, who had gone into the project with the understanding that the Italian actor would be the star. A couple of years later, Mastroianni reentered the scene, but then Fellini fell ill, and the actor didn't mind telling people that he saw that as a "bad omen" and pulled himself out. In 1979, Fellini and Mastroianni were seen conferring often enough to spark more speculation that the two of them were finally about to begin their voyage to the netherworld; instead, they ended up doing *La Città delle Donne* together. It was also around this time that Fellini acknowledged that several of the major set pieces scripted by him and Buzzati for *Il Viaggio di G. Mastorna* had in the meantime been inserted into some of his other films.

What appeared to be the final chapter of the story was written in the summer of 1992, with the disclosure that Fellini, once an artist for a satirical magazine, had decided to entrust the ethereal adventures of G. Mastorna to a comic strip executed with popular cartoonist Milo Manara. In designing the physical characteristics of the strip's hero, the director revealed, he had initially thought of caricaturing Mastroianni, but had then discarded the idea. After a couple of tries with the faces of John Barrymore and Ronald Colman, Mastorna assumed cartoon life with a significant resemblance to Italian actor-comedian Paolo Villaggio. Mastroianni conceded that he was surprised by the decision to turn the project into a comic strip but also observed that "an actor is lucky to play a fraction of the roles he is offered or dreams about doing."

24

A Second Wind

By the late 1970s, Mastroianni was well into his fifties and getting beyond the reach of producers who still wanted him to go back to being the Marcello of *La Dolce Vita*. The persistence of some in offering the roles of *aging* Lotharios was even easier for the actor to ignore. Instead, buoyed by the success of *Una Giornata Particolare* and by his new relationship with Tatò, he embarked on a series of characters that demonstrated his broad range as in no other period of his career except for the years immediately following *La Dolce Vita*. The only snag was that aside from one project with Fellini and another with Scola, his efforts went largely unseen outside the European Continent.

His immediate follow-up to *Una Giornata Particolare* was Marco Vicario's *Mogliamante* (Wifemistress), a somewhat odd soap opera laid at the dawn of the century that made publicity claims to being a feminist vision of marital and social relations. The basic story had Mastroianni in the role of a landowner who has to go into hiding because of a murder he didn't commit and whose absence allows his previously repressed wife (Laura Antonelli) to flourish as both the superintendent of the estate and a passionate woman. Whatever thematic agenda publicists claimed for *Mogliamante*, it was undermined by the thick melodrama of the tale as well as by the usual dedication of Italian filmmakers of the period to Antonelli's body. On the other hand, Mastroianni was widely praised for his performance as the alternately cold, enraged, and bewildered landowner.

With Steno's *Doppio Delitto* (Double Murder on Via Governo Vecchio), he was back to playing a homicide detective, but with a lot more wrinkles than the superficially similar character he did in *La Donna della Domenica*. Introduced as a fumbler who has been demoted to the police records room, Mastroianni's character vindicates himself by calmly piecing together the facts behind the murders of an aristocrat and an electrician in a Rome palazzo. His often antic methods are played off against an international cast (Ursula Andress, Peter Ustinov, Jean-Claude Brialy, Agostina Belli) representing the building's tenants. Although *Doppio Delitto* did not gain the world audience that the producers had counted on with the hiring of some of the performers, the picture was well received on the Continent as a respectable entertainment that owed much of its achievement to Mastroianni's lively portrayal of the policeman.

Ferreri's *Ciao Maschio* (Bye Bye Monkey) was something else again, and the actor didn't even know what that something was until he had arrived in New York, where the director had already begun shooting on another of his animal-keyed allegories. "I knew absolutely nothing about the role. Ferreri called me, and I flew to the United States, where we put the character together day by day."

By the director's own account, Mastroianni was a last-minute replacement in *Ciao Maschio* for Tognazzi, and precisely for that reason he enjoyed building up the role. As the director told an Italian television reporter at the time:

> Tognazzi wanted to do the film, but he was irritated because it turned out to be a much smaller role than he had thought. So when he said no and Mastroianni agreed to fly to New York without even seeing a script, I decided to irritate Tognazzi a little more by making the character more prominent.

Ciao Maschio centered around a Frenchman (Gérard Depardieu) who drifts around Lower Manhattan between jobs as an electrician for a wax museum and as a lighting man for an Off-Off-Broadway theater, lives in a basement overrun with rats and generally gives nothing to anyone except his occasional physical presence. Among the victims of his inertia are a woman (Gail Lawrence) he impregnates but shows no inclination to live with. The only exceptions to his emotional lassitude are a baby chimpanzee that he adopts and an eccentric Italian (Mastroianni) who lives amid the skyscrapers in Lower Manhattan tending to a garden and vaunting a self-delusional anarchism. Before the allegory has played itself out, the Italian will hang himself, the chimp will be eaten by the rats, and the Frenchman will die in a fire at the wax museum. The film's final image is of the woman and her young child sitting by the East River and munching on grapes.

Mastroianni has always listed *Ciao Maschio* among his best works—an opinion shared by numerous critics. Typical comments in the Italian press found his performance "refined," "of an infallible bravura," and a testimony to his "state of grace . . . as our most versatile actor." People involved with the production said that it was praise earned every shot along the way. In playing a character with

pronounced asthma, for instance, the actor found himself coming
down with some of the same symptoms whenever he had to do a
scene with the baby chimp. "The damn thing also seemed to like to
shit on me, which made Ferreri very happy."

Geraldine Fitzgerald, who had a key supporting role in the picture, also came away from it with at least one unpleasant memory.

> As a director, Ferreri was wonderful, even though he seemed to
> like to have people regard him as some kind of unintelligible eccen-
> tric. He knew exactly what he was doing every minute. But what
> bothered me was this oppressive palsy-walsy way that he had with
> some members of the production staff. They were always torment-
> ing the monkey in little ways, and then when they were through,
> they would just crate it up and have it taken off until the next day.
> I was very uncomfortable with that kind of behavior, but it seemed
> to be what Ferreri's technicians and assistants were accustomed to.
> It was like big little boys at play.

Were the actresses treated any differently than the actors, such
as charged by Catherine Spaak? Fitzgerald: "Well, I don't use big
words like misogynist, but I can understand why some people might
use it."

With *Così Come Sei* (The Way You Are), Mastroianni put himself in the hands of Alberto Lattuada, a contemporary of Visconti's
who had shot his first film in 1942. The picture also marked the first
time that he played his age in a drama about a love affair between a
teenager (Nastassia Kinski) and a man old enough to be her father. In
fact, the entire plot thrust of *Così Come Sei* was in discovering
whether or not the architect portrayed by Mastroianni was romanc-
ing his own daughter from a brief and almost forgotten affair. For the
most part, critical reaction to the film was harsh, with more than one
Italian reviewer suggesting that the sixty-four-year-old Lattuada had
made too many other films with such a motif for May-December
romances not to have become an obsession that was bankrupting his
directorial abilities. Mastroianni was also raked over the coals,
though for diametrically opposing reasons: If some critics found him
too young and ironic in the part of the architect, others pronounced
him on automatic pilot.

In the actor's opinion, *Così Come Sei* was far more important
thematically and much more graceful cinematically than most people gave it credit for. He has also acknowledged that the role of the
architect gave him considerable pause personally.

> The fact of the matter is that someone who has reached fifty years
> of age isn't the same person that he was. He doesn't have the same
> enthusiasms, the same generosity of soul, that he once had. He is

far more prone to settling within this great spiderweb that his years have woven around him. Very rarely is he capable of extricating himself from it.

The knocks that Mastroianni took for *Così Come Sei* were minor in comparison to the ones that he received for his subsequent project—Wertmuller's *Fatto di Sangue fra Due Uomini per Causa di una Vedova, Si Sospettano Moventi Politici* (A Bloody Event at Caminiti Between Two Men Because of a Widow, Political Motivations Are Suspected). The grotesquely windy title was about the only reminder of the films that had made Wertmuller an international sensation in the early 1970s and that had secured her an unprecedented long-term contract with a California studio. In *Fatto di Sangue*, Loren and Giannini flanked Mastroianni in a story that was described by one critic thusly:

> In a geographically improbable Sicily, against the background of the birth of Fascism (also improbable), three improbable characters meet, love each other, despise each other, then go their separate ways: a woman, a socialist, and an Italian-American gangster are symbolically reunited in death. All this is intermingled with post-card-like landscapes, dialogue rendered in an incomprehensible dialect, and with key scenes reminiscent of the worst kind of family melodramas and soap operas.

The rip by Gianni Rondolino found few dissenters. Several critics, in fact, came up independently with the same observation that the three leading players seemed to have been asked to parody roles that they had been celebrated for—Mastroianni for *I Compagni*, Loren for her Oscar-winning *La Ciociara* (Two Women), and Giannini for Wertmuller's *Film d'Amore e Anarchia* (Love and Anarchy). Unfortunately for all concerned, the film hadn't been intended as a satire, and it only further devalued the director's reputation. *Fatto di Sangue* also marked the tenth and last time that Mastroianni and Loren shared a marquee.

Ever since his return from France, the actor had let it be understood that he was open to proposals to return to the stage for what he called a "professional purgative." Despite some preliminary negotiating on more than one property, however, nothing was concluded. Instead, in 1978, he went in another direction by accepting an invitation from Petri to star in a television adaptation of Jean-Paul Sartre's *Les Mains Sales* (Dirty Hands). Not counting some appearances on variety shows, it was his first work for the small screen.

At times, Mastroianni made it sound as though he had agreed to do *Les Mains Sales* only because of Petri's involvement and because, as he was quoted by one reporter, "it won't take very much time."

But he has also admitted to having been intrigued by the central character of a left-wing intellectual who gets caught up in a conscience crisis over his Communist party loyalties. The play had in fact been a political cause célèbre since its Paris premiere in 1948, when the French Communists had inveighed against it as propaganda and Sartre had shelved it and forbade any other productions so as not to be exploited by either the Party or red-baiters. Given that background, the television production in Italy aroused various ideological expectations. But as it turned out, the shooting was overwhelmed by the national crisis precipitated by the assassination of Aldo Moro. "It was an absolutely hellish time," Mastroianni recalled.

> And to make it worse, Petri got it into his head that he was somehow a little responsible for the murder because of the assassination of the Moro character in *Todo Modo* a couple of years before. He stayed away from work for a few days, and was in tremendous crisis. You couldn't persuade him that, after all, the basic story of *Todo Modo* had come from Sciascia's book. The film had been seen by a lot more people than had read the book.

Not surprisingly, the resultant production of the Sartre work was much more correct than it was galvanizing. In a typically distant comment on the production, Mastroianni said that its principal merit was that "it demonstrated how much things had changed since the late 1940s and how facetious some of the charges of betrayal against Sartre had been." The experience didn't do much, either, for the actor's attitude toward television productions. "I felt suffocated by the ministerial office air of going to that studio every day. The atmosphere was completely different from making theatrical features. You had to go to one office to sign a contract, go to another one to get your money. I really hated it."

If Mastroianni had missed the helter-skelter of exterior shooting during *Les Mains Sales*, he retrieved it with interest in Comencini's *L'Ingorgo* (Traffic Jam), a star-studded coproduction about various characters caught up in a bottleneck outside Rome. Financing for *L'Ingorgo* came from Italy, France, Spain, and West Germany; in addition to Mastroianni, vignettes featured Sordi, Tognazzi, Sandrelli, Fernando Rey, Dépardieu, Annie Girardot, and Miou-Miou. The actor's role was of a very Mastroianni-like film star who proves to two members of his public that he is much less offscreen than his publicists have made him out to be. The story of the film star had originally been projected as the entire picture but was then telescoped into a long sketch by backers bent on having their own national stars figure more prominently. In the view of most continental critics, the recasting of the project only made the Mastroianni vignette look embarrassingly substantial in comparison to the other segments while simultaneously falling shy of a well-rounded tale. Otherwise, *L'Ingorgo* was mainly notable for being a rare Italian film that used direct sound.

More modest as a production but more successful as an entertainment was Sergio Corbucci's *Giallo Napoletano* (Neapolitan Mystery), in which Mastroianni portrayed a down-at-the-heels itinerant musician who gets entangled in a murder plot. Corbucci's open declaration that the film was inspired equally by Hitchcock and Totò was an open invitation to critics to suggest that the picture shifted uneasily between Hollywood-style intrigue and Neapolitan slapstick, but the consensus was that the star kept everything together with his raucous interpretation of the mandolin player. Mastroianni's most lasting memory of the project was a reminder that it hasn't been only Americans who have been exposed to his image as the Latin lover:

> One night, we're shooting a scene in the center of Naples. The police are holding back all the traffic, and I'm standing alone with my mandolin and in this atrocious makeup that makes me look like an old bum that's been scraped off somebody's shoe. I start strumming my mandolin, and suddenly out of nowhere comes this beat-up old car with two kids in it. And as they go driving by, one of them yells out, "Hey, look at the great cocksman Mastroianni! Now he's trying to get them with music!"

His next engagement was in Scola's *La Terrazza* (The Terrace), an intellectually ambitious undertaking that sought to illuminate the moral and emotional failures of middle-class professionals of Mastroianni's generation by delving into the lives of a group of friends gathered for a dinner party. Although Sandrelli, Carla Gravina, and other women were in the cast, the key figures were all men: Mastroianni as a newspaper editor who is no longer trusted even by his staff, Gassman as a Communist parliamentarian, Tognazzi as a producer, Trintignant as a screenwriter, Serge Reggiani as a writer turned television network functionary, and Stefano Sattà Flores as a politically correct critic. The roles and choice of actors to fill them made it obvious that Scola and co-scripters Age and Scarpelli were intent on reviewing their own place in the film industry as much as anything else; to underline the point, the background guests at the dinner party were portrayed by writers and other industry figures.

Given prerelease expectations that *La Terrazza* would be the *La Dolce Vita* of its time, the film had little place to go but down when it was actually seen, and that was where it went. Some reviewers backed Gassman's assessment that it "put too many irons in the fire," producing an overall "atmosphere of weariness" from the sheer repetition of stories that were too similar emotionally. Other opinion took Scola and the screenwriters to task for wallowing in their existential misery rather than focusing on it objectively. Except for Gassman, whose Communist deputy was indeed the biggest reach, most of the actors drew the same criticism; Mastroianni, in particular, elicited a wrong kind of comparison to *La Dolce Vita* with observations that his editor was merely an older variation on the reporter who had once run around the Via Veneto. The film's most ardent defender was cowriter Scarpelli, who complained to an Italian interviewer even years later that it had been sabotaged by media people left uncomfortable by recognizing themselves on the screen. Scarpelli:

> Whenever the *commedia all'italiana* was ironic about average citizens, the intellectual bourgeoisie (editorial writers, novelists, reporters) had no problem wondering about how accurate the picture of the people was. Gassman as a lumpenproletarian or Mastroianni as a cuckholded, drunken worker . . . you never heard any accusations about the inaccuracy of the type. Where workers are concerned, the more laughs the better, even with lies thrown in. But get accurate about those people. . . . The only invention in *La Terrazza* was the screenplay, not the people who inspired it.

The 1970s did not end happily for Mastroianni, and most of the problems coincided with the production of *La Città delle Donne*, which reunited him with Fellini for practically the first time in fifteen years. (There had been his brief appearance in *Roma* in 1972 in which he had played himself, but even that cameo had been cut from prints distributed abroad.) As in the cases of both *La Dolce Vita* and *8½*, there had been nothing automatic about getting back together with his avowedly favorite filmmaker.

La Città delle Donne, which turned out to be the most expensive picture ever made with European capital, had a tortuous preproduction history. As far back as the late 1960s, on the strength of the success of *8½*, Universal had agreed to underwrite what Fellini referred to as his "woman's film" as half of a projected feature that would have also involved Ingmar Bergman in a separate story. That deal began to unravel when the Hollywood company insisted on American actors for the two halves of the film—Katharine Ross for Bergman and Warren Beatty for Fellini. Although the Swedish director went along with the condition, Fellini effectively torpedoed everything when he held out for Mastroianni instead of Beatty. Over the next few years, other producers and money men came forward, only to go away again when agreement couldn't be reached on one point or another. Among them was *Penthouse* publisher Bob Guccione, who likewise insisted that the film star Americans and be shot entirely in

English. For his part, Franco Cristaldi, who had overseen other Fellini works, washed his hands of the project for the simple reason that he "didn't like it." It wasn't until Fellini struck a deal with Renzo Rossellini, nephew of the noted director, and Gaumont that financing became available.

Even with Gaumont behind him, Fellini had a casting problem because Gaumont was avid to have Dustin Hoffman play the protagonist; moreover, and in spite of his early championing of Mastroianni, the director wasn't all that averse to the idea of Hoffman, either. As he told Italian film writer Matilde Hochkofler, he didn't make his final decision until he was in a car one evening with Mastroianni:

> I have to admit that the notion of Hoffman seemed to me an exciting choice. Marcello listened to all this with a bare amount of attention. His attitude was that it had nothing to do with him, but that he was obligated out of friendship and courtesy to act vaguely interested. "It's a story," I said to him, "of a man who moves around women, looking them over from every conceivable angle, ending up fascinated and dismayed by what he sees. It is as though he looks at them without any real desire to understand them but just wants them to dazzle him, to arouse in him states of admiration, enthusiasm, discomfort, and tenderness. Maybe he is afraid, maybe he thinks that to find *the* woman, to reach her, is tantamount to going under, to disappearing, even to dying. So he prefers to continue searching for her without ever reaching her." I myself felt a sudden lurch outlining the story that way as we drove along. I kept driving, not saying anything. Marcello was very quiet, too. We avoided looking at each other for a very long time. It was in that silence that I think we both knew that we would be making *La Città delle Donne* together.

In retrospect, that turned out to be one of the easier moments in putting the film together. Aside from Mastroianni, the only significant male role in the picture was assigned to veteran character actor Ettore Manni. Two months after production had begun, in May 1979, Manni shot himself in the leg in a gun accident at home; the bullet split a vein, and before an ambulance could arrive on the scene, he bled to death. The tragedy prompted a shutdown of the set for almost six weeks, when it was decided that rather than scrap Manni's work and reshoot with another actor, a double of his same build would be used to complete his scenes by shooting him only from the back. No sooner had production resumed, however, than Mastroianni came down with a sty that necessitated medical treatment and rest, forcing another stoppage. Then, on November 12, still another blow fell with the death of the actor's mother.

She always insisted on living by herself. Every morning, she'd go out and take a bus somewhere, even at the age of eighty-six. She just liked riding around. Then in the afternoon, she'd go see a film. It was a routine that she rarely broke. I went over to see her, and the doorman tells me that she's been out as always. But when I went up to the apartment, there she was, just sprawled out on the floor, her eyeglasses a few feet away, a slipper off her foot. She'd always predicted to me that she was going to die alone. Yes, she was eighty-six, but a dog shouldn't die the way she did.

Even without the deaths of his mother and Manni, Mastroianni has confessed, *La Città delle Donne* had him in constant turmoil.

I felt like I was the only woman in an infantry barracks, except that the shoe was on the other foot. I was totally surrounded by women and I was alone. And they weren't the generous, amorous, or helpless women you could feel comfortable with. They were all extremely well prepared, each one different and creative, each one with a personality to assert, each one determined to live a life of her own. I felt completely besieged. It was suffocating. I was ill at ease from the first day. I couldn't help feeling that I had done something terribly wrong. I was totally intimidated, afraid of opening my mouth and saying something that would get everybody to ridicule me. It was the very first time, going all the way back to when I was an extra, that I didn't go around a set flirting with everybody, trying to be some kind of suave man-about-town. None of that. I thought I would've been killed if I tried it. The women that Fellini had surrounded me with all seemed to be there as investigating magistrates. Their main task, I convinced myself, was to carefully examine this little story that this suspicious director and his friend the actor wanted to tell about them.

The uneasiness also translated into his relations with other members of the crew.

I chased away the hairdresser whenever she came near me with her mirrors and brushes. "Are you insane?" I said to her. "You want all these women seeing this middle-aged idiot primping in front of a mirror like he was some kind of Valentino?" I also told the assistant director that I wanted my name taken off my chair and the name of my character—Snaporaz—put on instead. The last thing I needed to hear was some of the women seeing MASTROIANNI on the back of the chair and snickering to themselves. I wanted them to forget all about Mastroianni being there, which is what I suppose I wanted to forget, too.

La Città delle Donne amounted to Fellini's most concentrated cinematic pursuit of his "ideal woman," with Mastroianni's role of

Snaporaz the emblematic middle-aged Italian chasing, patrolling, surveying, and fleeing from every representative female type that occurred to the director. The main setting for the character's voyage is a fantasy hotel that Snaporaz reaches after leaving a train on which he has been riding with his wife. After his dreams have finally been exhausted, the protagonist reawakens on the train to find his wife still sitting across the compartment from him—her affectionate but also somewhat tolerant expression suggesting that perhaps she has been with him every step of the way in his fantasies.

Reaction to the film varied. Following its premiere at the Cannes Festival in May 1980, critics from several countries scored it in some of the same terms that had been applied to Scola's *La Terrazza*—that its case for the arrested development of the main character had been undermined by a lack of objectivity that ultimately excused rather than resolved a focal inertia and narcissism. Reflecting this view was Mira Liehm, who in her study of postwar Italian cinema entitled *Passion and Defiance* wrote off the film as "a *Reader's Digest* of Fellini's myths." According to the author, the repetitiveness of the myths "here loses all forward impetus, and the necessary link to reality is lacking." The Italian press was largely more sympathetic, though often with a tone that argued that the film had to be seen within the context of Fellini's works and that, at that level, it represented his most daring visual exercise. Response to Mastroianni's performance was equally divided: Some reviewers found him too captive to the essential passivities of Fellini's vision; others admired his ability to provide the film with a firm center.

By the time *La Città delle Donne* had reached America, it had already been the subject of several feminist protest demonstrations in Europe. Mastroianni has always expressed his dismay at such a reaction.

> The feminists thought that Fellini was attacking them, that he was speaking ill of women in general. Maybe they went to see another film, because there's nothing like that in the picture. What the movie is about is a *man*. A man faced with a new image of women and incapable of coming to grips with this image. So what does he do instead? He insists on pursuing his old ideal of a woman despite the fact that this doesn't exist anymore. Seems to me that it's the man, not women, who comes out looking the worse for wear.

> And as far as the women in the film who look ridiculous?

> Well, why not? That's normal. Everyone has his or her ridiculous side, including women and including feminists. We've got enough somber religions without adding more.

Amid all the controversy over *La Città delle Donne*'s sexual politics, Mastroianni went to work for his third woman director. Liliana Cavani's *La Pelle* (The Skin) was an adaptation of Curzio Malaparte's bitter novel about the postwar occupation of Naples; Mastroianni re-created the author's real-life role as a liaison between Italian authorities and the U.S. military. Despite a serious production and the presence in the cast of Cardinale and Burt Lancaster, the film was a disaster on just about every level. One problem was Mastroianni—a casting choice made by Cavani to play down the acrid personage of Malaparte that emerged from the novel. ("She wanted the Italian character to be more civil, elegant, and *simpatico*. In the end, this probably robbed the role and the story of a more painful, ironic thrust.") Even worse, especially for the Italian version of the film, was the decision to eliminate the Tower of Babel of languages spoken in the chaotic Naples of the period—the customary redubbing of everything depriving the picture of one of its requisite colors. In the words of one Italian critic, "The effective elimination of the background atmosphere only makes it more difficult to avoid what is going on in the foreground."

The response outside Italy was even worse. Regarding the film's relentless parade of images depicting the rampant prostitution and poverty in the occupied city, numerous reviewers chided Cavani for trying to liken postwar Naples to Sodom and Gomorrah. An indignant critic for *Variety* fumed that the film was "a poorly staged creepshow travesty with little to redeem it" and blasted Mastroianni for "resembling a tour guide for voyeuristic descents to human muck." After seeing the film at Cannes, *Village Voice* critic Andrew Sarris declared: "Should *La Pelle* ever get distribution in America—and I hope it doesn't—don't see it on a full stomach or a full mind. You're guaranteed to lose both." In fact, the film received next to no distribution in the United States.

Mastroianni would have another unhappy experience with Cavani a year later, but in the meantime he went back before the cameras for Risi, arguably the most noted Italian filmmaker with whom he has repeatedly come up short. *Fantasma d'Amore* (Ghost of Love) proved to be no more of a scintillating collaboration than *Il Viale della Speranza*, *La Moglie del Prete*, or *Mordi e Fuggi*. In *Fantasma d'Amore*, the actor played a married businessman who suddenly begins to have visions of a woman (Romy Schneider) he loved a number of years before. It emerges that the woman has in fact been dead for some time, her reappearance representing both a challenge to the businessman to break out of his social and emotional straitjacket and a foreshadowing of his own demise. One of the kinder words used to describe the film was "soppy," with more than one critic wondering how it had eluded Risi that the story's principal thrust should have been the protagonist's mental state, not his divided loyalties between his wife and his deceased lover. For his part, Mastroianni has conceded that *Fantasma d'Amore* was "less inspired" than some of his other work with Risi. At the same time, however, he has shrugged off theories that his generally mediocre efforts with the director were due to Risi's greater ease in working with "actors" like Gassman than with reactors like himself: "What it comes down to is that you can't make a masterpiece every time out. Wouldn't it be monstrous if you always knew ahead of time whether what you were doing was a good idea or a bad idea?"

His next project, *La Nuit de Varennes* (That Night at Varennes), turned out to be a good idea. As usual with director Scola, the film had one foot in history (the French Revolution) and a toe or two of the other one in sardonic cinema criticism. The inside joke this time was having Mastroianni do something of a takeoff on the way that Donald Sutherland had portrayed an old, debauched Casanova for Fellini a few years earlier. Fortunately for all concerned, the elaboration on the Sutherland endeavor did not get out of hand, and Mastroianni's performance became one of the most applauded of his career.

Written by Scola and Sergio Amidei, *La Nuit de Varennes* imagined what would have happened if the aging Casanova had found himself on the same road from Paris to Metz with Thomas Paine, Restif de la Bretonne, and other historical personages on the same evening that Louis XVI was fleeing the revolutionaries in the French capital. Principally through the eyes of Restif de la Bretonne (Jean-Louis Barrault), each of the historical figures is shown to be an emblem of the old and new worlds then in conflict, with the Casanova character coming off as far more interested in regaining his youth than in seeing the monarchy restored. In the end, the fabled lover is forced back to a role as court jester for a nobleman beyond the reach of the revolutionaries.

The actor's performance netted his best reviews since *Una Giornata Particolare*, with more than one Italian critic calling him "a national treasure" and reviewers abroad noting that he had lost none of his star quality by undertaking older roles. The endeavor also galvanized festival organizers in more than one European country into taking a longer look at Mastroianni's filmography and concluding that the time was ripe for retrospectives aimed at underlining his contributions to the screen. It was the kind of acknowledgment that he admitted to being somewhat queasy about ("I'm not dead yet, you know") and one that would require him to be even more gracious in public in the years to come.

25

Close-up:
The Lucky Amateur

As he entered his sixtieth year, Mastroianni began winning European acknowledgments for his career as a whole in addition to honors for individual performances. Retrospectives from France to Russia became commonplace. Lifetime-achievement awards were doled out by (among others) Italy's equivalent of the Academy of Motion Picture Arts and Sciences, continental film groups, and the organizers of the Cannes and Venice festivals. The actor's popularity and industry status also made him a predictable choice for prestigious committees representing Italy abroad at conferences examining European cultural and media problems.

Mastroianni's gratitude for such recognitions has not been without some elements of nervousness. Most obviously, every new tribute has prompted ironic remarks that he wasn't yet ready to be put out to pasture, that he considered his career an ongoing activity and not a remembrance suitable only for museums. As he told *Il Corriere della Sera* in 1984:

> The films that I have made are over with. As far as I am concerned, they don't count for anything anymore. I don't have a cult of the past. I don't have a library of my films or clips of my reviews or cassettes of my films. What I have are good memories of such films as *8½*, *I Compagni*, *Divorzio all'Italiana*, *Una Giornata Particolare*, and *Ciao Maschio*. Beyond that, I think only about what I could be doing next.

The industry salutes have also been unsettling in their implicit refutation of the actor's lifelong contention that he has been nothing more than "a lucky amateur" and spurred him to even more resolute defenses of that view. Following an announcement in 1988 that he

241

would be honored by an association of European producers, for instance, he declared: "There is something amusing about all these professionals wanting to honor an amateur. Maybe they have just run out of other professionals." Or, again:

> I've always been very lucky. That Visconti selected me for his theater company. That the company had so many big names and creative talents that I would work with in later years. That Gassman left in a short while and that I was the only one in the troupe who had the right age and look to replace him. That I got involved with *La Dolce Vita*. That none of the actors who received such scripts as *Il Bell'Antonio* and *Divorzio all'Italiana* ahead of me wanted to do them. It's all the luck of the draw in an actor's life. Only actors who delude themselves that they are engaged in some great scientific task will not admit the importance of luck in their careers.

For sure, there has been a decided element of luck in Mastroianni's career, particularly with regard to the roles that came his way in the early 1960s and that consolidated his international standing. Aside from Charrier not wanting to play the impotent lover in *Il Bell'Antonio* and Quinn (among others) objecting to some aspects of the role of the baron in *Divorzio all'Italiana*, there were also the cases of Sordi rejecting *I Compagni* and Olivier failing to persuade Fellini that he would have been a compatible co-worker on 8½. Even the episode of Mastroianni's insisting that Petri direct him in *L'Assassino* would not have taken place if Manfredi had been on tap to do the part, as had been planned originally. (Committed to making Sordi a household name on every continent, producer De Laurentiis had decided that Manfredi posed the greatest rival threat to his campaign, so he got the actor to sign a contract that effectively put him out of circulation for, among other films, *L'Assassino*.)

But fortunate as Mastroianni turned out to be in inheriting some of those roles, he was hardly an exception in an industry where dog-eared scripts were the norm and where "a Gassman film" could be quickly refashioned into "a Tognazzi film" if the former had better things to do and the latter announced his availability. Even the actor has acknowledged that he might have entered the 1990s in a similar professional position if, instead of doing the roles that he has become associated with, he had done some of the others that he had waived on and that later proved successful for other performers. In this sense, there has always been a whiff of the historistic to his adamance about having been lucky in his film career; that is, things came out all right precisely because that is the way they happened.

His protestations of being an amateur have also always had a limited application for his films; in fact, the more that he has elaborated on this belief, the more clearly it has emerged that it refers not to his preparations or talents as a performer but to his impulse in going from one project to another in an ambience where discrimination has been prized as a component of box-office survival and demand. As he told *La Stampa* in 1987:

> If I had become a serious professional, I would have made the correct choices, committed no errors, kept the number of my appearances very low instead of shooting films nonstop. I know this habit has disconcerted some people, made them edgy, but I don't really worry about that. I am very proud of being an amateur.

Or, again:

> Nobody could ever take me for a serious professional if they looked at how much I have worked. Only the amateur has a zest for acting that says, "Okay, I have made two lousy films, now let's see if I can make at least one of the next two good."

What Mastroianni has never been explicit about, however, is the "serious professionals" who supposedly committed no errors in making just a fraction of the films that he has starred in. This is not surprising insofar as they simply don't exist, even if, to cite two stars who have been extremely selective in their screen roles, they are called Warren Beatty or Al Pacino. Moreover, his nonstop work habits have rarely entangled him in the kind of exorbitant movie production where glitz was more important than story or role, where financial expectations preemptively blackmailed dramatic appeal, and where skimpy box-office lines branded performers with the industry's mark of Cain; even when he has done his *Ishtar* and his *Revolution*, and he has several times, they have been far less noticeable. For all those differences, it has been primarily Hollywood actors ("they need two years between every part"), in a context irrelevant to him, through whom he has most frequently confirmed his amateur's status by noting how much more he has worked. In this regard, it could be argued that in addition to all the other serious and whimsical reasons that he has given over the years for staying away from California, the adamant amateur has also felt the need to preserve a paper tiger.

But to judge from the sheer quantity of his comments going back decades, the actor's most reassuring evidence about both his luck and his amateur's status has come not so much from his experiences in the motion-picture industry as from his earliest days in the theater. If the perfect expression of his luck was in being spotted by Visconti's representative and being included in a company of talents that, individually, resurfaced in his projects ever afterward, he was never more of an amateur (literally) than he was when he was appearing with Masina in the university production of *Angelica*. Repeatedly, he has returned to these two events as the most formative of his adult working life—not solely as necessary stepping-stones to what ensued but as conditions of grace sufficient in themselves, as undertakings that would have kept their momentousness for him even without the films that followed. ("I am in many ways the same person that I was back at the university. I will always be that kind of an amateur.")

There has been more than nostalgia in this outlook. To begin with, going from the amateur theatrics of the university company to the most august troupe in the country within the span of a few months was very much luck for someone who not only didn't have stage credentials to speak of the evening that he was seen by Visconti's agent but who had elicited nothing better than a charitable response for his debut performance ("enthusiastic inexperience"). Using his own words, he was escorted through the "golden door" of Italian theater without having had to climb too many stairs to reach it. If that amateur wasn't lucky, none has ever been.

What followed was several years when he was reminded constantly of both states: an amateur because Visconti was never shy about telling him that was what he was, lucky because, simultaneously, there was the defection of Gassman from the troupe and his rise to starring roles. What this paradoxical situation encouraged in the development of his talent, it likewise discouraged in any solemn appreciation of those skills. *Doing* became the only imperative, as both a perpetuation and a vindication of his Lucky Amateur's status. Soon enough, the payoff for doing, what managed to sustain it beyond mere addictive exercise, was the fantasy world of the motion-picture set, where all the other lucky amateurs were to be found.

But the Lucky Amateur has not just shaped Mastroianni's work schedule; it has also helped to inform his attitude toward the film and theater businesses in general. For example, the doer has never been much of a watcher. ("Even if I wanted to be, where would I find the time? I start work early in the morning and go right into the evening often.") From most of his own testimony, he has gone to see films and plays only when they bore a direct relation to his work—a picture of his own at a festival or a theater director whom he wanted to scout. His cracks about being afraid of finding a superior actor have, within the context of the Lucky Amateur, been mostly revealing for their sardonic tone, the ever-so-slight suggestion that if he truly believed in comparing actors like racehorses or bottles of wine, it was unlikely that he would come across a better—unless his name was Gassman ("the best actor in Europe today"). This view, including the exception of Gassman, traces back to that embryonic actor who was fortunate enough to have landed with Visconti and who could not have possibly hoped to pick up vital insights outside his own training ground, which was recognized by everyone as the best there was.

In other words, aside from everything else, the boon of the Lucky Amateur contained with it the germ of an artistic arrogance— one that would only flourish with Mastroianni's regular appeal to other members of the Italian film and theater elite. At the same time, amateur that he considered himself to be within this circle, he had room to lash out at the industry with little trepidation of practical consequences, not only because the business was the crudity that many people besides him blasted it for being but also because it had never had much to do with his luck. Quite the reverse, when his fortunes seemed most on the verge of stalling over the years, it was the Viscontis (*Le Notti Bianche*), the Fellinis (*La Dolce Vita*), and the Scolas (*Una Giornata Particolare*), stalwarts of the elite, who came to his rescue *despite* what the industry's accountants and marketing soothsayers had to say.

All that said, one of the singular things about Mastroianni's career is that not even the Lucky Amateur's implicit sense of superiority has deafened him to the sound of gates clanking down around his sometimes restrictive choices. If his ties to the Viscontis and Fellinis have at times insinuated a lack of curiosity about who was doing what elsewhere in finished form, they have never deterred him from exploring work possibilities beyond their purview, from pursuing his own bent to do, even if that meant dealing with languages and cultures not his own. If anything, working in unfamiliar settings, with only his trust in the director as a guide, has ratified for him in new ways a profound conviction that there will always be a further opportunity for an amateur such as himself to have his enthusiastic inexperience molded into something cohesive. It is the sort of promise that, grateful as he might be to accept them, lifetime-achievement awards from film-industry professionals have not been able to give him.

26

Back to the Stage

Despite the horrendous reaction to *La Pelle*, Mastroianni was sufficiently impressed by Cavani's working methods to agree to another film with the director in 1982. The picture, entitled *Oltre la Porta* (Beyond the Door), was spared the savage reception accorded *La Pelle* mainly because, prior to being sold as a late-night TV entry featuring plenty of skin, even fewer people saw it.

In *Oltre la Porta*, Mastroianni played the part of a man serving a sentence in a Moroccan prison for killing his wife. His only visitor is a brooding blonde (Eleonora Giorgi), who may be his daughter or his stepdaughter but who is, in any case, tied to him through more than filial affection. The twin mysteries of the plot are the nature of the relationship (she turns out to be the stepdaughter) and how the wife really died (a suicide after discovering her husband and daughter together in bed). As with most Cavani films, however, the real focus was on the obsessions of the various characters: the wife who made her suicide look like murder, the husband who can't get his stepdaughter out of his mind, and the girl who suppresses evidence that would free her stepfather because she wants him dependent on her in his cell. Moving through the proceedings as well is an American engineer (Tom Berenger) who marries the daughter and ends up being another one of her sexual-psychological puppets.

Although Cavani had had a lot of practice in international films in which the actors all speak their native tongue (Michel Piccoli contributed his French in a supporting role), the unsynchronized results in many prints of *Oltre la Porta* lent even more tattiness to the production than that provided by the screenplay. Italian critics were practically unanimous in dismissing the film as being more exploitation melodrama than a penetrating study of sexual obsession. Mastroianni did not demur, voicing regret only that his satisfaction in working with Cavani had not been translated into something more noteworthy on the screen.

A father-daughter relationship was also at the nub of the actor's next undertaking, but far more incisively and to substantially greater critical approval. *La Storia di Piera* (Piera's Story) also marked something of a change of pace for director Ferreri, who for once abandoned animal allegories in favor of a fairly straight recounting of the formative years of Italian stage actress Piera degli Esposti. The film was based on a best-selling book in which degli Esposti and Dacia Maraini provided vivid details of the actress's parents—a father who aged from a romantically devoted husband and an energetic Communist party organizer to a shipwreck abandoned by everybody and a wild living mother who thought nothing of leaving her daughter for flings with the lover of the moment and who was eventually forced to submit to electroshock therapy to eradicate what was diagnosed as "nymphomania."

From the start, *La Storia di Piera* representated an odd combination of talents; even the veteran actress degli Esposti acknowledged that she had always thought of Ferreri "as the kind of ogre that your parents tell you will come and get you if you don't go to sleep then and there." As it turned out, however, it was the actress-cowriter who had to worry about being an ogre because of Ferreri's insistence that she show up on the set and show Hanna Schygulla how her mother had walked, talked, and even smoked. "I didn't want to do that. This wasn't some historical monument that had to be respected at all costs. I wanted the actors to feel free about what they were doing."

Degli Esposti also conceded that Mastroianni had not been her immediate image of her father and that he had been cast largely thanks to Ferreri. "The two of them were really very much alike. They were both a little like nuts—all hard on the outside and all delicate and sensitive inside."

While he had relatively brief screen time compared to Isabelle Huppert in the role of degli Esposti and Schygulla in the part of the mother, the actor made the most of it, winning applause for what one critic described as "a series of short, precise strokes that convey the entire span of a multicolored life." He and Schygulla also received the lion's share of the praise when the picture was presented at the Cannes Festival in 1983.

Immediately after *La Storia di Piera*, Mastroianni traveled farther afield for an assignment than at any time since he had gone to the Congo for *Tam-Tam Mayumbe*—agreeing to go to Brazil to costar with Sonia Braga in Bruno Barreto's *Gabriela*. The Jorge Amado novel inspiring the film was not new to the actor, since, a couple of years earlier, Ponti had contemplated teaming him with Loren in a screen version. What was new, on the other hand, aside from shooting in

South America, was doing his scenes in Portuguese—a challenge that he met with no little flair, according to both Barreto and the actor himself.

Some of *Gabriela*'s other challenges were not confronted so easily. What Mastroianni didn't know going into the project, for instance, was that the same story had been the basis for a tremendously popular television series in Brazil.

To distinguish the film from what had been on television, Barreto persuaded MGM/United Artists to shoot not in the chaotic Bahia port and market district where the novel is set but in a quaint little town between Rio and São Paolo called Parati. It was the kind of place that would have been suitable for a musical comedy, not a Jorge Amado story. It would be the same thing as going to Switzerland to shoot a story laid in Sicily. There was no sense of the sweat and heat and flies in what Amado had written. But all Barreto was worried about was not being accused of remaking the television series.

More trouble cropped up when a key generator on the production blinked out in the remote location, causing a week's delay in shooting. At that, Mastroianni and the other eleven Italians in the cast and crew had to consider themselves fortunate that they were on hand for any shooting at all following an announcement from the Brazilian Justice Ministry that they had eight days to get out of the country because they had gone to work with mere tourist visas instead of required working papers. Even when that bureaucratic problem had been resolved, according to the actor, there was a persistent problem between Italian and Brazilian members of the crew. "The Italians created the worst kind of confusion by always sticking together and spending all their time lamenting how much they missed home."

Gabriela cast Mastroianni as a café owner in 1925 Brazil who buys a cook (Braga), falls in love with her, and then, jealous of the attention she receives from his customers, marries her for the purpose of getting her out of circulation. When she revolts against his marital indifference and poses at respectability by taking a lover, he declares their marriage at an end. In the end, however, he realizes that he cannot live without her.

Critics had little good to say about the film outside of Mastroianni's performance, and some of them made a point of remarking on the "sterile atmosphere" bathing the proceedings. Despite such a negative reaction and all the production problems, however, the actor insisted that it was a "positive" experience.

First of all, I always liked the part. The café owner was like good bread. Unfortunately, in a world where people are more interested in drugs, who cares about good bread? But I also got the chance to go to Salvador, the capital of Bahia. It was like being in Naples. People in the street selling everything imaginable. Wild dogs. Coffin shops. Thousands of votary lights on all the churches. Whores everywhere you looked. There was confusion everywhere. It was wonderful.

The actor's taste for the exotic took him next to *Le Général de l'Armée Morte* (The General of the Dead Army), based on an Albanian novel by Ismail Kadare that had been read practically nowhere except in its country of origin and France. When a French producer who had held rights to the book since the mid-1970s couldn't interest backers in a package that would have starred Piccoli, he ceded his control to the French actor, who in turn tried to involve Ferreri as the director. Instead, Ferreri recommended that veteran cameraman Luciano Tovoli be given the directorial assignment. Piccoli and Tovoli then went to Tirana, where they managed the then-arduous feat of getting permission to shoot the picture in Albania. But then, a few weeks before the scheduled start of shooting, the hermetic regime withdrew its authorization because of some internal turmoil, leaving everything up in the air. Already extended too far financially, Piccoli agreed to share production reins with Enzo Porcelli and to settle for shooting in the Gran Sasso natural reserve in the Abruzzi region of Italy; with Italian money invested and with Ferreri lobbying him to help Tovoli succeed as a maiden director, Mastroianni stepped in to take on the leading role, while Piccoli kept an eye on his investment from a secondary part.

Le Général de l'Armée Morte gave Mastroianni one of his few military characters—in the role of an Italian colonel who goes to Albania to recover the remains of soldiers killed there during World War II. He is accompanied on the trip by a military chaplin (Piccoli), who is also a close friend of a rich widow (Anouk Aimée) who is particularly interested in finding the remains of her husband so that they can be reburied in the family crypt. The initially rigid colonel is little by little worn down by his wanderings through the death fields of Albania and comes apart altogether when he learns that the widow's husband was not killed during a battle but was murdered by the mother of a girl he had raped who had then committed suicide. The discovery prompts the disgusted colonel to throw all the bones that he has collected into a river and to start hallucinating about the horrors of war. In the end, he is forced to strike a deal with a German officer, in Albania for the same reason that he is, to come up with bones that he can pass off to the widow as those of her husband.

Mastroianni's own reading of his military character was that the man was "a fraud, a *pagliaccio*," and he intimated more than once that he would have liked to have done more with the part than he had. From a public standpoint, it all became academic when more money troubles from the distributors prevented the film from ever getting a proper release. The same distributor, Gaumont, was involved in his next project, leading to some unusual public explosions by the actor and to his return to the stage.

Enrico IV (Henry IV) was the first of two consecutive films for Mastroianni that were based on the work of Luigi Pirandello. Directed by Marco Bellocchio, *Enrico IV* provided him with the dream role of an aging man who has believed himself to be the monarch of the title for more than three decades, ever since the night at a costume ball that he discovered his beloved (Claudia Cardinale) betraying him. Weaving back and forth between flashes of dementia and canniness, the character of Enrico ultimately clings to his self-designed world against the shock-therapy attempts of family and friends to have him confront reality. For Mastroianni, parallels with his own professional life were only too obvious. "All actors *are* Enrico IV. Here's a character who thinks he's still only twenty-six years old, but then, in a spasm of sanity, shouts out at one point, 'One can't be twenty-six forever!'"

He told another interviewer:

It's a tremendous part, one that every actor should do at least once. He's the absolute protagonist, front and center from beginning to end, controlling the threads of the whole drama, making everybody else the pawns in his own game. The trick in playing him is not to seem like an actor who is pretending to play someone who is acting but to be absolutely in his world where he likes to act. He entertains himself, he suffers. The biggest difference in the film from the way the part is usually played on the stage is that we de-emphasized the bravura passages where the character lets go with everything he's got and wins applause in the theater. We made everything more intimate.

Mastroianni's performance earned him several awards and citations, including a Foreign Press Club Golden Globe prize for being Best Actor of the Year. But the acknowledgments only fueled further a months-long anger at the way that the film had been handled by Gaumont and the coproducing RAI Italian television network.

Gaumont released it at the end of May, when not even dogs go to the movies. They were up the creek with money problems and couldn't have cared less about us. Bellocchio shouldn't be treated that way, and neither should I. As for RAI, it likes to boast that it produces films, that it's a great defender of the cinema. But what does it really do for the cinema? It produces films to make money, and not very many of those. If it wants to be a defender of the cinema, let it produce fewer of those idiocies that it's always transmitting.

Outbursts of the kind did little to enhance *Enrico IV*'s circulation. On the other hand, the experience of doing such a theatrically rich role provided a final incentive for a return to the stage. The trigger for the return was a chance meeting in France with British director Peter Brook at the Quiberon thermal baths. Brook turned out to be another fan of François Billetdoux's bitter comedy *Tchin-Tchin*— the material that Mastroianni had once wanted to film with Magnani and that, even before that, American producer Harold Hecht had considered shooting with the actor and Angela Lansbury. Brook's idea was to mount a French stage production with his British wife, Natasha Parry.

Mastroianni's initial reservations about doing a French play with Italian and British costars in Paris were dissolved in short enough order. By his own account, there was a dinner with Parry during which the actress passed the "eye test" that he considered crucial before embarking on a professional venture. He was also won over by a production of *The Cherry Orchard* with old friend Piccoli that Brook had on in Paris at the time and by the French actor's urging him to undertake the project. Brook won additional points by noting that although the play, centering around the relationship between an Italian man and a British woman, had received nineteen productions around Europe up to that time, not once had it been mounted with an Italian actor and a British actress. Still another factor was that doing a play in Paris would have given him the opportunity to spend more time with Chiara, his daughter with Deneuve.

> All the signs were pointing in the same direction. Even the making of *Enrico IV* had been an argument in favor. Doing that picture had been a way of going back to the theater through cinema. In working with Bellocchio, I felt that I was doing a labor of love, out of respect for the author and out of respect for myself. All those feelings were a signal to me, an ambiguity that I was resolving to get to the realization that I really wanted to return to the stage.

The basic premise of *Tchin-Tchin* was the encounter between Cesareo (Mastroianni) and Pamela (Parry) after their spouses have run off with one another. At first intent on seeking ways of getting back their mates, they gradually become more interested in one another in a series of episodes marked by his alcoholic expansiveness and her phlegmatic reserve. By the end of the play, the two have come together, but in a pact that has reduced them to a frayed existence humanly even more than socially.

Mastroianni's attachment to the work (which would have still another chapter some years later in a film version) reflected his inveterate fascination with roles that had him pitting fantasy against some degrading landscape; he has even gone so far as to compare the part to a Shakespearean undertaking.

> I've always thought that Cesareo was far more difficult than King Lear. He has so many layers, but also, like a great many Italians, he comes down to this irresistible tendency to get lost in dreaming. His excessive imagination is something that is truly infantile.

As for working for Brook, he found the experience

> like getting back on a bicycle after a very long time. He was enormously inventive, refused to let me or Natasha get too entangled in the French language before we had the roles down. At one point, he insisted that I do the rehearsals in English and she do them in Spanish and German. It was a kind of direction that I felt totally at ease with.

If the actor had written the French press reviews himself, they could not have been more complimentary to the stars or the director. "*Formidable*" was the most used adjective, with the only doubts addressed to the point of Billetdoux's misanthropic exercise. As he had hoped, a secondary reward of the play's run was being able to pick up the eleven-year-old Chiara from school every day. ("It wasn't ideal, but I tried to give her more.")

Following *Tchin-Tchin*'s successful limited run, Mastroianni again teamed up with Monicelli for *Le Due Vite di Mattia Pascal* (The Late Mattia Pascal), adapted from the Pirandello novel *The Late Mattia Pascal*. The long and complicated production involved several European television networks, with a small-screen miniseries version later telescoped into a theatrically distributed feature. In the title role, the actor portrayed a librarian who is kicked around by family and friends, wins some money gambling at Monte Carlo, but then discovers that everyone has thought him dead. His attempts to create another identity for himself fail, leaving him suspended between a physical existence and a spiritual death.

Mastroianni had little sympathy for the role and not much more for the intricacies of the television coproduction.

> My character is really a corrupt double-crosser who wants to get away from everyone and everything. He really doesn't know how to do anything, even make another life for himself when all the

conditions are there for him to do it. He plays the victim all the time, but at bottom he's somebody who, as the Romans say, cries for the dead and screws the living.

As for why he played the part, it came down to his need for money after the theater run of *Tchin-Tchin* and the opportunity to work with Monicelli.

It has always been a pleasure to work with somebody so intelligent and so in control of what he is doing. But I don't think there is very much to say about the film itself. You might as well ask some office worker about a task that he performed a couple of months ago. The only thing he can tell you is that he balanced a few accounts. That's what actors have to do sometimes, too.

The actor's expectations were much higher when he went into Scola's *Maccheroni* (Macaroni), costarring Lemmon. As it turned out, however, his main rewards were a deeper appreciation of the American star and some good personal notices that contrasted sharply with a general panning of the film.

Maccheroni told the story of a dour American businessman (Lemmon) who returns to Naples for the first time since the end of the war for a conference and gets overwhelmed by an amateur playwright (Mastroianni) who has turned him into something of a legendary figure over all the intervening years; among other things, the playwright has been faking letters to his own sister, once the American's lover, in the businessman's name, the missives filled with picaresque adventures of life in the United States. The businessman becomes helpless before the affection shown to him by the playwright's family, gradually thawing from his own bitter life and even managing to rescue the playwright's son from misadventures with local gangsters. The film (sort of) ends with the death of the fantasy-obsessed playwright, but then the businessman remembers his Neapolitan friend's stories of how he had returned from the dead twice before and, in his new sense of hope, wants to believe that there will be yet another resurrection.

For both Mastroianni and Lemmon, the making of the picture was a small revelation about the other. Mastroianni:

He's exactly what he is on the screen—adorable. Everybody knows what a good actor Lemmon is, but his modesty is something very precious. He adapted himself immediately to the Italian way of doing things. There were none of these Hollywood airs that stars of his rank usually bring to Italy. And mind, shooting in Naples, in particular, can be hell. But not once did he object to anything. When he wasn't needed, he would just go over to some corner and settle down with these big crossword puzzle books he had. The call would come for his next setup, and he would be totally prepared. He was fantastic.

According to Lemmon, the only difficult moments in shooting in the streets of Naples came when he *wasn't* working with Mastroianni.

You get all this stuff about the Latin Lover, which he truly hates, and what it hides sometimes is that he happens to be one of the really great actors. When we would be shooting, for instance, we would do the scene first in English, then in Italian. Even when we were doing it in Italian (I'd do it again in English), I never had the least doubt where I was with him in cues because his eyes said everything. The only other Italian actor I know who has that same perfect communication is Virna Lisi. When I got into trouble over timing, it was usually in scenes that I had to do with the Neapolitan extras. That's the only time I asked Scola if we could do it over again.

For the American actor, the atmosphere on the set was epitomized by an incident involving Mastroianni's reluctance to do the film with a prop mustache.

Marcello didn't want to go through the picture with something fake on his face, so he asked Scola if he could arrange the shooting so that he would have time to grow a real mustache. Scola had no problems with that, so we went ahead for two weeks without Mastroianni while he stayed in Rome growing the mustache. Finally, one night, he arrives, and he has a perfect mustache. We go out for dinner, we say good night at the hotel. The next morning, I have a couple of things to do before Marcello's first scene around noon. Noon, one o'clock, no Marcello. Finally, there's a murmuring from the crowd. Here comes Marcello. But as he walks over to us, he keeps his head all the way down. Only when he sits down next to me does he look up. There's no mustache! I said to him, "What happened?" He's so embarrassed he's ready to drop. "Jack," he says, "I'm a creature of habit. When I get up in the morning, if I don't have an *espresso* or two right away to get my eyes opened, I don't know what the hell I'm doing. So I just got out of bed, went into the bathroom, and shaved." I couldn't believe it. Two weeks of rearranging everything, and he just shaves! Then Scola comes over, and I think to myself, Oh, oh, he sees this, and he's going to have a fit. But I forgot I wasn't in Hollywood. Scola takes one look at Marcello's face and almost falls on the ground, he laughs so hard. Needless to say, Marcello wore a fake mustache for the film.

Among the numerous problems that critics had with *Maccher-oni* was its title, since there is absolutely no reference to pasta in the story. When the picture was released, Scola's explanation was that it was meant to signify the opposite of fast food and the kind of society that the American businessman represented. By Lemmon's account, however, the title had an altogether different origin.

> Scola came to me and my wife one night and asked us to give him a disparaging word in English for Italians because that's what he decided was going to be the title. I told him we could think of two words, but we weren't going to tell him because we thought his idea was really lousy. But we keep talking, and he finally gets us to admit that one of the words is Wop. He couldn't have been happier. "That's what we'll call it," he says. "The film will be called *Wop*." I said no way. Even if you somehow managed to get that title through, you'd have every antidefamation organization and Italian-American club in the United States on a picket line outside the theaters. I don't think that bothered him particularly, but then Felicia said that another word in English for putting people down was to call them noodles. He loved that even more than Wop, and as far as I know, that's where the title was born.

With the signal exception of Mastroianni's performance, however, it was *Maccheroni* itself that was branded a noodle, especially by American critics. Vincent Canby of the *New York Times* called the film "gummy, joyless, and simple-minded," then added:

> It's one thing for Americans to make such movies about overscheming Americans, but something else for Italians—it's as if they have begun to believe the publicity that we've sent them in the form of movies like *Summertime* and *It Started in Naples*.

Andrew Sarris of the *Village Voice* echoed Canby, declaring:

> I was somewhat surprised to see an Italian film maker treating Neapolitans as vital, quaintly eccentric "life givers" on the condescendingly colonial model of the stage-set Okinawans in *Teahouse of the August Moon*.

Reviews of the kind doomed the film commercially in the United States; European reaction was more benign, with the two stars praised for their chemistry. In Mastroianni's eyes, the American response was overwrought and perhaps somewhat insular.

> The film was about an American in Naples, but it could have just as easily been about a Swede in Milan or even an Italian executive

in Milan. The main point was to set up the contrast between the man who has lost all touch with humanity for his professional career and people who, for whatever reason, have never lost their ability to live day by day. Americans in Naples don't have a monopoly on that kind of dramatic conflict.

27

Close-up: Middle Age

One curious aspect of Mastroianni's screen career is that notwithstanding the huge number of films that he has made, he was for many years hardly ever cast as a father. Prior to *Allonsanfan* in 1974, in fact, the exceptions and near exceptions were as striking as the rule: In *Tragico Ritorno*, he had a son who didn't know him and whom he left; in *Tempi Nostri*, he sought to abandon his child; in *Padri e Figli*, he had to be reconciled to the fact that he would never have a natural heir; in *Matrimonio all'Italiana*, he had to accept marriage because he didn't know which of his lover's children was his; in *Ça N'Arrive Qu'Aux Autres*, he had to cope with the death of a child; and in *L'Événement Plus Important Depuis Que l'Homme A Marché sur la Lune*, he achieved fatherhood only by also attaining motherhood. As either the ingenuous taxi driver of his early years or the personification of everything from dissoluteness to dementia in his middle period, he simply wasn't perceived as a parent on the screen. Even the "breakthrough" father roles of the 1970s, in *Allonsanfan* and *Così Come Sei*, carried an asterisk—the former film presenting him as a father who has to take care of a son he barely knows, the latter making him a family elder principally to set up the situation of his passion for a friend of his daughter's.

For Mastroianni, there has been little mystery in such a record. While conceding that it was "odd" that the sheer number of his roles had not turned up many more father figures before the 1980s, he has also noted how often he was asked to play "self-absorbed" characters.

> There has to be a basic altruism in parenthood, the notion that your sons and daughters may be more important than you. Most characters I have played, whether because of their youth or their pretensions, have started with just the opposite kind of attitude.

Over the last decade, with the actor moving away from his sixties and toward his seventies, the situation has changed somewhat. Not only has he played fathers with a central dramatic importance as such more regularly, but he has taken on the kind of generically paternal roles that, once upon a time, he had also been extraneous to. "It is all part of growing into things. Mind you, I say growing *into*, and not just growing old."

This distinction noted, it remains a fact that Mastroianni's personal and professional agenda at sixty-eight (as he was in 1992) is not the same as it was at thirty-eight. Newspaper obituary columns alone in recent years have brought some brutal reminders of the aging of his generation. Undoubtedly, the most famous Italian film name to pass from the scene was Tognazzi, who had often joked that he had cobbled his career together from the parts that Mastroianni had declined. Even bigger blows to the actor were the deaths during the 1980s of Petri and Buazzelli, the latter a friend since the university theater. By the end of the decade, other associates had moved away from Rome into retirement and semiretirement because, as screenwriter Tonino Guerra put it, "we suddenly realized we had gotten old."

From his own promontory of middle age, Mastroianni has looked more regularly into the past and ahead to the future and confessed to not being thrilled by either vista. At the same time, he has seldom granted an interview of any length since his sixtieth year in which he has not emphasized the even greater significance of his work to him; another frequently reiterated theme has been the importance of his daughters. As he told Curtis Bill Pepper in 1987: "Everybody loves Chiara. If I had known it was going to be like this, I might have had more children by the others."

The "others," of course, were the lovers who had come and gone, either because they had never been meant to stay or because he couldn't get around to asking them to remain. To the actor's own admitted amazement, reaching his seventh decade had done little to extinguish at least the fantasies about there being still more others. As he also remarked to Pepper:

> Fellini always said that when we got past sixty, there would be less trouble, more peace. Women are beautiful, but they complicate life. At night, you don't sleep, you talk, you argue, you make love at five in the morning, then you drag yourself off to the studio—a madhouse! But now there is still no peace, it's even worse. Sunday morning, down at the beach at Ostia, I see these pretty girls in bathing suits. I go crazy. With my fantasies, it'll never end, even at one hundred!

But what has at least slowed down is the urge to act on the fantasies.

> Love affairs, adventures—these things become less important. It's your work that mainly gives you an illusion of staying young, so it assumes far more importance. When you're younger, you're always chasing after something that has nothing to do with your work. But the older you get, the more time you have at your disposal to hone your craft.

Although he has given every indication of having established a modus vivendi with any guilt feelings arising from his well-chronicled love affairs, the actor has acknowledged on several occasions in recent years some regrets that take in a much broader territory than marital remorses.

> One thing in particular that sometimes stops me in my tracks lately is when somebody says, "Oh, you've made so many films without a break." When I hear that now, I can't help thinking sometimes, *Ow*, Marcello! When have you really lived? Because when I look back, I don't really have so many memories from what you might call real life. Almost always, my deepest memories are of some film, of meeting some director or actor. . . . When you are one person today and somebody else tomorrow, it seems sometimes that you no longer know who you are. You begin to think that you have lived only between takes, that the sound of the clapboard has determined everything. You see it in your relationships with everyone around you—mother, father, wife, and children. Have I really given others love and affection? Most of the time, it seems to me, I've said something like "I'll be back later" and never really returned until about twenty years later.

Not all his unease has been about the past, either.

> I have no real fear of death. But getting older means getting feeble, and what I'm afraid of is turning into another crabby old man who goes around babbling and complaining all the time. To work as much as I have required pretty good health, and aside from a little bronchitis here and there, I've been lucky. But the older you get, the more prone you are to getting sick, to forgetting the simplest things. A young man is not going to wait for an elevator if he's in a hurry; he'll run up the stairs. But the old man? He realizes one morning that he can't even bend over to tie his shoelaces. Who the hell needs it? It just isn't fair. There may be a God up in heaven, but I'll be damned if I can understand why old people can't end their lives well, why they have to be reduced to weak, tired, and horrid creatures before somebody shovels dirt over them.

Or, again:

No matter how hard you try to gloss it over with euphemisms, old age comes down to meaning that you fall apart physically and mentally. It isn't true that you have the wisdom of the ages in your head just because you lived a long time. There's nothing in the least wise about some old man who has to stop at a street corner and look up and down three times before he dares step off the sidewalk. He's not wise, he's just afraid, resigned to what he sees as his limitations.

He has also confessed to anxieties about the impression that enfeeblement makes on others.

You don't have to be a film actor to worry about something like that, but I suppose it could reinforce the fear. However much we love some old person, isn't there always a part of us that can't wait for him to kick off? Obviously, I don't look forward to the day when people will think about me in such a way.

But Mastroianni's increased reflectiveness in recent years has produced more than ruefulness about the past or melancholy about the human condition. With advice not to "close the coffin on me yet," he has spoken even more enthusiastically about the challenges of his profession and maintained a work schedule that, while not quite as hectic as that of the 1950s or 1960s, has still left few weeks of rest between the end of one project and the beginning of another. Equally striking, all but two of the films that he has taken on since 1990 have involved lengthy location work in other countries and on other continents, and even one of the exceptions committed him to three months of journeying around Italy from Sicily to Milan.

If there's one thing that I sometimes find irritating, it's when somebody comes up to me and says, "I guess after all the films you've made, you don't really find the joy in your work that you once did." Some of them don't even ask; they just assume that's true. But in fact the joy is even greater; it grows! It's your work that furnishes the dynamic illusion of life, of being useful. The older actor's work is far more satisfying, more precise. As an older man, I've found much richer, more complex characters to play. Maybe what bothers some of the people who come up to me is to see this person with a ten-year-old's brain still going after all these years. *Pazienza.* A long time ago, I stopped wondering why, after some of the crap I have made, people didn't come up to me on the street and spit in my face. Instead, I ended up taking prizes for some of those things. How could I not be satisfied by such a way of making a living? How could I not be even more grateful for it now?

Suggestions that work has become a religion on which he has grown only more dependent in his later years have never bothered the actor; on the contrary, it is an observation that has struck him as "only too obvious after all this time."

> Like the old ladies in the church who are afraid of being forgotten when the time comes? Well, why not? They do it their way; I do it mine. I was raised as a Catholic, but as an Italian Catholic. Maybe always with that little wink that tells the priest, "Hey, I know what you're up to, and you know what I'm up to, so why don't we leave it like that?" I don't begrudge people who take comfort in religion. I wouldn't be so arrogant. What the hell are they supposed to believe in—television quiz shows, some hypocritical politician who walks around expecting everyone to salute him as *Onorevole*? But as far as me personally, it's to hell with those neon signs of God, Country, and Family. Ideals like that don't cover it anymore. Why should I tie myself to shibboleths that have caused so much disaster in the world?

Or again, in his 1987 conversation with Pepper:

> I'm not religious. If they ask me about God, I don't know what to say. I think God is all that life has to offer us—my friends, things close to me, people I love, nature—everything. There you can feel the presence of God. As for a hereafter, I don't believe in it.

On a droller note, Mastroianni has made it part of his interview repertoire for years to recount a hoary Italian joke about Jesus and Joseph. As the tale goes, Jesus arrives in Nazareth and asks a passerby where he can find Joseph the carpenter. Directed to a house, he walks in the door to see Joseph sawing away at a piece of wood. "Papa!" Jesus cries out. Joseph turns around, beams at the sight of his son, and replies, "Pinocchio!"

Asked about the upbringing of his daughters, the actor has replied that he was

> very thankful that they have been able to grow up without all the mumbo jumbo about Madonnas and St. Peters and some of the other things that were around me when I was growing up. They have never had time for that kind of thing, and that's fine with me.

On the other hand, he has had more time for his daughters— Barbara, a furniture designer in her forties, and Chiara, an aspiring actress who turned twenty in 1992. Concerning Chiara's ambitions, Mastroianni has described them as "understandable. She knows that it's a demanding profession, that if one goes at it rigorously it can be exciting, but that if she doesn't go at it that way, it can be the most miserable thing in the world, bringing constant humiliation at having to wait by the telephone for some producer to call." It was also Chiara who pulled him off to see Kathy Bates in *Misery* when he was trying to make up his mind about ending his boycott of American pictures by appearing with the actress in *Used People*. "Daughters are like generous lovers who never criticize, who give only love. I've always felt that Barbara and Chiara accept me as I am because they know that I love them more than anything else in the world."

It has been a security that has not only underwritten the father—and even grandfather—roles that the actor has taken on more regularly over the last decade, but that has also ensured that even these parts would not be sentimental banalities, would not compromise his creative taste for the unusual in the name of a more acceptable bourgeois image on and off the screen. In fact, although he has played fathers more frequently, none of the roles has been of a classic *padre di famiglia*. In one film, he was a parent who waited only for his daughter to be married off before undertaking a spiritual journey that ended with his committing suicide with bee stings; in another, he was someone who made up for his lack of natural children by abducting kids off the street; in a third, he was a grandfather who fell in love with his daughter-in-law.

And beyond even these roles?

> The part that I really look forward to, that I hope Fellini will call me to take on some day, is of an old coot who doesn't understand anything anymore. With a character like that, I could really let myself go. It would be a true triumph!

28

Closing Circles

In the mid-1980s, Mastroianni began dotting some *i*'s and crossing some *t*'s in his career. Among other things, he took his first film role opposite Giulietta Masina, who had been so instrumental in helping him beyond the university theater; he got as close as he could hope to get to Fred Astaire, one of his earliest screen idols; he revisited two of his biggest triumphs, *I Soliti Ignoti* and *La Dolce Vita*, in a working capacity; he appeared in the Chekhov play that he had planned to do with Visconti before going off to make *La Dolce Vita*; and he finally succeeded in starring in a film version of *Tchin-Tchin*. No less noteworthy, he also ended decades of resistance by agreeing to make his first Hollywood picture.

On Italian television, as Valentino in *Ciao, Rudy*, and in several films (for instance, *Le Notti Bianche*, *Una Giornata Particolare*, *La Città delle Donne*), the actor had been only too eager to show off his dancing skills. It was only in Fellini's *Ginger e Fred* (Ginger and Fred), however, that he realized "the dream that a lot of us had to be up there with Ginger Rogers."

The film dream wasn't quite the same as the boyhood dream. In a story that many people viewed as a Fellini reflection on his long marriage with Masina and that wags redubbed *Ginger e Federico*, *Ginger e Fred* took a bittersweet look at two aging ballroom dancers who are reunited for a television show after years of estrangement. The title stemmed from the fact that Amelia (Masina) and Pippo (Mastroianni) had attained celebrity in their day by adopting the names of the American stars. In the course of their sponsored reunion, they go back over all the hopes and conflicts that characterized their personal and professional relationships and that still has the broke and sour Pippo endeavoring to find work as a third-rate emcee. In the end, the pair rediscovers the old magic only in the precious few moments when they are performing for the television cameras.

Even before its release at the beginning of 1986, the film sparked some political disputes in Italy and France for its depiction of a philistine television world in which the likes of Amelia and Pippo were regarded not merely as relics but as less than human within the priorities of the medium. Fellini, for one, was on the defensive for months denying that the film was intended as a commentary on the increasing privatization of European television. "I made this film because I liked the story," he told one reporter for the Italian news agency ANSA, "not because I want to attack television. If there are a few polemical points in it, fine. But what *Ginger e Fred* is, and what it was intended to be from the start, is a love story. Over and out."

For Mastroianni, the character of Pippo was another addition to his gallery of favorite roles.

> He's like the dregs of war, a battered jeep that refuses to go to a demolition lot. He's sixty-eight years old, and he's done everything in life: traveling salesman, pitchman, lover, actor, lifeguard, you name it. He's the classic Italian victimized by his compulsion to fantasize at all costs.

To do the part, the actor even agreed to shave his hair, giving him a look that, from some angles, couldn't fail to suggest his director. "When some people saw what I looked like with my hair shaved, they said that Fellini had destroyed me. But I didn't have any doubt. To me, it just underlined how desperate this wreck of a man was."

To help get into the role, he had a pair of special shoes.

> I decided to go to Lobb in Paris to find what I thought would be the shoes Pippo would wear. The damn things cost me a fortune, but as soon as I saw them, I felt like I was holding a Stradivarius.

After all the controversy over the story's television background, critics found it the most obvious part of the film—hardly more biting than the identical setting used for a similar American picture, *The Sunshine Boys*. Fellini also came in for some knocks for not maintaining his usual spirited rhythm of images. Mastroianni and Masina, on the other hand, drew raves, not least for their climactic dance number. Typical was *Time* magazine's finding that the two stars were "lovely, observant, original, and infinitely appealing." Mastroianni added to his trophy room with another Nastro d'Argento and another David di Donatello from the Italian academy.

The actor's next project, *I Soliti Ignoti . . . Vent'Anni Dopo* (Big Deal on Madonna Street . . . Twenty Years Later), was mainly a trip down memory lane to keep his creditors happy. As suggested by the title, it picked up the story of some of the surviving hapless thieves from the Monicelli hit of the late 1950s, following them into new misadventures. This time around, Mastroianni played the head of the band instead of Gassman because of the latter's theater commitments. ("Vittorio told them he could work only five days, and they had to accept that or be without a film altogether.") Most critics agreed that *I Soliti Ignoti Vent'Anni Dopo* labored for long stretches without any satirical relief and principally illustrated that director Amanzio Todini was no Monicelli.

Nothing was less of a joke than Theo Angelopoulos's *O Melissokomos* (The Beekeeper), an extended dirge about an old Greek Communist's voyage back through his past toward suicide. Before the film was completed, the actor would be dubbing himself in Greek, continually reassuring his neophyte costar that she was up to the task, and getting attacked by dozens of bees for three days running.

If Mastroianni had been looking for any ominous signs of what was to come, he would have found them easily enough in Angelopoulos's declarations before and during production that he had been mainly inspired by Antonioni, and specifically by the Italian director's *La Notte*. It was in the same spirit, according to the Greek filmmaker, that he had wanted Mastroianni for his protagonist.

> To me he represented the cinema of our fathers. The character that he was playing might have been his brother. More than that, he seemed to me to be the only actor in either Greece or Italy who could have carried this film. The role absolutely excluded any display of virtuosity. It demanded that all the acting be esoteric and silent. I was afraid that the Greek actors I knew would have been crushed by it. When we started talking about Italians, we realized that most of them have a tendency to externalize everything, just what we *didn't* want. That left it up to Marcello, who is not only a good actor but who has the kind of image weight to carry a role that really had to sustain the entire film.

According to the director, Mastroianni didn't even read a script before agreeing to the project.

> I just met with him, explained what I was after, and he said okay. During the shooting, we would sit down and have a drink the night before every setup, and I would tell him what I had planned for the next day. The next day, he would stay in his trailer for ten minutes before we were ready to go, then come out, and be exactly what I was looking for.

Despite its somber southern European mood, *O Melissokomos* was actually based on a Swedish novel by Lars Gustafsson that formed part of a fictional cycle aimed at probing ideological disillu-

sionment in the Europe of the 1960s and 1970s. By the time Angelopoulos and cowriter Tonino Guerra got through with it, however,
only the skeleton of the story remained. The key confrontations in
the tale are those of Mastroianni's character with a dying political
comrade from the old days (Serge Reggiani) and a young hitchhiker
(Nadia Mourouzi). In the end, the protagonist returns to the island
where his father and grandfather had raised bees for two generations
and exposes himself to the insects because, according to Angelopoulos, "it is his act of confession that he has been cut off from nature his
whole life."

Along with the production's other travails of shooting in some
of the most desolate regions of Greece, there were problems of confidence with Mourouzi, a young stage actress who was making her
motion-picture debut. Angelopoulos:

> She was terrified of working with Mastroianni, who had been a
> screen myth in Europe for so long. He grasped that immediately and
> sat her down day after day, calming her down, telling her hilarious
> stories about filmmaking, and giving her all the confidence she
> needed. He did the same thing with a couple of the other Greek
> actors. He was magnificent.

By his own account, Mastroianni had no problems with anything besides the bees. As he told Matilde Hochkofler:

> The stinging scene was left to the very end because, as I said to the
> director, "then if you have to cart me off to the hospital, you'll still
> have your film completed." "Don't worry about it," he says,
> "because what we're going to do is put hives with robber bees on
> one side of you and the hives with the honey and worker bees on
> the other side. When you kick over everything, the robber bees will
> fly right past you to get at the honey. You'll just be in the middle,
> and they won't bother you. I won't wear a mask, either."

But no sooner had Angelopoulos called for filming to begin than
the director himself took off to shake a bee that had been attracted to
his bald head.

> I'm supposed to be showing all this anguish of a man committing
> suicide, but I can't help seeing out of the corner of my eye Ange-
> lopoulos tearing around like a hare. Finally, he yells for the cam-
> eraman to cut and asks me how I thought it went. "Perfectly," I
> said, because the last thing I wanted to do was to have to reshoot
> everything. It was only then that I realized that after I had kicked
> over the hives, some of those maddened beasts had gone straight for
> my neck.

Mastroianni's announced satisfaction with the sequence not-withstanding, it took three full days before Angelopoulos was equally satisfied with the scene, prompting the producers to have a doctor give the actor cortisone shots.

People ask me, "Why would you take such a risk?" Well, we were in Greece, not in Hollywood, where they probably can give commands to bees through radios. You have to just throw yourself into things sometimes. Of course, there was also my vanity as an actor that was whispering to me, "When audiences see this scene up on the screen, they'll see that it was really me in the middle of all those furious bees. Even if they don't like the film or my performance, they'll have to admit I was pretty good with the bees."

Difficulties didn't end even with the completion of photography, since it was only then that Angelopoulos admitted that he had been unable to find the right Greek voice for dubbing Mastroianni. This was no minor problem: For one of the only times in his career, the actor appeared in every single scene of a film.

I finally told him, "Look, you and I will stand next to one another. You'll say the line to me, and I'll do it until I get it right—like we do with extras in Italy." But then the language per se turned out to be the least of it. When we went back to some of the locations, months had passed. What had been winter was now spring, and we had no visual help for timing the dialogue or anything. We ended up doing everything with a single microphone and *imagining* how long every scene would run. Still and all, that was really me speaking Greek up there, and I was a little disappointed that more critics didn't comment on it.

What the critics did comment on was the visual spareness of *O Melissokomos*, with some finding it too bleak by half and others congratulating the work's cinematic rigor. Depending on tastes, the inevitable (and widespread) comparisons to Antonioni's *La Notte* were cause for complaint or praise. For his part, Mastroianni netted solid reviews for finding more than joylessness in his essentially joyless character and for again showing that he was Europe's foremost player when it came to less being more. The British film magazine *Sight & Sound* was not alone in terming his contribution "extraordinary."

Less as more was also the keynote of the actor's next two endeavors—both with Russian director Nikita Mikhalkov and both inspired by the writings of Anton Chekhov. In teaming up with Mikhalkov for *Oci Ciornie* (Dark Eyes), in fact, Mastroianni took as much of an initiative as he had taken since *Divorzio all'Italiana* in launching a project by writing personally to the filmmaker to ask whether he would be interested in their working together; the letter was triggered by his enthusiasm for the director's screen version of *Oblomov*. After months of meetings in Italy and the Soviet Union, during which Mastroianni and Mikhalkov settled on Spanish as their common language, producer Silvia d'Amico Bendico put together the deal for the picture that would bring the actor his third Oscar nomination and practically a sweep of European acting honors in 1987.

Although steeped in such Chekhov stories as *The Lady with a Dog* and *The Birthday Party*, *Oci Ciornie* was actually a Chekhovian hybrid put together by Mikhalkov, Alexander Adabachian, and Suso Cecchi d'Amico. The story revolved around Romano (Mastroianni), a shipboard waiter who corners a Russian diner (Vsevolod Laryonov) with the lugubrious details of his life. What it all comes down to is that Romano never made one bad choice when it was possible to make two—living lovelessly with his rich wife (Silvana Mangano) while frittering away his ambitions as an architect, falling in love with a Russian woman (Elena Sofonova), whom he pursues from Italy to Leningrad, returning to his wife but lacking the courage to break up with her, watching his hopes for the consolations of a leisurely life disappear when the wife loses her inheritance, and turning down the opportunity to scurry back to his Russian love on the assumption that she has long since forgotten him. The final bitter twist comes in the diner's revelation that he has just married a woman whom he pursued for years but who had put him off waiting for her Italian lover to return.

The presence of longtime friend and associate Cecchi d'Amico on the writing team made it less than a coincidence that some of the particulars of Romano's life, including his profession as an architect, approximated Mastroianni's.

> Of course, there are many things in the character that resemble me. Somebody with constant fantasies, really a superficial person. He's not a bad man, but he's so indecisive he has to fail.

Aside from capturing him another Oscar nomination, the actor's performance in *Oci Ciornie* produced the top prizes of the year at Cannes and in both the Nastro d'Argento and David di Donatello competitions in Italy. When the picture was chosen to inaugurate the twenty-fifth Lincoln Center Film Festival, New York dailies took the occasion to link the fortunes of the annual screenings with the performer's career. According to the *New York Times*,

> Mastroianni's performance . . . is itself a celebration of the first quarter-century of the New York film festival inasmuch as it was

24 years ago that Mastroianni assured himself a place in cinema history with his role in Federico Fellini's *8½*. . . . Since then, both Mastroianni and the festival have had their highs and lows, and today they are again in the forefront with Mastroianni still on the scene truly triumphant.

In the words of the daily *Newsday*: "Italian cinema is virtually in crisis because Italians today prefer to turn on their television sets, but, fortunately, Mastroianni survives." Even the normally iconoclastic weekly *Village Voice* observed that there was "nobody better than Mastroianni" for launching Lincoln Center's silver anniversary screenings.

Even before *Oci Ciornie*'s international success, Mastroianni had been playing with the idea of returning to the stage in an early unfinished play of Chekhov's titled *Platonov*, which he had been scheduled to do with Visconti just prior to going off with Fellini for *La Dolce Vita*; in fact, during negotiations for *Oci Ciornie*, he had even received an offer to do the drama in the Soviet Union. In his turn, Mikhalkov was approached to direct the play in Italy. When the director made it clear that he would consider such a venture only with Mastroianni, the die was cast for *Pianola Meccanica* (Player Piano).

While largely based on *Platonov*, *Pianola Meccanica*, similar to *Oci Ciornie*, also incorporated elements from other Chekhov writings, giving Mastroianni another fundamentally self-destructive character who tries to conceal his inadequacies behind a barrage of witticisms and ironies. If there was any surprise for critics in another roundly lauded performance, it was in the fact that, in contrast to his generally easy readings on the screen, the actor was a far more emphatic figure on the stage, often bellowing to unexpected dramatic effect. The play had limited runs in Rome, Paris, Milan, and Turin, where the consensus was that Mastroianni had probably become Europe's most authoritative interpreter of Chekhov outside the Soviet Union. The one sour note in the proceedings was the refusal of the RAI state television network to air the play after its theatrical runs, as had been the original plan. Although various official reasons were given for the decision, the project had clearly not been aided by the high visibility of Silvio Berlusconi, the country's most prominent private television entrepreneur, during Rome performances of *Pianola Meccanica*.

Mastroianni revisited the days of *La Dolce Vita* more directly in agreeing to appear as himself in Fellini's *Intervista* (Interview). Made to celebrate Cinecittà's fortieth anniversary, *Intervista* was a film within a film in which Fellini is depicted at the studio in the process of shooting a screen version of Franz Kafka's *Amerika* when he is approached by a Japanese television crew intent on making a documentary on his career. Mastroianni enters the scene when he is spotted in a magician's costume doing a detergent commercial for Japanese television. Later on, Fellini drags Mastroianni, an actor playing the director as a young man (Sergio Rubini), and the Japanese crew to Anita Ekberg's home. One in-joke follows another as everybody watches some scenes from *La Dolce Vita*, and the aged Mastroianni and Ekberg re-create the dance scene from the film in which he rhapsodized on the Swedish actress as the ideal woman. All of this nostalgia wears heavily on Ekberg, who may or may not be acting in crying before the realization that she is no longer the young woman from the Trevi Fountain. The film ends with Fellini at work in Cinecittà on his adaptation of *Amerika*.

Intervista did not enthuse either critics or audiences in Italy. While some people were exasperated by its Chinese-boxes structure, a few reviewers also took Fellini to task for his allegedly cruel treatment of Ekberg, who had not worn her years from *La Dolce Vita* particularly well. In Mastroianni's opinion, the latter attacks were completely out of order.

> Why cruelty? [What *Intervista* showed] was simply human. That's the way it's been for Ekberg and me. We're not what we used to be. And at bottom, as long as you keep your ability to laugh at yourself, nothing is ever over.

The film fared better in other parts of Europe. At Cannes, it received a special award in connection with the festival's fortieth anniversary; at the Moscow festival, it was honored with a jury prize as best film of the year. In the United States, on the other hand, *Intervista* was regarded as so arty and specialized that it couldn't even get into Manhattan's foreign-film houses until Martin Scorsese helped promote its distribution in late 1992. Critical reaction was generally good, with the *Village Voice* calling the film "a joy" and concluding its review: "*Intervista* bravely confronts time's ravages with the puny consolations of art. And wins."

Aside from giving him an opportunity to visit Budapest, Mastroianni found little that was gratifying in his next venture, Pal Sandor's *Miss Arizona*. Drawn to the project by the Hungarian director and Hanna Schygulla, the actor played a 1930s cabaret performer who realizes a dream by opening a successful music hall in Budapest. But just as Sandor and Mitzi (Mastroianni and Schygulla) seem to have given birth to a Moulin Rouge East, the Nazis invade Hungary. Sandor, who is partly Jewish, is shipped off to a concentration camp, and Mitzi becomes part of the human flotsam of war.

Miss Arizona came in for a critical lambasting just about everywhere it was shown, not least in Hungary itself. The daily *Magyar Hirlap*, for example, called it "two hours of static nothing" and asserted that Mastroianni and Schygulla were an "ill-matched couple." The Budapest paper even cited the Hungarian dubbing as "unintentionally hilarious." Even less forgiving was the weekly *Elet Es Irodalom*, which cited only Mastroianni as "having anything to do with life in this overly glossy view of a story that is supposed to end in Auschwitz." The magazine also took Schygulla to task for "simply not being credible."

Mastroianni has seconded such judgments, but has equally insisted that the main culprit arose after he and Schygulla finished their assignments.

> When I went to see it, I was shocked by how much they had cut it. There was absolutely no coherence to what came off the screen. While I was watching it, I don't know how many times I said to myself, "Now where the hell did this come from?" It was supposed to have run two hours and twenty minutes, but was well under two hours. You just can't cut things that way.

According to the actor, the one saving grace of the experience was his opportunity to get to Hungary. "But sometimes when you float off somewhere, there's a hole in the raft."

His next three projects—a television series in which he again appeared as himself and two films—saw him back on more familiar territory with Scola in Italy. But even when he wasn't shooting abroad in the mid-1980s, he was conspicuous as an Italian delegate to international gatherings for promoting cultural causes. It was at a world conference of artists and scientists in Moscow in 1986, for instance, that he met Soviet President and Communist party secretary Mikhail Gorbachev.

> Everybody was there—Norman Mailer, Gore Vidal, Gregory Peck. I was with Silvia d'Amico and Carlo Lizzani. During a luncheon at the Kremlin, I saw Gorbachev talking to some people in a corner. I ambled over to hear what he was saying, and he saw me and waved for me to get closer. "*No* Mastroianni," he said, which means something like Maestro Mastroianni. It was the first time I had ever heard that, and I was a little taken aback. While we're shaking hands, I babble something like "I'd like your autograph." He nods and takes out a piece of paper but has no pen. I ask Lizzani for his, and Gorbachev just writes his name on the paper, tells me that he's seen all my films, and walks away. I'm standing there proud as a peacock when Lizzani yanks on my arm and says that Gorbachev has walked away with his pen. "It's real gold," he says, "and you

have to get it back for me." "What's the matter with you?" I say to Lizzani. "I thought you were a real Communist." But he didn't want to hear anything but the pen. Too bad for him because Gorbachev was already gone. It was a shame because I really wanted to tell him that Lizzani was a bad Communist, was too interested in gold.

It was a couple of years later in Brussels that Mastroianni, as an official representative of Italy, put his name to a document warning against the "colonization" of European culture by the mass media of the United States. Two of the document's key points were the flooding of continental networks by such American television shows as "Dallas" and the long-festering problem of having to shoot feature films in English to satisfy the North American market. Mastroianni's endorsement of the English-language threat represented a 180-degree turn from previous declarations on the issue. In 1981, for instance, he told the American monthly *Attenzione* that people were getting upset unnecessarily over English-language shoots that prompted awkward redubbing and only approximate lip synchronization.

> So who looks at lips? I look at the eyes of an actor, not his lips. Oh, maybe I'll look at the lips of a beautiful woman every once in a while. I kind of peek at them, you know? But it'd be a beautiful thing, wouldn't it, if we all started looking at each other's mouths while we were talking! A passerby would think we had a screw loose!

In Brussels, however, the actor held forth at a widely covered press conference in which, among other things, he declared:

> Just about every continental film in which I was involved where we were compelled to speak English turned out badly. This was inevitable because you just can't have Italians in an Italian setting stuttering along on their idea of English. It's not merely a question of language, either, because all your gestures get affected when you're struggling to speak in this foreign tongue. When we were doing *Maccheroni*, the producers went so far as to insist that the Neapolitan extras who were playing Neapolitans speak in English. The irony is that not even the Americans seem to want all this artificiality, because when the picture went to the United States, even they wanted to hear the track with the Neapolitans speaking their own tongue. So who is all this for, then?

For quite some time, Mastroianni had been the first to agree that his reliance on established directors had done little to encourage aspiring Italian filmmakers; simultaneously, he had pointed a finger at producers for not coming to him with more projects involving young directors. Thus, he was not in much of a position to say no when Scola asked him to make token appearances as himself in a cycle of six television movies aimed at promoting young directorial talent. The cycle, entitled *Piazza Navona*, had Mastroianni doing little more than talking on the telephone with his attorney Giovanna Cau but provided something of a thread for the otherwise disparate stories. The telefilms did not uncover any new Fellini, and the actor himself voiced doubts that the byplay with Cau made sense to anybody who didn't know them.

Scola's interest in history and film history was again on display in *Splendor*, which recounted the ups and downs over the years of a movie-house manager (Mastroianni) in a small town outside Rome. The picture costarred Massimo Troisi as a projectionist and Marina Vlady, with whom Mastroianni had not worked since De Santis's *Giorni d'Amore* in 1954, as an usherette and the manager's lover. *Splendor* (the title was the name of the movie house) covered more than fifty years in its largely nostalgic review of the trials of a motion-picture exhibitor, starting from when the Mastroianni character as a boy accompanied his father around the countryside with the latest films to the flush days of the 1950s, when American movies kept the theater packed every night, to the modern era, when falling attendance because of television prompts the manager to contemplate bringing in strippers as a coattraction with films. In the end, the theater operator is forced to sell out to a buyer who intends to raze the old palace, but he manages something of a moral consolation in insisting that the deal also include his right to slap the buyer in the face in front of all the town's cultural leaders.

Splendor drew notices that were more respectful than enthusiastic; most of the praise was reserved for Scola's small historical touches and for the chemistry between Mastroianni and Troisi. Still, the film might have fared better if not for the coincidence that it was shown at Cannes only hours after *Cinema Paradiso*, which also focused on a theater as the symbol of a village's hopes and tribulations. Faced with pictures that were so similar, American distributors went for the cheaper *Cinema Paradiso* and promoted it into an Oscar for Best Foreign Film.

During the making of *Splendor*, Mastroianni, Troisi, and Scola hatched plans to team up again immediately afterward for *Che Ore È?* (What Time Is It?), a project that the director had had on the shelf for some time. In *Che Ora È?*, Mastroianni played an affluent attorney who visits his son (Troisi), a draftee at a military post, in an attempt to mend a few fences. Although the father tries to overwhelm the boy with elaborate gifts, including a car and an apartment, the only present that is truly appreciated by the son is his grandfather's watch, which reminds him of how he once nagged the old man to tell him what time it was. After spending a day together, the father realizes that the son has established his own friends and interests and cannot simply be reeled back in after years of emotional neglect. The film ends on a tenuous note of hope when the father, already on the train that will take him back home, asks the son the time and the latter pulls out the watch to tell him.

Che Ora È? was an atypically svelte film for Scola, with historical references very much in the background. Some critics found this positive; others decided that it deprived the picture of nuances that would have made it less predictable. The divided opinion did not prevent *Che Ora È?* from picking up several sectarian and association awards in Italy or Mastroianni and Troisi from sharing Best Actor recognition at the 1989 Venice Film Festival.

In *Stanno Tutti Bene* (Everybody's Fine), the actor again portrayed a father, but this time a much more elderly one beginning to show a sign or two of senility. Directed by Giuseppe Tornatore, the maker of *Cinema Paradiso*, it follows the Sicilian Matteo as he leaves home to visit his five grown children scattered around Italy, his object being once again to have them all around the same table. The journey takes him to Naples, Rome, Florence, Milan, and Turin— each stop strengthening his suspicion that his sons and daughters are trying to keep something from him. In fact, they are concealing two things: that each is a failure in his or her own way and that the youngest son committed suicide some months earlier. Matteo returns home, where his anguish gets the best of his heart. When he wakes up in the hospital, his surviving children and a grandson are around the bed—as close as he will ever get to having everyone around a dinner table again. The film ends with the old man visiting his wife's grave and assuring her that the children are all fine.

Actor Victor Cavallo was struck by two things in Mastroianni's behavior during the shooting of *Stanno Tutti Bene*. The first was his relationship with Tornatore.

> For a long time, you heard a lot about how Marcello avoided young directors. But he was incredible with Tornatore. Total generosity, absolutely did what he was asked to do, never a trace of that attitude of some older actors that says "Hey, I'm in this business since before you were born, so I know what's best in this scene." I think Tornatore himself was flabbergasted by the enthusiasm and cooperation he got.

But on a darker note, according to Cavallo, there was also Mastroianni's reaction to a scene that the two actors had to do near the Trevi Fountain.

A couple of years earlier, there was a lot of talk about how Ekberg had been broken by having to do Fellini's *Intervista*, having to see herself so much younger. Well, Marcello wasn't exactly broken, but when we were shooting that scene he became so quiet that it was a little frightening. I never felt such a profound melancholy from another person. You didn't have to be a genius to figure out that he was going through some of the same things that Ekberg went through during *Intervista*.

In good part because of the hopes raised by *Cinema Paradiso* for the arrival of a new generation of Italian directors, both Tornatore and *Stanno Tutti Bene* received largely benevolent reviews for a tale that was far more trite than either *Splendor* or *Che Ora È?*; the film also contained some of the crudest paternalisms to be found in a Mastroianni film since the 1950s. For the actor, the best part of the assignment was getting to travel from one end of Italy to the other over a period of three months. The worst part?

I had to wear eyeglasses that were thicker than bottles. I could barely see through them, and they gave me headaches almost every day. When we rehearsed for a scene, I had to count off steps all the time because, once the cameras started going and I had the glasses back on, I really didn't know where I was going. If nothing else, the experience gave me enormous respect for the way blind people can move around on the street.

Making up for lost time with his previous neglect of young Italian directors, Mastroianni next went to work for another tyro, Francesca Archibugi, in *Verso Sera* (Toward Evening). A tight psychological study of unrealized desires, *Verso Sera* cast him as a retired university professor who is forced to take care of his granddaughter after his son and daughter-in-law break up. Eventually, the daughter-in-law also moves in with him, and it isn't long before he is feeling more than father-in-lawly toward her. She moves away with her daughter, however, before the relationships get more complicated. The professor, who has narrated the story in a letter to his granddaughter, leaves it up to the young girl to say the last word about her mother and grandfather.

Mastroianni's studied performance of the professor's being gradually drawn out of a shell of sixty years of stodgy habits elicited a number of critical raves and moved one reviewer to note that "he brings the same total professionalism and uncanny conviction to his work, whether he is being directed by somebody named Fellini or somebody named Archibugi." In what was becoming almost an annual habit, he also won another Nastro d'Argento as Best Actor.

At the beginning of 1990, Mastroianni finally realized his years-long ambition of filming Billetdoux's *Tchin-Tchin*, the play that he had done successfully in Paris with Natasha Parry. The deal was put together by Arturo La Pegna, a specialist in television commercials who had the backing of Italy's biggest brewery. In an attempt to assure the film's success with the American market, Julie Andrews was hired for the role of the Englishwoman, and Gene Saks was brought in as the director. By Saks's recounting, there was only one reason he agreed to get involved in the project:

> I was never a fan of the material. I found it nasty and degrading, basically a paean to alcohol, with these two characters just sitting around and slugging it down. What I was a fan of, on the other hand, was Mastroianni, whom I consider one of the great actors of the second half of this century. If he was involved, I told myself, maybe we could get something good out of it all.

In the event, the good that Saks got out of it was what he might have counted on—Mastroianni. Just about everything else went wrong.

> Marcello and I agreed with La Pegna that we were going to lighten everything up, not make it this sour work of misanthropy that Billetdoux had written. We aimed everything at irony instead of self-hatred. We had several ideas for a screenwriter, but we couldn't find the person we really wanted. What we ended up with was somebody who never showed the slightest bit of interest in the project. All he was interested in was his contract, which obligated him to two drafts and a polish. After that he was gone, and I think the lumps in the screenplay show it.

During production in Paris, Biarritz, and Quiberon, La Pegna was no help, either, with his constant wranglings with the mixed French-Italian crew over money matters. The tensions came to a boiling point midway into production when the French discovered that they were making less than the Italians and threatened to walk off unless they received the difference that was owed them; La Pegna retaliated by calling a halt to production in the middle of a scene and announcing his own plans to scrap everything. While a compromise that allowed the filming to go on was eventually reached, the incident was memorable to Saks particularly because of Mastroianni's reaction.

> Here you have him in close-up, and suddenly La Pegna walks on and announces that's the end. Marcello didn't lose his calm for a second. He just looked at me and shrugged and said something like "They'll work it out."

The American director also confirmed the opinion of numerous European directors that the first Mastroianni was usually the best Mastroianni. "I've never seen an actor that good on the screen in a first take. He'd just get right into it. After a little while, I realized that the more takes we did of a scene, the less effective he was."

Tchin-Tchin was practically sneaked into Italian and French theaters in the summer of 1991 and left next to no trace either critically or commercially. Under the title of *A Fine Romance*, it reached the United States in the fall of 1992, where it was written off as "tired and predictable." The best that the *New York Times* could say for it, for example, was that "there was some pleasure in watching two indomitable troupers going through familiar paces with an obvious relish." The naysayers included playwright Billetdoux, who saw the film before its release in Europe and, infuriated by the changes from his drama, demanded that his name be removed from the credits. Mastroianni wasn't very happy about the changes, either. While conceding that "modern audiences might be made uncomfortable by all the alcohol consumed in the original" and that the film's resolution (in which the cuckolded pair take back their adulterous spouses only to begin a secret affair of their own) might be "more ironic," he has also bemoaned the "lack of bite" in the screen version. "What came out was really some kind of Cary Grant light comedy that misfired."

One of the factors involved in the actor's decision to work with Angelopoulos in *O Melissokomos* was his belief that the Greek film industry was "as young and creative" as Italy's had been in the 1960s. With the same reasoning, and despite his misadventures with the bees, he returned to Greece and Angelopoulos in the fall of 1990 to make *Le Pas Suspendu de la Cigogne* (The Suspended Step of the Stork). Once again revealing his admiration for Antonioni, the director this time not only had the male star and screenwriter (Guerra) from *La Notte* but also the female star (Moreau). What he also had were political and religious obstacles that ultimately required the intervention of the Greek Defense Ministry to make sure that the film was completed without attacks by saboteurs.

Le Pas Suspendu de la Cigogne, like *O Melissokomos*, had a relatively simple plot: A television journalist (Gregory Karr) travels to the northern Greek town of Florina to do a report on the thousands of Balkan and Middle East refugees who have been kept there—most, for years—in the hope of gaining admission to Greece. While there, he spots an old man (Mastroianni) who resembles an idealistic Greek politician who dropped from sight years before after announcing his disillusionment with politics. Sensing a scoop, the journalist brings in the politician's abandoned wife (Moreau) to confirm his identity.

But though she realizes that it is her last chance to reconcile with the man she loves, the woman denies that the old man is her husband, leaving him to his anonymity, herself to isolation, and the television journalist to professional frustration.

The plot line of *Le Pas Suspendu de la Cigogne* was only a pretext for Angelopoulos's uniquely lyrical denunciations of the borders separating people and the perilous futilities of nationalistic sentiments. The director also encouraged a secondary reading that the ultimate frontier outside a town such as Florina was death; in fact, the title was inspired by a scene in which one of the characters stands with one leg raised on the line between Greece and Yugoslavia, noting that if he were to lower his leg, he might be shot by the neighboring border guards watching him. One critic who was convinced that Angelopoulos was making more of a political than a metaphysical statement was the Greek Orthodox bishop of Florina, who sought to prevent the film from being shot on the grounds that it was a "subversive attack" on the refugee center, sought to portray the city as a prison for foreigners, and showed contempt for the "pride of Greek nationality." To show how serious he was, the cleric organized protest demonstrations and warned that any resident who aided the production as either an extra or even a caterer would be excommunicated. Encouraged by the inflammatory atmosphere, a phantom group of terrorists threatened bomb and fire attacks against the troupe if it came to Florina.

The bishop's belligerence set off a storm of protest across Europe, with actress and Greek socialist deputy Melina Mercouri rallying continental cultural organizations and the Italian and French governments applying pressure on Athens to ensure the safety of their nationals. Greek government officials guaranteed that the filming would proceed as scheduled in Florina, under army protection if necessary. The bishop made a retreat, but not before excommunicating all the Greeks connected with the picture. Mastroianni found the whole incident "comic and ridiculous," while Angelopoulos pointed to it as "further confirmation that politicians are interested only in career opportunities, no matter the cost in human life and civility."

After all the furor stirred by its filming, *Le Pas Suspendu de la Cigogne* impressed critics on both sides of the Atlantic as being among Angelopoulos's minor works, and it failed to get far beyond festival screenings in Cannes, New York, and San Francisco. (Its pacing was not helped by a peculiar soundtrack that had Mastroianni again dubbing himself in Greek but France's Moreau speaking English behind the glib dialogue explanation that her character "had never learned Greek.") A typical comment was that of Caryn James of the *New York Times*, who declared in part:

> ... the work suffers from a major, disastrous decision. Its center-piece is the reporter, a bland, banal character unable to offer any intriguing perspective on the politician's identity. As played by Gregory Karr, this mournful-eyed journalist dissolves suspense wherever he turns. He can turn a silent, eyes-across-the-table seduction into an unintentional parody of an Angelopoulos scene. Only when the film focuses on Mr. Mastroianni, who towers over everyone else here, does it capture the mystery, ambiguity, and poignancy of this man's situation, whoever he turns out to be.

Of all Mastroianni's "paternal" characters, none was more unorthodox than his role in his next assignment, *Le Voleur d'Enfants* (The Colonel's Children). Based on a French novel, the actor had been attracted to the project since 1986, at one time telling friends that "this colonel seems to have been written with me in mind." But he then cooled on the idea when British money got involved and plans were laid to shoot a screen version in English. Only when Sergio Gobbi, an Italian producer working in Paris, took over did he agree to do the film in French.

Le Voleur d'Enfants cast Mastroianni as an exiled Argentinian military officer in 1925 Paris who makes up for his lack of children by abducting them off the streets. With the collusion of his wife (Angela Molina), he sets them up in his luxurious mansion, regaling them with war stories and fitting them out with clothes so identical that they resemble uniforms. The one lack in his menagerie is a girl, and this he fills when a local puppeteer (Piccoli) sells him his daughter (Virginie Ledoyen). But though enthusiastically welcomed by all the boys, the teenaged girl precipitates a double crisis, first by stirring desires in the old colonel that he doesn't want to face, then by awakening the sexual hunger of the oldest boy among the kidnapped children. When the latter rapes the girl, the colonel throws him out of the mansion. Only too aware of his own desires as well, however, the old man then jumps into the Seine out of shame. Only as he is about to go down for the third time does he remember that his pocket contains the last will and testament signing over all his property to the children. Returning home, he learns that the raped girl is pregnant. The film ends with the colonel sailing back to Argentina with his whole brood; midway across the Atlantic, the girl gives birth to a healthy son. Everyone agrees that it is a good omen for the family's fortunes in South America.

Critics generally congratulated director Christian de Chalonge for keeping *Le Voleur d'Enfants* fabulistic enough to stave off deeper considerations of the story's premise. Aiding this effort in no little way, according to a consensus of reviewers, was Mastroianni's subtle depiction of the colonel—a performance that called for him to keep negotiating between a patriarchal self-confidence and a basic dementia. For the actor, one of the greatest rewards of the film was being able to work in scene after scene with the children. Contradicting the usual older actor's wisdom about appearing on the screen with minors, he told one interviewer:

> From the second day of shooting, I would arrive on the set and the kids would all come running up to me, saying, *"Bon jour, Papa."* I put myself immediately into the role. It was a wonderful game, as though I had become as much of a child as they by being in the middle of them. I really felt a wrench when the film was over and I had to leave them.

What he left them for was something that he had avoided his entire career—a true Hollywood movie. According to Beeban Kidron, the director of *Used People*, if Mastroianni was ever going to end his boycott of a wholly American production, it was going to be for her film.

> We had already cast all the women in the picture, and what I didn't realize immediately was that they all represented something to Marcello. All I knew was that I was desperate for him to do it, despite what some other people had in mind. Only when a mutual friend told him who else was in the cast did he agree to a meeting in Paris.

The actresses who made the difference were: Shirley MacLaine, whom Mastroianni had met on his first trip to Hollywood in 1962 and with whom he had almost worked in the stillborn *Cosa Nostra* for Joseph E. Levine; Jessica Tandy, who had starred on Broadway in *A Streetcar Named Desire* only shortly before the same Tennessee Williams drama had thrust the actor into prominence in Italy; and Sylvia Sidney, a screen fixation when he had been a boy. As Kidron observed:

> It was all bizarrely symmetrical in his life. We talked about this and that, but I really had the feeling that I was his last real question mark before saying yes. Finally, he turned to this friend of his and said, "She has intelligent eyes." And that was really it.

Used People, which opened in New York in December 1992, cast Mastroianni as a longtime secret admirer of a middle-class Jewish woman (MacLaine), who decides to announce his affections on the day that she is burying her husband. The woman's perceptible openness to being courted is enough to send her Queens family into conniptions about her insensitivity, this in turn giving way to various examinations of conscience.

Mastroianni's one complaint about the film, which was shot in New York and Toronto, was Kidron's insistence on a couple of weeks of rehearsal before going before the cameras.

> She's a little Fellini, no doubt about her talent. But although she's British, she also went along with the American practice of sitting around a table for endless talk about the characters. It was pretty boring. Okay, if you want to sit down with a director, get to know one another. But after all the analyzing of this and that, I started going crazy. You have to be spontaneous making a film, too. You have to allow for the impact of eye movements, images, pacings. But I tried to be the good soldier. It was another experience—something new for me to talk about around some restaurant table in Rome.

Kidron conceded that "he almost killed me" over the rehearsals. "Shirley, in particular, wanted to have a very precise idea of the dimensions of the roles. With Marcello, it was a little more like talking about restaurants in Venice. Different people require different things for their energy."

At the same time, however, the director laughed at the notion that Mastroianni wanted no more preparation than a telephone call in the morning to his hotel to wake him up.

> Don't let him fool you. When we had our first script meeting, he arrived with a completely written out description of his character. He had foreseen changes from the original script that I hadn't mentioned to him but that he had intuited. There were a few other things that I wouldn't permit, and still other ideas of his own that I found enormously gratifying. The man is a giant of an actor—an incredibly sensitive machine. And once we got started, he just did what I asked.

Unfortunately, what Kidron asked wasn't nearly enough in the eyes of New York critics. *Used People* was roasted by both daily and weekly reviewers, even the most charitable notices calling it "*Moonstruck* without the magic." At the center of most of the commentary was simple incredulity that the Mastroianni character could have been attracted for so long to the sour, oppressive figure played by MacLaine. The *New York Times*, among others, also took the picture to task for its stereotypical treatment of both Italians and Jews in New

York. While Mastroianni and Tandy escaped with some backhanded compliments, the actor got bruised for his heavily accented English.

None of this stopped Mastroianni. Asked continually during the shooting of *Used People* why he had decided to end his boycott of Hollywood productions after so many years, he usually mentioned his attachment to the story, Kidron's blandishments, and/or the opportunity to work with three Oscar-winning actresses (MacLaine, Tandy, and Kathy Bates) on the same project. At the same time, however, he made it clear that he did not consider the assignment as the closing of some final professional frontier; on the contrary, during the filming in Toronto and New York, he returned again and again to stories of how he had been trying unsuccessfully for years to get a director from Mali to send him a project that they could work on together in the African nation. In any event, his next film following *Used People* did not call for location work in Mali but in Uruguay and Argentina. "I have never really seen those countries," Mastroianni said.

Afterword:
In the Abstract

M arcello Mastroianni's preeminence among European actors has
not been at issue for some time. Others might have given
equally affecting performances in this or that role, but nobody else
has come close to putting together the gallery of memorable characters that he has created over more than forty years. Others might
have attained an identification with their film industries comparable
to his with Italy's, but none has been readier to work across the borders of the Continent, in the process gaining almost as much of an
association with a second national industry (that of France). Others
might have achieved a star power that has translated itself into magazine covers from the English Channel to the Urals, but only Mastroianni can pile new covers atop those that began yellowing with age
decades ago. As a European motion-picture star, he has been the contemporary of everyone from Jean Gabin to Gérard Depardieu, with
all the Philipes, Jurgenses, Werners, Delons, Montands, and Belmon-
dos in between.

Away from Europe, Mastroianni has generally been more star
than actor—except when his films are shown and audiences and critics can remind themselves that image makers haven't exactly been
selling a pig in a poke. In the United States, his has been the only Italian male film persona that owes nothing to the screen Mafia or the
ingratiating immigrant. In Argentina, distributors practically dis-
pense with the titles of his films as very secondary to the fact that he
is back and that audiences can have him. In Brazil, one popularity
poll in the 1980s established only Loren and Leonardo da Vinci as
equally famous Italians. In Japan, he has been commonly referred to
as Maiki the Magnificent.

The parallel longevity of Mastroianni as both a gifted actor and
a star has stumped more than one film theoretician over the years not

because of doubts that he was both but because of the lack of some instant formula to explain the phenomenon. In taking his turn at the question several years ago, Britain's Alexander Walker might have come as close as anyone when he wrote:

> He has one of those no-faces like Sir Alec Guinness's or Peter Sellers's whose proportions and planes can be scrambled at will to let him take on new identities—often by as little as a flake of makeup, occasionally by a complete transformation like his *professore* in [*I Compagni*]. Inside him, less explicably, whirs the gyroscope of what one can inadequately call "screen presence"—the force that one senses without seeing in the great film actors, that holds a performance perfectly in balance however rocky the rest of the film. It is a quite different thing from "star quality," an emotion beamed outwards and often unconnected with a performance. When the two are present in the same artist, then one can speak of a great actor being also a great star. One can say that in certainty about Mastroianni.

The actor himself has never attributed much importance to such distinctions. When he has touched on the subject at all, he has downplayed the significance of his ability to "scramble proportions and planes" in the manner of an Alec Guinness or Peter Sellers, placing far more emphasis on the nimbleness of Marcello Mastroianni in discovering another facet of Marcello Mastroianni within the bones and psyche of the character of the moment. His estimation of his own talent has normally been a fiercely subjective one, nowhere more evident than in his acknowledgments of being a constant captive to his fantasies. The concessions to his objective status after more than forty years on the theater screen have by and large been deferential—in irony ("I have been working steadily, so it looks like someone likes something"), in self-deprecation (the lucky amateur), or in gratitude (the lessons he learned from Visconti and other directors). At the same time, however, his modesty has never crossed into self-abnegation, as epitomized by his avowed pride in being able to deliver himself in a pristine state to filmmakers so as to allow them to make of him anything that they would. In fact, it has remained one of Mastroianni's more beguiling accomplishments over the years that just as he has frequently made his solipsisms sound like more than egotism, he has often made his luck sound like less than accident.

Few directors who have worked with him have passed up the opportunity to plot Mastroianni's place in the motion-picture firmament. The customary starting point has been some variation on Fellini's remark that he offered untold possibilities because his was a face "without personality." John Boorman's version of this was that he was "completely plastic," Mauro Bolognini's that he was "the essence of pliable." It was from this premise, according to Antonioni in 1960 and according to Angelopoulos thirty years later, that the actor's presence was converted into a force field on the screen, endowing everything around him with an energy that even his scripted character sometimes lacked. If this didn't always mean making "apathy irresistible," as a critic said of Mastroianni's antihero roles in the 1960s, it usually made it clear why there was a dramatic black hole in many of his films when he was off the screen.

If only through hindsight, Mastroianni's status as an international star seems more obvious than his standing as one of the world's most profoundly versatile actors. Mastroianni the Star was born in the right film (*La Dolce Vita*) at the right time. He was adopted by image makers who, however much they might have irritated him personally, created a figure for the long haul that, as has been observed by Jack Lemmon and others, has always attracted publicity out of all proportion to the number of people who have actually seen him work. The mix has also included the actor's own developed instincts for promotion, his highly visible association on and off the screen with the most glamorous actresses of his day(s), and the professional strategies that have kept him away from titanic projects that would have demanded he go down with them. If Mastroianni the Star did not *have* to perdure for as long as he has, neither has he done too much to undermine a star's image. Indeed, after so many years of declaring his hostility to it, he has managed the difficult feat of compounding the image that initially appealed to audiences on both sides of the Atlantic—no longer the Latin Lover so much as the Film Actor Who Insists That He Is Not a Latin Lover.

On the other hand, Mastroianni the Actor, even in retrospect, doesn't always seem so logical, seems to have defied an awful lot of the shibboleths pertaining to artists who have grown over as long a period in public as he has. Most immediately, there has been little slow-up on any level. The parts that he has taken over recent years have been just as risky from a box-office standpoint as the title role in *Il Bell'Antonio* once seemed to be. Comparable only to such idols of his own as Gable and Astaire, he has stayed Mastroianni while broadening his repertoire to embrace aging fathers and grandfathers—but unlike Gable in his final pictures, there has been no sense of the fading performer playing out the string, and unlike Astaire, it has not meant accepting character cameos. Never having accorded primary place to words in the development of his roles, he has challenged himself still further in his search for characters over the last decade by rendering them in foreign languages.

Just as Mastroianni has never seen a need for exercise to

refreshen his sorely tried body, he has not felt a need to replenish his imaginative stores by withdrawing from the scene for any significant amount of time to commune with the moon or the local butcher at a more leisurely pace. Over the last four decades, he has done very little *except* make movies, *except* mingle with fellow professionals in the industry, *except* be treated as everybody's privileged and honored guest. Even his often vaunted travels abroad have been limited in their renewal properties, drawing as they have steady complaints that he was unable to see much of Poland, the Ukraine, Jerusalem, because of work schedules and official commitments. That such a rarefied atmosphere has not dried up his creative springs but, on the contrary, seems to have reinvigorated him at regular junctures says more than a little about his imaginative capacities and less than a little about the belief that artistic range is something of a correlative to a *curriculum vitae* that lists driving a truck, running guns, or spending a couple of years in a South African prison as unsheltered life experiences.

Mastroianni has also been there ahead of his critics to denounce his psychological stagnancy with many of the people closest to him, not least the women in his life. He has been the first to demonstrate that his self-criticisms are not always the stuff of galvanizing self-awareness and admits the possibility that he has even manipulated the former to preclude the latter. When he has articulated his notion of an ideal theater role, it has been to talk of a man "bitter in the realization that time passes on but (he) always finds himself stuck at the exact same point"; in describing his ultimate film role, he has mused about a character who understands absolutely nothing. And yet, except in his own negatively cited examples, such as *La Notte* and in the conflict around his interpretation of the protagonist in *Lo Straniero*, bleak lassitude has rarely been up on the screen; perhaps in the film around him but not in his work on his character.

Once at work, Mastroianni the Actor has usually found a great deal more than Mastroianni. He himself has seen nothing mysterious in this, considers it his trade—something more than a job but less than an art. If he has managed to grow as an actor, he has always been prompt to underline, it is because the fantasies of his earliest years—within a universe that extended from Fontana Liri to Hollywood, from his solid sense of family to the japes that had to be endured because of his uncle's outrageous taste in clothes, from stealing knives to stealing looks at the maid in the house across the road—have continued to regenerate themselves in forms adaptable to his rigorous theatrical training, not because he has matured beyond the infant touched by the Madonna. To a significant degree, in fact, the question is not so much how he has kept in touch with the realities outside the relatively exclusive world in which he has been circulating for so long to render the variegated characters that he has but how he has succeeded in exploiting the limitations of his professional ambience for giving conviction to such a wide array of roles.

A couple of things suggest themselves:

The intensity of Mastroianni's imagination and of his technical skills in channeling it into specific assignments has sometimes obscured the intelligence governing the process, leading some critics over the years into dissections of his talent that do not sound remarkably different from the fable of the Madonna and her magical finger. For some time, the actor even felt compelled to address the canard that he did little more than improvise off dialogue before the camera, some writers having taken him too much at his word that he was lazy. But Mastroianni's industriousness in preparing for a role has never been questioned by his directors, nor has he ever been a naïf. Indeed, second only to his emotional and physical malleability, filmmaker after filmmaker has singled out his astuteness as his major acting asset. "He has made a lot of specific choices about his character before showing up on a set," Monicelli has said. "His spontaneity has been thoroughly earned." According to Fellini, "Nobody is more conscious of what he is doing." For Kidron, the actor's, preparations were even typed out in a biographical sketch of his character. Or, as Saks has put it:

> You don't arrive ready for a first take the way he does if you're just hoping to be inspired by a thunderbolt out of the sky once the camera begins rolling. The man does his homework.

In general, the Mastroianni arsenal for making choices is stocked no differently from any other actor's, the most important weapons being observation, the relevance of what is observed to what can be felt, and the techniques for effecting the transition. The resultant approach to rendering what has been absorbed, however, is not all that common and points to at least one prominent intersection between Mastroianni the Actor and Mastroianni the Star.

In once contending that Mastroianni's closest forebear among American actors was the emphatically theatrical John Barrymore, Petri was not so much comparing the expressive styles of the two actors as he was taking note of their joint antagonism toward a naturalistic mode of performing. Petri has hardly been alone in deciding that Mastroianni had very little in common with such naturalistic heroes of his as Cagney and Bogart. On more than one occasion, Fellini has seconded the view—most conspicuously, by casting Mastroianni as his dream-treatise protagonist in several films, by regarding the regularly epiphanic Olivier as the only serious alternative to the Italian for a couple of his most ambitious projects, and even by procrastinating between images of Barrymore and Mastroianni for a comic-strip representation of "G. Mastorna." In going after the actor for *O Melissokomos*, Angelopoulos made it clear that one of his principal considerations was that he wanted somebody who was not only a star but a star not given to the naturalistic tendencies of most Italian (and Greek) performers. Directors as otherwise diverse as the Taviani brothers, Antonioni, and Mikhalkov have sought a similar quality in their collaborations. If Mastroianni has never been "bigger than life" in the Barrymore way, the consensus has been, his approach to character has been complicitly unnaturalistic enough to make himself *smaller* than life when that has been required.

As with so many other things, Mastroianni's attitude toward naturalistic forms of acting was shaped to a decisive degree during his years with Visconti. For the director, the compulsion for naturalistic detail within his elaborate theatrical productions extended well beyond props visible to an audience. In *Death of a Salesman*, for example, he abandoned an original idea of using an offstage recording of a car motor because it didn't sound right; instead, in the interests of heightening the suggestibility of his actors to Arthur Miller's milieu, he had a real car parked in the wings throughout the play's run, assigning a stagehand to rev up the engine whenever it was called for. In his staging of *The Three Sisters*, he had a live band in the wings every evening for nothing more than a bar or two of offstage music. In filming *Le Notti Bianche*, on the other hand, Visconti switched gears for a deliberate mounting of artifice as suggestion to the actors (an atmosphere carried over to some extent in Mastroianni's other cardinal success of the period—*I Soliti Ignoti*). Within both the formalities of theater and the realisms of film, in other words, the director's main tack with actors was to broaden their horizons beyond the orthodox structure of the medium they were working in.

The contiguity of the purposely artificial and realistic in filmmaking was no less pronounced with Fellini. This was true not only of the director's decision to move the Via Veneto to Cinecittà but of his tactic of incorporating scenes and dialogue abstracted from actual situations and conversations involving Mastroianni and other performers. Even the most realistic looking and sounding screen moments were conscious distillations of real happenings—a fact hardly lost on the participants in the original scene and in its cinematic sequel. As illustrated by the story of Mastroianni's forgotten coat, not even the self-enclosed reality of Fellini's film was safe from violation under the pressures of practical necessity.

For the actor, such experiences were not only part of admittedly technical (Visconti) and emotional (Fellini) educations but of an intellectual one as well. And their importance was reinforced by other factors. Rome itself took on equivocal connotations. In going into the streets to do something like *La Dolce Vita*, Mastroianni did not sally forth in the same spirit as, say, Marlon Brando did in going down to the Manhattan piers and to Hoboken to shoot *On the Waterfront* or that even Mastroianni himself did in going to Battery Park for *Ciao Maschio*. The Italian capital's suggestiveness was only *too* familiar for somebody who had not merely been brought up in its environs but had come to appreciate personally its parallel dimension as a fictional city for filmmakers.* While certainly more natural than the creations of the set designers at Cinecittà, the piazzas and markets of Rome had gained their own filter to what was "real"—that of the repeatedly used location. In effect, the city posed a double reality that actors had to compress for the purposes of character—one a standard physical invitation to realism, the second a prepossessive reminder of the artificial made to look real.

Nobody has been more equipped than Mastroianni before the task of compressing such a double reality within a given role. It has been the kind of challenge that has called for more than the naturalism that his most trusted mentors were never satisfied with but also more than formalisms that, they made clear, they found equally inadequate. It has in fact been before such challenges that the actor has most forcefully brought into play the intelligence indicated by practically all his directors as his most overlooked asset—a very precise methodology that, for lack of a better word, might be termed abstractionist.

He has provided clues. His mastery of lines has been an assumption, not a goal. He has never tried to be a perfectionist where dialects are concerned but has been content to plumb the general "musicality and rhythms" of regional speech and go from there. He has continually shown his impatience with facsimile characterization. He has exalted his relationships with directors (notably, Ferreri) who have taken for granted not only his interest in their metaphorical quests but also his ability to fashion character out of the hunt with a minimum of guidance. In giving absolute priority to directors over scripts in choosing projects for so long, he has also implicitly been attributing greater importance to the *idea* behind a proposal than to the written development of story and character, including his own. Simi-

---

*Symptomatic of the local consciousness of this phenomenon, foreign tourists almost had a collective heart attack one evening in the early 1970s when army tanks suddenly sealed off all avenues leading into the Piazza Navona; only Romans continued to sip their Camparis calmly before pointing out that a film set during World War II was scheduled to be shot in the square the following morning.

larly, most of the stillborn projects that he has lamented have attracted him as ideas indebted to only the most expedient notions of a representational place, to the point of fancying an aging Tarzan limping around in Siberia.

The actor's gift, of course, has been in his skill in setting off from such general ideas toward the specific attitudes and behaviors of character. Being an actor and not an ideologue, his initial idea has normally prevailed only until a character has begun to take shape as an autonomous psychological entity. But the initial idea has never disappeared entirely. It has lurked in the background as take after take has worn out the actor's deeper discoveries of emotional particulars, reclaiming the high ground with Mastroianni anxieties and melancholies in direct proportion to the growth of a director's dissatisfaction. As an articulation of purpose in doing a role, the original idea has recurred even more dominantly in discussions of the part with interviewers months later, no matter the actual intervening acting experience. It is because of this that his dissections of his roles for the media have often sounded like a broken record, making such different characters as the deadbeat in *L'Assassino* and the military officer in *Le Général de la Armée Morte* seem identical, and have ultimately done a disservice to what he has usually accomplished on the screen. What that achievement often is has been the disavowal of his own consoling, intellectual self-perceptions and an embrace of the fantasies that have, paradoxically, allowed him to cross into flesh and blood.

Converse evidence of the abstractionist has not lacked, either. When Mastroianni has flopped most spectacularly, it has almost always been in roles that, rather than encouraging him to break through some concept into marrow, have themselves existed only as gossamer conceits. A classic case was the symbolic figure of the Latin Lover in Polanski's *Che?* Another was Demy's hastily inspired pregnant man in *L'Événement le Plus Important Depuis Que l'Homme A Marché sur la Lune*. On another level, there was Scola's reverential continuation of the journalist character from *La Dolce Vita* in *La Terrazza*—a point of reference that, for all the anguish and interia of the personage, was more aesthetic than anything else. Other actors with less cerebral impetus than Mastroianni might have actually milked such roles more entertainingly, might have found their essential abstractness a well-marked destination; in starting off from such a point, however, there was little artistic journey involved, least of all that of heading into flesh and blood. In a way, it was like the young Mastroianni receiving Holy Communion twice during the same mass—overpresence rather than meaningful observation.

Throughout his career, Mastroianni has made a clear distinction between filmmaking as his life and filmmaking not being itself life. It is a distinction that has taken on a special resonance from within his own social orbit, where not only have his fantasies been encouraged and his skills been appreciated but where his abstractions of characters from other walks of life have received regular endorsement as sufficient for getting on with it. In Italy, especially, even after forty years, there is no such thing as "a Mastroianni film" in the sense that Sordi's immersions into the specifics of loud little men created expectations of "a Sordi film." All of Mastroianni's instincts, from his imaginative capacities to his intellectual control of character, have always aimed for more—and less—than that. It is in this connection as well that Pietro Germi, the director of *Divorzio-all'Italiana*, the film that more than any other established Mastroianni as both an actor and a star, once sought to explain the international drawing power of his one-time leading man. Germi declared:

> What he is is not quite exactly anything. He has Italian qualities that make him very accessible to foreign audiences, because he contains them, makes them less folkloristic than other actors. He is Italian enough, but also less than an Italian really is. Maybe he's just a little bit of everything, and maybe he is so popular because everyone wants to be like that.

Filmography

Mastroianni made his screen debut as an extra in the 1938 musical *Marionette* (Marionettes). Over the next few years, he appeared in background spot roles in what he has estimated only as "an awful lot" of features shot at the Cinecittà studios. What follows is the list of films in which he had a speaking part:

1947

Tempesta su Parigi (the second part of *Les Misérables*). Director: Riccardo Freda. With Gino Cervi and Valentina Cortese.

1949

Passaporto per l'Oriente (A Tale of Five Women). Director: Romolo Marcellini. With Bonar Colleano and Gina Lollobrigida.

1950

Una Domenica d'Agosto (Sunday in August). Director: Luciano Emmer. With Franco Interlenghi and Massimo Serato.

Vita da Cani (A Dog's Life). Directors: (Stefano Vanzina) Steno and Mario Monicelli. With Aldo Fabrizi and Gina Lollobrigida.

Cuori sul Mare (Hearts at Sea). Director: Giorgio Bianchi. With Jacques Sernas and Doris Dowling.

Contro la Legge (Against the Law). Director: Flavio Calzavara. With Tino Buazzelli and Fulvia Mammi.

1951

Atto d'Accusa (The Accusation). Director: Giacomo Gentilomo. With Lea Padovani and Andrea Checchi.

Parigi È Sempre Parigi (Paris Is Always Paris). Director: Luciano Emmer. With Aldo Fabrizi and Lucia Bosè.

1952

L'Eterna Catena (The Eternal Chain). Director: Anton Giulio Majano. With Gianna Maria Canale and Marco Vicario.

Le Ragazze di Piazza di Spagna (Three Girls from Rome). Director: Luciano Emmer. With Lucia Bosè and Cosetta Greco.

Tragico Ritorno (Tragic Return). Director: Pier Luigi Faraldo. With Doris Duranti and Dante Maggio.

Sensualità (Sensuality). Director: Clemente Fracassi. With Amedeo Nazzari and Eleanora Rossi Drago.

Penne Nere (Black Feathers). Director: Oreste Biancoli. With Marina Vlady and Guido Celano.

1953

Gli Eroi della Domenica (Sunday's Heroes). Director: Mario Camerini. With Raf Vallone and Cosetta Greco.

Il Viale della Speranza (The Boulevard of Hope). Director: Dino Risi. With Cosetta Greco and Liliana Bonfatti.

Febbre di Vivere (Fever for Living). Director: Claudio Gora. With Massimo Serato and Anna Maria Ferrero.

Non È Mai Troppo Tardi (It's Never Too Late). Director: Filippo Walter Ratti. With Paolo Stoppa and Isa Barzizza.

Lulu. Director: Fernando Cerchio. With Valentina Cortese and Jacques Sernas.

1954

Tempi Nostri (Anatomy of Love). Director: Alessandro Blasetti. With Lea Padovani and Nando Bruno.

Cronache di Poveri Amanti (Chronicles of Poor Lovers). Director: Carlo Lizzani. With Anna Maria Ferrero and Cosetta Greco.

Schiava del Peccato (Slave of Sin). Director: Raffaello Matarazzo. With Silvana Pampanini and Camillo Pilotto.

Giorni d'Amore (Days of Love). Director: Giuseppe De Santis. With Marina Vlady and Lucien Gallas.

Casa Ricordi (House of Ricordi). Director: Carmine Gallone. With Paolo Stoppa and Gabriele Ferzetti.

Peccato Che Sia una Canaglia (Too Bad She's Bad). Director: Alessandro Blasetti. With Sophia Loren and Vittorio De Sica.

La Principessa della Canarie (The Island Princess). Director: Paolo Moffa. With Silvana Pampanini and Gustavo Rojo.

1955

La Bella Mugnaia (The Miller's Beautiful Wife). Director: Mario Camerini. With Sophia Loren and Vittorio De Sica.

Tam-Tam Mayumbe (Mayumbe Drums). Director: Gian Gaspare Napolitano. With Pedro Armendariz and Kerima.

La Fortuna di Essere Donna (Lucky to Be a Woman). Director: Alessandro Blasetti. With Sophia Loren and Charles Boyer.

Il Bigamo (The Bigamist). Director: Luciano Emmer. With Franca Valeri and Vittorio De Sica.

1957

Padri e Figli (The Tailor's Maid). Director: Mario Monicelli. With Vittorio De Sica and Marisa Merlini.

La Ragazza della Salina (The Girl of the Salt Works). Director: Frantisek Cap. With Isabelle Corey and Peter Carsten.

Il Momento Più Bello (The Most Wonderful Moment). Director: Luciano Emmer. With Giovanna Ralli and Marisa Merlini.

Le Notti Bianche (White Nights). Director: Luchino Visconti. With Maria Schell and Jean Marais.

Il Medico e lo Stregone (The Doctor and the Witch Doctor). Director: Mario Monicelli. With Vittorio De Sica and Marisa Merlini.

1958

Un Ettaro di Cielo (A Piece of the Sky). Director: Aglauco Casadio. With Rosanna Schiaffino and Polidor.

I Soliti Ignoti (Big Deal on Madonna Street). Director: Mario Monicelli. With Vittorio Gassman and Totò.

Racconti d'Estate (Love on the Riviera). Director: Gianni Franciolini. With Michèle Morgan.

Amore e Guai (Love and Troubles). Director: Angelo Dorigo. With Valentina Cortese and Richard Basehart.

1959

La Loi (Where the Hot Wind Blows). Director: Jules Dassin. With Melina Mercouri and Yves Montand.

Tutti Innamorati (All the Lovers). Director: Giuseppe Orlandini. With Jacqueline Sassard and Gabriele Ferzetti.

Il Nemico di Mia Moglie (My Wife's Enemy). Director: Gianni Puccini. With Giovanna Ralli and Vittorio De Sica.

Ferdinando I Re di Napoli (Ferdinand I, King of Naples). Director: Gianni Franciolini. With Eduardo De Filippo and Vittorio De Sica.

1960

La Dolce Vita. Director: Federico Fellini. With Anouk Aimée and Anita Ekberg.

Il Bell'Antonio. Director: Mauro Bolognini. With Claudia Cardinale and Pierre Brasseur.

Adua e le Compagne (Love à la Carte). Director: Antonio Pietrangeli. With Simone Signoret and Sandra Milo.

1961

La Notte (The Night). Director: Michelangelo Antonioni. With Jeanne Moreau and Monica Vitti.

L'Assassino (The Lady Killer of Rome). Director: Elio Petri. With Micheline Presle and Salvo Randone.

Fantasmi a Roma (Ghosts of Rome). Director: Antonio Pietrangeli. With Vittorio Gassman and Eduardo De Filippo.

Divorzio all'Italiana (Divorce Italian Style). Director: Pietro Germi. With Daniela Rocca and Stefania Sandrelli.

La Vie Privée (A Very Private Affair). Director: Louis Malle. With Brigitte Bardot and Gregoire von Rezzori.

1962

Cronaca Familiare (Family Diary). Director: Valerio Zurlini. With Jacques Perrin and Salvo Randone.

1963

8½. Director: Federico Fellini. With Claudia Cardinale and Anouk Aimée.

I Compagni (The Organizer). Director: Mario Monicelli. With Renato Salvatore and Annie Girardot.

Ieri Oggi Domani (Yesterday, Today, and Tomorrow). Director: Vittorio De Sica. With Sophia Loren and Aldo Giuffré.

1964

Matrimonio all'Italiana (Marriage Italian Style). Director: Vittorio De Sica. With Sophia Loren and Marilù Tolo.

1965

Casanova '70. Director: Mario Monicelli. With Marisa Mell and Enrico Maria Salerno.

La Decima Vittima (The Tenth Victim). Director: Elio Petri. With Ursula Andress and Elsa Martinelli.

Oggi, Domani, Dopodomani (Today, Tomorrow, and Day After Tomorrow). Directors: Marco Ferreri, Eduardo De Filippo, and Luciano Salce. With Catherine Spaak, Virna Lisi, and Pamela Tiffin. (Note: Released in the U.S. in a drastically re-edited version, minus the Ferreri episode, as Kiss the Other Sheik.)

1966

Io, Io, Io . . . e gli Altri (Me, Me, Me . . . and the Others). Director: Alessandro Blasetti. With Walter Chiari and Gina Lollobrigida.

The Poppy Is Also a Flower. Director: Terence Young. With E. G. Marshall and Trevor Howard.

Spara Forte, Più Forte . . . Non Capisco (Shoot Loud, Louder . . . I Don't Understand). Director: Eduardo De Filippo. With Eduardo De Filippo and Raquel Welch.

1967

Lo Straniero (The Stranger). Director: Luchino Visconti. With Anna Karina and Georges Geret.

1968

L'Uomo dei Palloni (The Man with the Balloons). Director: Marco Ferreri. With Catherine Spaak and Ugo Tognazzi. (Note: This is a lengthened version of Ferreri's "L'Uoma dei Cinque Palloni" episode originally in the 1965 Oggi, Domani, Doppodomani. It was released as Break-up in France.)

Amanti (A Place for Lovers). Director: Vittorio De Sica. With Faye Dunaway and Caroline Mortimer.

1969

Diamonds for Breakfast. Director: Christopher Morahan. With Rita Tushingham and Maggie Blye.

1970

I Girasoli (Sunflower). Director: Vittorio De Sica. With Sophia Loren and Ludmila Savelyeva.

Leo the Last. Director: John Boorman. With Billie Whitelaw and Calvin Lockhart.

Dramma della Gelosia: Tutti i Particolari in Cronaca (The Pizza Triangle). Director: Ettore Scola. With Monica Vitti and Giancarlo Giannini.

Giochi Particolari (The Voyeur). Director: Franco Indovina. With Virna Lisi and Timothy Dalton.

La Moglie del Prete (The Priest's Wife). Director: Dino Risi. With Sophia Loren and Venantino Venantini.

1971

Scipione Detto Anche l'Africano (Scipio the African). Director: Luigi Magni. With Vittorio Gassman and Silvana Mangano.

Permette? Rocco Papaleo (Rocco Papaleo). Director: Ettore Scola. With Lauren Hutton and Tom Reed.

1972

Correva l'Anno di Grazia 1870 (1870). Director: Alfredo Giannetti. With Anna Magnani and Mario Carotenuto.

Ça N'Arrive Qu'Aux Autres (It Only Happens to Others). Director: Nadine Trintignant. With Catherine Deneuve and Serge Marquand.

La Cagna (Liza). Director: Marco Ferreri. With Catherine Deneuve and Michel Piccoli.

Che? (What?). Director: Roman Polanski. With Sydne Rome and Hugh Griffith.

1973

Mordi e Fuggi (Sting and Run). Director: Dino Risi. With Oliver Reed and Carole André.

Rappresaglia (Massacre in Rome). Director: George Pan Cosmatos. With Richard Burton and Leo McKern.

L'Événement le Plus Important Depuis Que l'Homme A Marché sur la Lune (A Slightly Pregnant Man). Director: Jacques Demy. With Catherine Deneuve and Micheline Presle.

La Grande Bouffe (Blowout). Director: Marco Ferreri. With Michel Piccoli, Philippe Noiret, and Ugo Tognazzi.

Salut l'Artiste (Salute the Artist). Director: Yves Robert. With Françoise Fabian and Jean Rochefort.

1974

Touche Pas à la Femme Blanche! (The True Story of General Custer). Director: Marco Ferreri. With Catherine Deneuve and Ugo Tognazzi.

Allonsanfan. Directors: Paolo and Vittorio Taviani. With Lea Massari, Laura Betti, and Claudio Cassinelli.

1975

La Pupa del Gangster (The Gangster's Doll). Director: Giorgio Capitani. With Sophia Loren and Aldo Maccione.

La Divina Creatura (The Divine Nymph). Director: Giuseppe Patroni Griffi. With Laura Antonelli and Terence Stamp.

Per le Antiche Scale (Down the Ancient Stairs). Director: Mauro Bolognini. With Françoise Fabian and Marthe Keller.

La Donna della Domenica (The Sunday Woman). Director: Luigi Comencini. With Jacqueline Bisset and Jean-Louis Trintignant.

1976

Culastrisce Nobile Veneziano (Lunatics and Lovers). Director: Flavio Mogherini. With Claudia Mori and Flora Carabella.

Todo Modo (One Way or Another). Director: Elio Petri. With Gian Maria Volonté and Mariangela Melato.

Signore e Signori, Buonanotte (Ladies and Gentlemen, Good Night). Directors: Nanni Loy, Luigi Magni, Ettore Scola, and Mario Monicelli. With Vittorio Gassman, Nino Manfredi, and Ugo Tognazzi.

1977

Una Giornata Particolare (A Special Day). Director: Ettore Scola. With Sophia Loren and John Vernon.

Mogliamante (Wifemistress). Director: Marco Vicario. With Laura Antonelli and William Berger.

Doppio Delitto (Double Murder on Via Governo Vecchio). Director: (Stefano Vanzina) Steno. With Peter Ustinov and Ursula Andress.

1978

Ciao Maschio (Bye Bye Monkey). Director: Marco Ferreri. With Gerard Dépardieu and Geraldine Fitzgerald.

Così Come Sei (The Way You Are). Director: Alberto Lattuada. With Nastassia Kinski and Francisco Rabal.

Fatto di Sangue fra Due Uomini per Causa di una Vedova, Si Sospettano Moventi Politici (A Bloody Event at Caminiti Between Two Men Because of a Widow, Political Motivations Are Suspected). Director: Lina Wertmuller. With Sophia Loren and Giancarlo Giannini. (Released in the U.S. in 1979 as *Blood Feud.* Later recut and retitled *Revenge.*)

1979

L'Ingorgo (Traffic Jam). Director: Luigi Comencini. With Stefania
Sandrelli and Ugo Tognazzi.

Giallo Napoletano (Neapolitan Mystery). Director: Sergio Corbucci.
With Ornella Muti and Michel Piccoli.

1980

La Terrazza (The Terrace). Director: Ettore Scola. With Vittorio Gassman, Ugo Tognazzi, and Jean-Louis Trintignant.

La Città delle Donne (The City of Women). Director: Federico Fellini.
With Anna Prucnal and Ettore Manni.

1981

La Pelle (The Skin). Director: Liliana Cavani. With Burt Lancaster
and Claudia Cardinale.

Fantasma d'Amore (Ghost of Love). Director: Dino Risi. With Romy
Schneider and Eva Maria Meineke.

1982

La Nuit de Varennes (That Night at Varennes). Director: Ettore Scola.
With Jean-Louis Barrault and Hanna Schygulla.

Oltre la Porta (Beyond the Door). Director: Liliana Cavani. With Eleonora Giorgi and Tom Berenger.

1983

La Storia di Piera (Piera's Story). Director: Marco Ferreri. With Hanna
Schygulla and Isabelle Huppert.

Gabriela. Director: Bruno Barreto. With Sonia Braga and Antonio
Cantafora.

Le Général de la Armée Morte (The General of the Dead Army). Director: Luciano Tovoli. With Anouk Aimée and Michel Piccoli.

1984

Enrico IV (Henry IV). Director: Marco Bellocchio. With Leopoldo
Trieste and Claudia Cardinale.

1985

Le Due Vite di Mattia Pascal (The Late Mattia Pascal). Director: Mario
Monicelli. With Flavio Bucci and Laura Morante.

Maccheroni (Macaroni). Director: Ettore Scola. With Jack Lemmon
and Daria Nicolodi.

Ginger e Fred (Ginger and Fred). Director: Federico Fellini. With Giulietta Masina and Franco Fabrizi.

1986

I Soliti Ignoti . . . Vent'Anni Dopo (Big Deal on Madonna Street . . . 20
Years Later). Director: Amanzio Todini. With Vittorio Gassman
and Tiberio Murgia.

O Melissokomos (The Beekeeper). Director: Theo Angelopoulos. With Nadia Mourouzi and Serge Reggiani.

1987

Oci Ciornie (Dark Eyes). Director: Nikita Mikhalkov. With Silvana Mangano and Elena Sofonova.

Intervista (Interview). Director: Federico Fellini. With Anita Ekberg and Federico Fellini.

Miss Arizona. Director: Pal Sandor. With Hanna Schygulla and Gabor Zsoter.

1988

Splendor. Director: Ettore Scola. With Massimo Troisi and Marina Vlady.

1989

Che Ora È? (What Time Is It?). Director: Ettore Scola. With Massimo Troisi and Anne Parillaud.

1990

Stanno Tutti Bene (Everybody's Fine). Director: Giuseppe Tornatore. With Michèle Morgan and Marino Cenna.

Verso Sera (Toward Evening). Director: Francesca Archibugi. With Sandrine Bonnaire and Lara Pranzoni.

Tchin-Tchin (A Fine Romance). Director: Gene Saks. With Julie Andrews and Jean-Pierre Castaldi.

Le Pas Suspendu de la Cigogne (The Suspended Step of the Stork). Director: Theo Angelopoulos. With Jeanne Moreau and Gregory Karr.

1991

Le Voleur d'Enfants (The Colonel's Children). Director: Christian de Chalonge. With Virginie Ledoyen, Angela Molina, and Michel Piccoli.

Used People. Director: Beeban Kidron. With Shirley MacLaine, Jessica Tandy, Kathy Bates, and Sylvia Sidney.

Mastroianni also appeared as himself in cameo roles in Fellini's *Roma* in 1972 and in Scola's *C'Eravamo Tanto Amati* (We All Loved Each Other So Much) in 1974.

Bibliography

Books

Alpert, Hollis. *Fellini—A Life*. New York: Atheneum, 1986.

Argentieri, Mino. *La censura del cinema italiano*. Rome: Editori Riuniti, 1974.

Aristarco, Guido. *Miti e realtà nel cinema italiano*. Milan: Il Saggiatore, 1961.

Assessorato alla Cultura del Comune di Roma, ed. *La città del cinema*. Rome: Napoleone, 1979.

Berthome, Jean-Pierre. *Jacques Demy: Les racines du réve*. Nantes: L'Atalante, 1982.

Betti, Liliana. *Fellini*. Zurich: Diogenes Verlag, 1976.

Biarese, Cesare, and Aldo Tassone. *I film di Michelangelo Antonioni*. Rome: Gremese, 1985.

Bondanella, Peter. *Italian Cinema*. New York: Continuum, 1991.

Brunetta, Gian Piero. *Storia del cinema italiano*. Rome: Editori Riuniti, 1979.

Camerino, Vincenzo. ed. *Il cinema di Giuseppe De Santis*. Lecce: Elle, 1982.

Ciment, Michel. *John Boorman*. Translated by Gilbert Adair. London: Faber and Faber, 1986.

Crowther, Bruce. *Burt Lancaster—A Life in Films*. London: Robert Hale, 1991.

DeSanti, Pier Marco, and Rossano Vittori. *I film di Ettore Scola*. Rome: Gremese, 1987.

De Sica, Emi, and Giancarlo Governi, eds. *Vittorio De Sica: Lettere dal set*. Rome: Sugarco Edizioni, 1987.

DeTassis, Piera, Tullio Masoni, and Paolo Vecchi, eds. *Il cinema di Antonio Pietrangeli*. Venice: Marsilio, 1987.

Eastman, John. *Retakes*. New York: Ballantine, 1989.

Faldini, Franca, and Goffredo Fofi, eds. *L'avventurosa storia del cinema italiano (1935–1959)*. Rome: Feltrinelli, 1979.

Faldini, Franca, and Goffredo Fofi, eds. *L'avventurosa storia del cinema italiano (1960–1969)*. Rome: Feltrinelli, 1981.

Faldini, Franca, and Goffredo Fofi. *Il cinema italiano d'oggi* (1970–1984). Milan: Mondadori, 1984.

Ferrara, Giuseppe. *Il nuovo cinema italiano.* Florence: Le Monnier, 1957.

Gili, Jean. *Le cinema italien à l'ombre des faisceaux.* Perpignan: Institut Jean Vigo, 1990.

Gori, Gianfranco. *Blasetti.* Florence: La Nuova Italia, 1983.

Governi, Giancarlo. *Nannarella.* Milan: Bompiani, 1981.

Gromo, Mario. *Cinema italiano, 1908–1953.* Milan: Mondadori, 1954.

Hochkofler, Matilde. *Marcello Mastroianni: Il gioco del cinema.* Rome: Gremese, 1992.

Hotchner, A. E. *Sophia: Living and Loving.* New York: Morrow, 1979.

Huffhines, Kathy Schulz, ed. *Foreign Affairs.* San Francisco: Mercury House, Inc., 1991.

Hunter, Allan. *Faye Dunaway.* New York: St. Martin's Press, 1986.

Kaufman, Hank, and Gene Lerner. *Hollywood on the Tiber.* Milan: Sperling and Kupfer Editori, 1980.

Leyda, Jay. *Voices of Film Experience: 1894 to the Present.* New York: Macmillan, 1977.

Liehm, Mira. *Passion and Defiance: Film in Italy from 1942 to the Present.* Berkeley and Los Angeles: University of California Press, 1984.

Lizzani, Carlo. *Il cinema italiano, 1895–1979.* Rome: Editori Riuniti, 1979.

Mahad, Michel. *Marco Ferreri.* Paris: Edilig, 1987.

Marcus, Millicent. *Italian Film in the Light of Neorealism.* Princeton, N. J.: Princeton University Press, 1986.

Nowell-Smith, Geoffrey. *Visconti.* New York: Viking, 1973.

Orto, Nuccio. *La notte dei desideri (il cinema dei fratelli Taviani).* Palermo: Sallerio, 1987.

Parisi, Antonio. *Il cinema di Giuseppe De Santis: Tra passione e ideologia.* Rome: Cadmo, 1983.

Pisano, Isabel. *Appuntamento con il cinema italiano.* Rome: Edizioni dell'Ateneo, 1980.

Ponzi, Maurizio. *The Films of Gina Lollobrigida.* Secaucus, N.J.: Citadel Press, 1982.

Schifano, Laurence. *Luchino Visconti: The Flames of Passion.* London: Collins, 1990.

Spinazzola, Vittorio. *Cinema e pubblico: Lo spettacolo filmico in Italia, 1945–1965.* Milan: Bompiani, 1974.

Tassone, Aldo. *Parla il cinema italiano.* 2 vols. Milan: Edizioni Il Formichiere, 1980.

Thomson, David. *A Biographical Dictionary of Film.* New York: Morrow, 1981.

Tinazzi, Giorgio, ed. *Il cinema italiano degli anni '50.* Venice: Marsilio, 1979.

Verdone, Luca. *I film di Alessandro Blasetti.* Rome: Gremese, 1989.

Walker, Alexander. *The Celluloid Sacrifice.* London: Michael Joseph, 1966.

Wexman, Virginia Wright. *Roman Polanski.* Boston: Twayne Publishers, 1985.

Witcombe, R. T. *The New Italian Cinema.* New York: Oxford University Press, 1982.

Periodicals

Over the years, interviews, feature stories, and reviews touching on Mastroianni and his work have numbered in the thousands. The most useful daily newspapers included:

ITALY:

Avanti, L'Avvenire, Il Corriere della Sera, Corriere d'Informazione, Corriere Lombardo, Corriere Mercantile, Il Giornale, Il Giorno, Il Manifesto, Il Mattino, Il Messaggero, La Notte, Paese Sera, Il Popolo, La Repubblica, Il Resto del Carlino, Il Secolo XIX, La Stampa, Il Tempo, L'Unità, La Voce Repubblicana.

THE UNITED STATES:

Boston Sunday Globe, Chicago Sun-Times, Daily News (New York), *Film Daily, New York Herald Tribune, Hollywood Reporter, Newsday, New York Journal-American, New York Post, New York Times, Il Progresso, San Francisco Chronicle.*

Among weekly and monthly publications, the most helpful sources:

ITALY:

Cineforum, Cinema, L'Epoca, L'Espresso, L'Europeo, Oggi, Panorama, Rinascita, Rotosei, La Settimana Incom Illustrata, Settimo Giorno, Tempo, Vita.

OTHER EUROPEAN:

Cahiers du Cinéma, Cinématographie, Du, Elet Es Irodalom, Films and Filming, Film Dope, La Revue du Cinéma, Sight and Sound.

UNITED STATES:

Attenzione, Cue, Esquire, Holiday, The New Yorker, New York Times Magazine, People, Saturday Review, Variety, Village Voice.

Index